THE D.I.V.A. HERSELF

I SURVIVED MY MESS!

THE D.I.V.A. HERSELF

A MEMOIR

I SURVIVED MY MESS!

HOW TO CONQUER:
The Guide to Keep on Living

Dr. La Shawn Denise Witt

The Global Strategist™
@the_global_strategist

**The D.I.V.A. Herself: I Survived My Mess!
How to Conquer: The Guide to Keep On Living
By The Global Strategist, LLC**

Copyright © 2024 by The Global Strategist, LLC.

All rights reserved. No part of this book may be reproduced in any form or by any electronic or mechanical means, including information storage and retrieval system, without permission in writing from The Global Strategist, LLC, or Dr. La Shawn Denise Witt, except by a reviewer who may quote brief passages in a review, permitted by the copyright law. Any person who does any unauthorized act in relation to this publication may be liable to criminal prosecution and civil claims for damages.

This book is a non-fiction work and is intended for informational and educational purposes only. The content provided in this book is based on the author's research, personal experiences, and professional expertise.

First Printing: 2024

ISBN: 979-8-9917508-0-6 (Hardback)
ISBN: 979-8-9917508-2-0 (Paperback)
ISBN: 979-8-9917508-1-3 (E-book)

Cover design by: Panagiotis Lampridis, Book Design Stars
Cover photo by: Rick Collins, Collins Visual

Published in the United States of America.
Visit the following websites for further information:
https://theglobalstrategist.info OR https://drlashawndenisewitt.com
Email: lashawn@drlashawndenisewitt.com

Dedication

To my darling daughter, Morgan Airriel-Josephine Williams "KTA":

Snooks,

You are the best gift that God has entrusted me with. You are my everything. You inspire me every day to be better, to dream bigger, and never give up. For the last 27 years, you have brought great joy to my heart.

Thank you for praying Mommy back to life and being my soldier during my mess. Let this book remind you to "dream big," baby girl, and don't stop until the dream comes true. I'm so proud of the incredible person you are. Know that mommy is always so proud of you!

I love you more than you will ever know,

Momma KTA

Notes to My Four Angels

Dear Granny,

Life without you has been challenging, but I am forever grateful for the lessons you taught me. You told me when I was a little girl that I would write a book that would change lives. As a little girl, I had no idea what you meant. The book is written—and I dedicate this to you. You told me my voice would reach many; here we are. Lastly, you taught me the importance of praying and reading Scripture, which ultimately saved my life more times than I care to count. Granny, your prayers are still being manifested. I treasure the mantle you passed on to me. I pray I have made you proud!

Love and miss you so much,
Shawnie

P.S. You should see me in the kitchen, honey! Please don't play with me. I do my best to keep the family legacy going … but you know your kids.

In memory of my grandmother,
Josephine Charlesetta Butler.
February 4, 1924–September 14, 1996.

Dear Brother,

I have no words. I did not expect our last time together to be spent three weeks before you left me. Words cannot express the void that I feel with you being gone. A girl's second heart belongs to her big brother. I got the book done, finally. Thank you, Daywalker, for loving me as your little sister and caring for me while you were here. Although we were divided as siblings, you saw to it that we had a bond when I was old enough to understand. During your passing, I learned more about you than I ever knew. You always bragged about your sister and how awesome I am, but now I will forever brag about my big brother and the amazing man of God you truly were. I can't wait to see you again—and little sister does have some bones to pick with you. LOL. Know that I will continue to honor your legacy and always hold Kathy and Caden in my heart.

Love and forever miss you,
Your sweetheart

P.S. I remember the last thing you told me before we left Dallas: "Sis, I got your back, and we are going to work this out!" Those words forever changed my life.

In memory of my brother,
William Joseph Witt.
September 3, 1965–August 13, 2023.

Dear Aunt Mollie,

My sweet, sweet Auntie Ma, my biggest cheerleader, my soror; I miss you and that porch! I finally got this book done. Thank you for being one of my biggest inspirations and encouraging me when I felt alone. Thank you for stepping up to guide me when my grandmother passed. From childhood through college to my journey to Delta land, you always held a special place for your California niece and made sure everyone knew I was your favorite! I miss your wisdom; I miss our talks. I miss you so much!

Love you always,
La Shawn

In memory of my Auntie,
Mollie Margret Tompkins Witt.
April 22, 1941–February 4, 2021.

P.S. I took your advice ... Balance is so important because, ma'am, I was worn out.

Dear Uncle Gregory,

I miss your chitterlings, and I miss you! I finally got this book done. Now we are 1:1. I often pick up your book, *Not This Time Around*, and say to myself, "Wow! My Uncle Gregory would always say, 'My niece Shawnie needs to write a book.'" Well, it's finally done. Just the other day, I laughed at the time I said, "You b****." I was really something else. Well, we're still here on earth; your family is still dramatic, per usual, but I am doing my best to hold it down. You're forever and always in my heart!

Love you more than you know,
Shawnie

In memory of my uncle,
Gregory Reynaldo Ratliff.
February 9, 1949–January 12, 2019.

"As black women, we're always given these seemingly devastating experiences—experiences that could absolutely break us. But what the caterpillar calls the end of the world, the master calls the butterfly. What we do as black women is take the worst situations and create from that point."

—Viola Davis

"Give a girl the right shoes,
and she can conquer the world."

–Marilyn Monroe

Message to My Readers

Dear Sister/Brother,

This is not the end—there's more after this. God will restore and sustain you. I speak to the overcomer in you, the conqueror through Christ Jesus. Keep moving forward because you have a powerful testimony ahead. This is not how your story ends! Persevere, stay faithful, and keep living! It's time to move on. How long will you dwell on this mountain? You have to decide how you're going to feel and push forward.

In 1 Kings 19, we see the prophet Elijah at a low point, vulnerable and in despair. As he rested under the broom tree, God told him to eat because the journey ahead was long. This shows that even in our weakest moments, God comes to us, providing exactly what we need for the road ahead. His presence and guidance often come in unexpected ways, reminding us that doubt and weakness can visit even the most faithful.

It's no accident that Apostle Paul connected "rejoicing in hope" with "being pat2ient in trouble." In tough times, you'll be tempted to think, *The setback is too big. This health issue won't get better. My career took a hit. It's over!* But none of this surprises God. He already knows the solution and the direction He's taking you. Be patient in the trouble and be prayerful. The trouble is not permanent, and it's not the final chapter of your story. God wouldn't allow the difficulty if He didn't plan to bring you out stronger.

Scripture says, "God makes everything beautiful in its time." Trust His timing and give Him space to work things out. Just because you don't see progress doesn't mean He's not working. Behind the scenes, He's aligning every piece you need for His bigger, better plan—a plan more rewarding than you can imagine.

Walk in your purpose, my friend! I appreciate you!

All my love,

Dr. La Shawn

Message to My Family and Friends

Dear Family and Friends,

You may read this book and know who you are or know who it is. Remember, this is my testimony, and I will always protect your identity.

Love you,

Dr. La Shawn

Table of Contents

Preface 1

THE D.I.V.A. HERSELF 8

My Life 20

Part 1: Lil' Shawnie 23

Chapter 1: Hey, Shawnie! 24

Chapter 2: Lost! What a Life! 42

Part 2: The Destruction 51

Chapter 3: Out of Control 52

Chapter 4: Deal with You! 68

Chapter 5: "My Mr. !" 79

Chapter 6: Move Forward! 95

Chapter 7: "If it don't make cents, it don't make sense!" 103

Chapter 8: Loving My Daughter Out Loud: A Mother's Journey 138

Part 3: My Reckoning 145

Chapter 9: Stripped to Rise: My 'Job Season' of Faith, Failure,
and Redemption 146

Chapter 10: From Trumps to Triumph: Finding Your Purpose
in the Journey 167

Part 4: My Purpose Defined 177

Chapter 11: "YOU ARE MORE THAN A CONQUEROR!" 185

Chapter 12: Embracing Deliverance: Living Free From Rejection And Rediscovering Worth 195

Chapter 13: "KEEP ON LIVING!" 200

Chapter 14: "Disciplines of the Heart: Embracing Deliverance and Rejection-Free Living," 204

Chapter 15: Bring It On Home: This Is Where We Come Alive! 236

Epilogue: Building Your Spiritual House 284

Acknowledgements 288

About the AuthoR 291

PREFACE

> *"God is in the midst of her; she shall not be moved:*
> *God shall help her, and that right early."*
> *–Psalm 46:5 (KJV)*

My story can only be told by me! For years, I have struggled with the question, "What is my story?" Before you start wondering about the uncertainty I harbor, let me ask you this: "Have you ever heard things about yourself that have shocked you to the core?" Do you often ask yourself where in the world do they get such information? I've been there and have done that!

The narratives about me that were out there were so convoluted. At times, I couldn't even relate to some of what was being circulated. I would question, "Why are they trying to tell my story?" I recall my grandmother telling someone, "When they tell my story, I hope they tell how good I was to them." My grandmother's sentiment about being remembered for the kindness she showed to others is a touching reminder of how our actions and relationships shape the stories that are told about us. This often makes me think about those who have come and gone in my life over the years and the words that they spoke to slander my character, making me think, *Wow!*

It's not uncommon for others to attempt to tell your story or interpret it in ways that may not align with your own narrative. Just recently, I learned that individuals who were once friends had pulled some inaccurate information about certain things from my professional past. They even spread false narratives and information within various organizations I belong to. What was the reason for broadcasting these false narratives? Do you ever wonder what folks gain from that? Well, I do, and I have spent many restless days wallowing in the pain it induces. This reminds me of yet another incident when a past client conjured up a story and spread it amongst some of our mutual associations. As expected, the rumor spread like cancer. Most of those folks were once friends but no longer, as they chose to believe something that had no truth in it. When I finally processed what the lie was, it hurt me for years that my allies had fallen for such falsities. For the life of me, I am baffled as to why people do that, especially to someone like me, who is extremely transparent about everything in my life.

My grandmother always told me, "You won't have many friends. Look at your right hand and count your fingers. That's the number of real friends you will always have." All those years ago, I didn't understand why she said that, but at 47, I know better. Let me tell you my own story about what I did when I faced such situations. Intrigued? If you have had a sour experience, sit tight and hold it until you reach the end of this book.

I have always been the one to care about what people thought of me or even heard about me. I am not sure about the reasoning behind the sentiment, but it ruined me for years. Now, I can honestly say I have finally been delivered from that spirit. Yes, it's a spirit. God showed me how validation and pleasing others to befriend me was a demonic spirit living within me. Those relationships led to betrayals that were beyond my imagination.

At some point in life, we all have to face people who don't like us. When interacting with such people, you can spend time wondering how to amend things and worrying about the outcome. However, you should never let yourself feel cornered. Stand by your values, and good things will happen. David writes that in times of trouble, God will hide us. Mind you, it doesn't say we won't have troubles. Difficulties may come, but God's promise is that He will shield us from them. He's going to make you invisible to the enemy. He will see us through.

Amidst my crisis, I kept hearing a voice say, "Write the book!" However, self-doubt used to make me question, "How can my story give hope to anyone who has been through multiple hardships?" I have faced way too many adversities over the years. Soon, I realized that the question was not "How big do you see your problem?" but, rather, "How big do you see your God?" Exodus 14:14 says, "The Lord will fight for you; you need only to be still." I know that problems are inevitable. People will spread a lie about you or mistreat you, trying to pull down your confidence. But let me debunk this for you. I have learned over the years that these problems will be a blessing and catapult you to new levels. While I was still trying to weigh the pros and cons of writing the book, I came across the phrase, "**Favor ain't fair.**" Sometimes, you have to go through levels of pain to get to where God needs you to be. That's when the light bulb turned on. If you can just read how someone else got through the sorts, you can be encouraged that your story will change for the better too!

I am here to tell you that Jesus bore your shame in your dire situations and longs to lift your burdens. Though others may look at what you've done or define you based on your past, God sees your inner beauty; that's the real you, my friend. He exchanged your imperfection for his perfection and called you beautiful. You are everything to Him.

The shackles that once bound you to heavy weights of disgrace, guilt, and shame have been unlocked by the kindness of the One with nail-scarred hands. My friends, on this journey, I have learned that you no longer need to carry the stigma of your past. Perfect love has awakened your heart, wiped away your sin, and set you free. Once you embrace the truth of who you are, you won't strive to prove it to anyone; you will be at peace with who you are. You shall be infused with confidence that doesn't need validation from anyone other than our Father in Heaven.

When I started this writing journey in 2017, I thought I could do it because I had just written my almost 400-page dissertation. To get into the groove of writing, I enrolled in multiple book writing classes and hired professionals to assist me with my book. But none of them panned out. I felt discouraged, as I was left with no book. I had penned down portions of the chapters but didn't have anything that was reflective of the vision God gave me. This led to utter disappointment.

There was no motivation behind the story. It wasn't until God began sending destiny partners to guide me that I got serious and started typing. I owe a debt of gratitude to Prophetess Taquila Coleman's book class, "How to Write a Book." It provided the crucial push I needed to complete this book project. Thank you, Prophetess Coleman, for your guidance—without you, I would still have been trying to figure this out.

During the book-writing workshop, the common theme was that writing a book about your life can be a way to engage in self-reflection and gain a deeper understanding of your own experiences, choices, and personal growth. Initially, I wondered why I'd want to revisit past mistakes. Then, the facilitator's words resonated: "Sharing a story can provide a sense of closure and catharsis." I thought, *Ma'am, it's gonna make something rise out of me and knock the hell out of someone!* Then it hit me: *La Shawn, you still have some healing to do!* #Thetriggerwason.

For the past seven years, I've been in a cycle of writing, stopping, and rewriting this book. My inner critic has fueled a pattern of write-stop-delete, as I've struggled to decide what stories to reveal and what secrets to keep. The list goes on! I often asked myself, "What can I safely share with the world? Will this revelation change how people perceive me? Will that honesty offend someone?' Well, it is now 2024. God needed me to write this book in my voice and from my perspective. Honestly, as I wrote, I needed to remind myself that people are not always fascinated by one's story. Instead, they are fascinated by a God who cares about ordinary people, regardless of their circumstances. Writing a book was just not on my to-do list, but I knew that God was testing my obedience. Here I am now, ready to share my personal experiences, struggles, achievements, growth, transformation, and reflections on my journey, hoping that someone will be blessed.

Let's be honest; God said there was a need. He wanted me to share how I overcame my challenges and found my purpose; He wanted me to talk about self-discovery and the importance of faith and perseverance. I am here to remind you that you are in control of your life. No one takes your life from you but you! I don't care if you see things as perfect right now or maybe there are some challenges you are facing. Guess what? Keep on living! Job 22:27 reminds us, "When you pray, God will answer you ..." Jeremiah 33:3 says, "Call to me, and I will answer you and show you great and mighty things, which you do not know."

Various motivations and personal reasons can drive the decision to write a book about your life. However, as you will see, writing this book triggered a lot of emotions in me. This book is raw and may be very difficult to read, but it truly comes from my heart. You may have to put it down a few times, and that is okay, but just be sure to finish it. If you know me personally, you will probably call me and say, "Girl! La Shawn! Say what!" It's like that. I want you to be inspired to share your story with others. Friends, this is my life, my story, for the sole purpose of inspiring you to be intentional about your life and to walk in your purpose. If my experiences can spare you from even a fraction of the trials I faced, I will be deeply blessed. Now, I pass the torch to you. Take hold of your pen and write a story that will illuminate the path for others. I have no doubt that your story will be a beacon of hope, guiding others through life's challenges.

We often hear people say, "Walk in purpose and live the life that you were created for." But how do we know what that is, especially if we have endured so much disappointment, delay, pain, and whatever else over the years? No matter what adversities come your way, know that you have a purpose that must be lived out. If I could change my life, I wouldn't. There would simply be no testimony to bless you with. Quite honestly, I probably wouldn't live such a public life if God didn't save me or use me the way He does.

The year 2023 will forever be etched in my memory as the most challenging season I've ever endured. I honestly believe it was punishment for not walking in the path God prescribed for me, hence the delay in getting this book done. When you're believing for a bigger purpose in life, you've got to go through hell to get there. I recently read the entire book of Job. The book of Job was named after the main character. It is believed that Job lived during the patriarchal period when men had long life spans. In Job 42, we learn that all we go through, lose, and experience is for the greater good. God allowed Satan to test Job's faithfulness. Job lost everything he owned:

animals, children, and even his health. But, eventually, God broke into all the drama and challenged Job and his friends to judge His sovereign will. In the end, God graciously restored to Job all he had lost and even more. The message is simple: no matter how terrible the suffering, we are to cling to our hope in the Lord and never lose faith. God uses suffering to purify His children.

As God works in our lives, let us surrender to His sovereign will, trusting with unwavering certainty that He refines us like gold. As Job declared, "When He hath tried me, I shall come forth as gold" (Job 23:10). Upon reading this scripture, I heard God say to me, "It is time."

You have to trust the process and understand that your plan isn't God's plan. May we emerge from the refining fire with faith renewed and hearts transformed.

THE D.I.V.A. HERSELF

I knew that *The D.I.V.A. Herself* was the most appropriate title for my first book. And this is just the beginning—more books are on the horizon. I have always been known as the DIVA of all things: spreading love, serving, and making people happy. I love entertaining, supporting, and helping others. To begin, D.I.V.A. is an acronym that represents a Divinely Inspired, Victoriously Anointed woman of God. When people hear me say DIVA, they immediately think it is derogatory or negative, especially the saints. They will tear you down over the word DIVA. However, I'm here to redefine what it means to be a DIVA. Far from being derogatory, being a DIVA embodies wonderful qualities: strength, resilience, faith, and inspiration. To me, being a DIVA represents the epitome of biblical femininity, as described in Proverbs 31. Being a DIVA is about living a life of purpose, integrity, and compassion—a life that honors God and inspires others.

Proverbs 31 provides a comprehensive portrait of a godly woman, outlining qualities like wisdom, kindness, and faithfulness. Initially, I felt overwhelmed, believing that failing to embody every trait would disqualify me from God's blessings. Years of reading this passage left me feeling discouraged, focusing on my shortcomings. However, as my relationship with God deepened, I gained a new perspective. I realized that this woman is an aspirational figure, a model of godly character, not a benchmark for perfection. Embracing this truth freed me to celebrate my unique strengths and those of other women, recognizing that our diversity is a reflection of God's creative design. One day, while studying the passage, I heard God say, "You are you, and that's a good thing. I will work with you and in you so the qualities shown will become an integral part of who you are.

Don't expect perfection; strive for daily progress and ever-growing maturity. In times past, my prayer was always, "God, work diligently in me so that I can come close to the woman you have called me to be." Coming into my full self, early-40s, I accepted the woman who God called me to be. I set out with attributes that I knew I wanted to be known for. God made me trustworthy, resourceful, hardworking, industrious, entrepreneurial, business-minded, compassionate, generous, wise, prudent, family-centered, and—most importantly—fearful of Him. These were things I prayed to be. I didn't have the privilege of growing up with positive role models or experiences that people often talk about. Yet, deep within me burned a desire for something more. But how could I become what I'd never seen? How could I achieve what I didn't know existed?

As I matured and grew in my purpose, I felt an inner nudging that there was something else that I needed to put a stamp on my calling. Someone from my past gave me the brand name "The Global Strategist." I wasn't quite sure how I would fit into this name. The name was derived from my many talents and how I navigate a global platform. But after much prayer, I quickly figured out the multi-talented woman behind The Global Strategist brand. These varied and diverse talents have led me to become a serial entrepreneur:

- I am the CEO of Divine Diva Events and Travel. I have been a wedding and event planner for 30 years, establishing a legacy of exceptional service that leaves lasting memories. I literally started planning events as a senior in high school. I added travel to my brand shortly after hosting my 40th birthday in Cabo.
- I am the CEO of Diva's Fabulous Fixins'. During the holidays, I prepare side dishes, desserts, and breads. Cooking has become my therapeutic outlet, helping me cope with life's losses and nourishing my soul. This tradition reminds me that even in darkness, there's always something to be grateful for, and sharing love through food brings light to those around me. #SheCooks.
- I am the CEO of Dr. La Shawn Denise Witt. I am a well-noted transformational speaker, engaging mistress of ceremonies, and highly sought keynote speaker, captivating audiences with impactful messages and unforgettable experiences. Adding to my distinguished portfolio, I am now an accomplished and best-selling author. My words have the power to shape realities, and I boldly speak things into existence—a principle you'll learn more about within these pages of this book.
- I am the CEO of My Sister's Keeper Ministries. This is my ministry, where I host the annual "Wonder Woman Conference." Soon, I will be breaking ground on my transitional housing project, Charity House. This is the legacy that I have prayed to birth in honor of my father, who has a passion for ministering on skid row, and my mother, who has a passion for ministering to drug addicts. I am also passionate about ministering to women who, like me, are on their second chance of life. Lastly, committed to serving the vulnerable, I've launched Rahab's Daughter, a community outreach program in

Los Angeles, specifically ministering to sex workers on Figueroa Street. Our mission is to offer hope, resources, a supportive community, and a path to restoration.

Just recently, I launched Witt & Associates, LLC. I am a consultant to non-profits, school districts, and churches. I possess strong administrative skills, enabling me to effectively support diverse groups and audiences. **At Witt & Associates, I focus on leadership training and personal development, especially for women and professionals in educational settings. I approach each client providing tools, strategies, and mindset shifts necessary to lead themselves first, empowering them to then lead others effectively. It's about fostering a growth mindset, resilience, and clarity of purpose—key principles that we instill in our workshops and coaching programs.**

As you can see, The Global Strategist is a visionary serial entrepreneur with a multitude of passions and gifts, connecting with people worldwide to fulfill God's purpose. At the end of the book, I share how all of this builds the brand of where my passion lies. In addition, I have four degrees, the highest of which is a doctorate. But what does this all mean? As we navigate my journey together, you'll discover the intersection of faith, education, and entrepreneurship and how these elements have shaped my life.

God's instruction to write a book was swiftly followed by a cascade of prophetic declarations. The message was clear and consistent: the stories, wisdom, and insights within me were destined for print. The reverberating call to authorship left no doubt—I was to share the books God had placed in my heart. I spent time praying and fasting regarding this book, and as I mentioned earlier, even starting it and stopping it over the years. I was pondering how to share and be open about who I am and my life as I have come to realize and understand it. However, with humility and obedience, I surrendered to God's call, embracing the journey of authorship as a sacred trust. My desire is that my vulnerability will inspire others to embrace their own authenticity, recognizing the beauty in imperfection and the power of resilience.

For the purposes of this book, I am La Shawn, not Dr. La Shawn, not Dr. Witt. I have been through many different and difficult seasons, and I have come to hold my head high despite those things. I am not proud of all my decisions, but I am thankful for the experiences. I try to stay humble with those things I am proud of so as to always stay low before God. As I began to deal with becoming the woman I am today, there were layers of things that had to be peeled back and removed from me.

In May 2023, my life changed. God shut me all the way down for over a year and stripped me of everything I thought defined me and brought value to my life. I knew it was time to really live the life that He called me to fully. Disobedience sent me into a season where I was all alone and shut in the house for months, with not a soul to speak into my life, direct me, guide me, advise me on what I should do, etc. All I could do was hear from God. It made sense why this book was delayed and why it was written in this season. I had another season to go through before I could really share and birth breakthroughs with those I would have a voice to speak audibly to or by written word.

In this most recent season, God took me through another level of purging in relationships that I had built recently. These were relationships that I valued and held in high esteem. However, I didn't quite think some were just for a season. God showed me that some relationships had reached their seasonal endpoint, and it was time to reassess and adjust my connections. A few of them should have never happened. I had entrusted intimate spaces to people who were siphoning my spiritual energy and anointing, contrary to God's will. I was in a place where I was trying to draw from them in order to make moves in my life for places that God was positioning me for. Did I seek God to establish these relationships? Clearly, I didn't because they are no longer in their respective positions. As God took me through my most recent season, I understood why I was rescued. Oftentimes, you reflect the community of people that are around you. I was being groomed to make moves, but those folks weren't adding to that preparation. You can only receive from others based on where they are in their journey. Sometimes, individuals cannot pour into you due to their own struggles, insecurities, or limitations. In the simple words of my uncle, "They ain't got no stroke!" This is why it is important to surround yourself with people who inspire and uplift you; don't be afraid to seek mentors or a community that can provide spiritual nourishment.

Over the years, in my 20s and 30s, I was shy and hidden because of what I was dealing with. I mastered hiding the real me from people. I lied my way out of many things and lived a life of walking out the door with it all together and crying myself to sleep almost daily. Who was I? Broken, empty, and far from purpose. With everything I've gone through, I look at my life now and see a vision of a trophy–it's been one triumph after another. I see gold medals, someone who has the victory. My transformation began when I hit rock bottom. It was the beliefs I held about myself during that darkest hour that sparked an inner triumph, propelling me toward breakthroughs and purpose. This journey ultimately set my life on a path of self-discovery, revealing the true meaning and potential that lay within me. Often, we struggle to make sense of our struggles, wondering, "Why did I endure that?" and "How did I end up here?" But in the midst of chaos, it's challenging to see the bigger picture—the intricate tapestry of life's seasons, each woven together to shape us into who we're meant to be. Let me tell you that what you have been through is for someone else. Your biggest testimony will free the very people who will be called to you. You will triumph over all that you have encountered.

My life is about perseverance, the sacrifices I made when I did not have the wisdom to choose better, and how God restored me. There were different seasons where I constantly did things for others to validate myself, them, and the nature of our relationship. I have pushed and pulled on relationships that I thought I needed to get me to the next stage of my life. I have forced relationships because I did not know the perfect love of God and did not love myself. I have come to realize that life is so much better when you seek to remain in God's love and love yourself. Don't get me wrong; I have made mistakes along this new journey, but keeping God at the helm allows me to seek Him before investing in relationships that are not good for me.

Over the years, I masked my pain a lot through spending money. I bought myself things I could not afford or did not truly need. Not only did I buy them for myself, but I bought them for others as well because that was my way of persuading people to be my friend; that was my way of hiding (like I was so accustomed to doing since childhood) behind and falling victim to the pride of life and vanity. I had become successful and made good money, but still, I was so bitter that I could not truly enjoy my money. Instead, I had a dis-ease, a displeasure deep within that caused me to be wasteful and vain. This dis-ease made it difficult for me to enjoy life and the things God had blessed me with. I had no peace. I used money as a form of masking and hiding, and I truly did not believe my life had much value. According to Ecclesiastes 6:1–2 (NKJV), "There is an evil which I have seen under the sun, and it is common among men. A man to whom God has given riches, wealth, and honor, so that he lacks nothing for himself of all he desires; yet God does not give him power to eat of it, but a foreigner consumes it. This is vanity, and it is an evil affliction."

There is something about believing you have value simply because Jesus exchanged His life for yours. No number of accomplishments can give our lives greater value than the love of Christ, and no amount of sin can lessen the value of our lives because the only prerequisite we need is the love of Christ. Because I had not yet reached this breakthrough, I made a lot of monetary decisions to earn a place in people's lives and prove to myself that I belonged. I borrowed money that I didn't have, bought men things just so they would be with me, opened a lot of credit card accounts and maxed them out, hosted extravagant parties, purchased cars for men, gave expensive gifts to people, etc. You name it; I did it all. I felt like I had to buy these things so that people could see what I wanted them to see. The point of hiding behind money was to lie about who I really was to obstruct the view of my dis-ease about life. When we fail to uncover the truth of God's perspective on our lives, we miss out on the transformative evidence of faith that brings clarity and purpose to our experiences. The evidence of faith is the hope that God has for us. It is the hope of God and hope in God that causes us to believe that our lives are good, and we then begin to search out the good, which is God, in our lives. When you seek God with your whole heart, you will find Him and begin to uncover the treasure—the value—that is in your life.

God has graciously given me a second chance at life. He has restored my life, brought order to my mind, and begun bringing correction to wrong thought patterns that kept me in a self-sabotaging cycle. Now, I am happy to say I have steady multiple income streams. I'm taking control of my finances by saving and investing, steadily paying off debt, and committed to avoiding past financial pitfalls. I believe I have a gift of giving; I give money freely. If there is a ministry, organization, or cause that I feel prompted to support, I have no problem with giving. If you know me, you know that I am a giver. But I have now learned how to say "No" or not be bullied into giving money away. My parents always got on me about being a giver. I would give my lunch money away at school. I would steal food from the cafeteria and feed the homeless when I got off the school bus. One time, my mother bought me a new pack of underwear; I took them to school to give to my friend because she needed underwear.

The power that the love of money once had over me is broken because I know who I am and who God is. I am not rich yet, but I am proud of where I am, and the fact that I am now a good steward of my finances and able to give to others is a major accomplishment that I thought I would never see. Now, as I reflect on life, I thank God for what I was able to accomplish, the beauty that came from the ashes.

After a seven-year journey and a three-year hiatus of being kicked out of my doctoral program, I pushed through and received my doctorate. I grew in management in my professional career and job. I've uncovered another precious aspect of my identity—I am an intercessor, blessed with a depth and richness that comes solely from God. I have developed a love for talking to God. I enjoy praying for God's people. I consider that an accomplishment because I acquired this special ability through the goodness of God. I stumbled upon this fulfillment accidentally. It wasn't something I put on a vision board or petitioned God for; instead, it was birthed in me because that is what God hoped for me and said was good for me. The mere fact that I had the courage to chase after God's righteousness is, in itself, an accomplishment. It shows I had a genuine longing, and now, I reap the ultimate reward: being satisfied and filled with His goodness. "Blessed are those who hunger and thirst for righteousness, for they will be filled" (Matthew 5:6, NIV). He filled me.

One of my most cherished accomplishments to date is becoming a mother and nurturing an amazing daughter. Morgan is my pride and joy! I had my daughter at the young age of 20. At that point in time, it was very difficult for me because my dad was an assistant pastor and a law enforcement officer. I was also a student at a PWI (Predominantly White Institution), so it was a very shameful experience. People always told me that I had ruined my life and that my dreams were over. They also told me that I wasn't going to amount to anything. I absolutely love my daughter. She is my heart. We grew up together. I sometimes felt like I wasn't the best mom because I was in school at night, worked three jobs, and had to get people to watch my daughter while I took care of things. I felt as though I neglected her because life had to keep going, but I believe and know that I love my daughter and tried my best to do right by her and give her the life she deserves. I never told her "No." Oftentimes, at night, I'd just hold my daughter and cry because I was trying so hard to do the right thing, as I was learning along the way.

To see my daughter bloom into the bold, beautiful, and compassionate woman she is today fills my heart with awe and gratitude. I'm humbled and grateful to have been entrusted with the privilege of guiding and nurturing her on her journey. I love my baby girl publicly and proudly and believe that her life's journey is a testament to who God has called her to be. Nothing compares to a mother's love for her child. My daughter is so intelligent and outgoing. Those who know and follow me can attest to the fact that we are a dynamic mother-and-daughter duo. I am grateful for the work God has begun in my daughter because He is faithful and just to complete it, and I am thankful for who I have become because He entrusted her to me. I will be sharing more about my daughter later in this book.

I want to remind you that you are in control. No one takes your life from you but you! So, decide to keep on living. The Bible says it's the glory of God to conceal a thing, but the honor of kings is to seek it out. You are royalty, so seek it out! Seek out the meaning of your life. Seek out the purpose of your life.

There is an "after this." This is not the end. God will restore and keep you. I speak to the conqueror in you. You are more than a conqueror through Christ Jesus. You have to keep going because you have a story to tell (testimony). This is not how the story ends. You have to persevere, stay faithful, and keep on living. Move on! How long are you going to dwell on this mountain? You have to tell yourself how you want to feel. Elijah was at the tree, and God came to him and told him to eat because the journey was long (1 Kings 19:7).

God finds you wherever you are, even if you feel that no one notices how much you are suffering right now. No matter how imprisoned you are, you are loved by someone who cares about your freedom—and makes freedom possible. Many people don't know what you've been through, but the God you serve is mighty! He is faithful to restore and prosper you. My prayer for you at this time is that God blesses you so exponentially, so abundantly, that your mind is blown, and you know that He truly loves you and wants to bless you! Everyone will see the blessing in your life and will know you received your miracles.

Just so you know, this book details my journey woven with challenges and triumphs. Throughout these pages, you will find song lyrics, quotes, decrees, scriptures, and prayers that have sustained me during difficult times. I also outline the plan that has guided me through various aspects of my life. I wanted to share, but I also wanted to teach my audience. What is a book if you don't learn from it? You will discover the principles I built upon and the lessons I learned through my experiences with the Bible and heartfelt prayer. It is my hope that these reflections and insights will minister to you in your time of need or resonate with someone you may share this with.

Now, it's time to tell my story! I want you to hear someone being transparent about their life without shame. My journey has helped me evolve into the 47-year-old woman I am today, and my life is good. My life is beautiful. I know this because God is good. I hope my story will change your life. God is good. He has given you a purpose, and your duty as royalty is to seek it out. I survived my mess, and now I have a beautiful, one-of-a-kind life! That's why I know how important it is for me to tell my story to you. It hasn't been easy. There was a lot of processing that needed to be done. I am not by far perfect, but I am healed, whole, and a conqueror. If you're reading this book, then God has given me something for you, and you have now been invited to seek it out. Let me remind you again … there is an end. Enjoy!

MY LIFE

If there were a theme song for my life, it would be "My Life" by Mary J. Blige. Originally released in 1994, this song literally saved my life. My iTunes play count says that, as of date, I have played this song 1,706 times. As I journeyed through some of the many adversities of my life, this song was my guiding light; its lyrics spoke directly to my heart, mirroring my struggles and offering comfort. This is a confirmation that life is shaped by the choices we make and how we respond to difficult moments. Let me break down the revelation I received from the lyrics of the song:

1. **Overcoming challenges with authenticity**: The lyrics emphasize not pretending or hiding your feelings when you're feeling down. This connected with my journey of embracing my truth, acknowledging my feelings, and seeking genuine growth, even through those tough times.
2. **Finding inner peace and trusting in faith**: The song guided me to be true to myself and let go of negativity so that I would find peace. It highlighted the importance of spiritual grounding—trusting God ("the Man up above") to provide love and peace. Faith helped me to navigate my path and find peace within myself.

3. **Taking life one day at a time**: The lyrics reminded me to take my time and not rush, acknowledging that everyone struggles. I am no different. This aligned with my diverse roles—running multiple businesses, empowering women, applying for various leadership roles, and managing my personal life. It's a reminder that progress is a journey, and patience is key.

4. **Hope and resilience**: The repetition of "If you looked in my life and see what I've seen" spoke to the idea that others may not fully understand your experiences, but there's resilience and hope that comes from knowing your own story. Know that you've seen challenges but also found strength in your purpose and faith.

5. **Encouragement to keep moving forward**: The song's message of hope—trusting in a higher power, believing things will turn out fine, and moving forward with faith and determination—mirrors my own commitment to personal growth, leadership, and transformative change in life and work.

I found comfort when I acknowledged that my life encountered some difficulties and challenges. I realized that everyone encounters struggles. Throughout the song, there is a sense of personal growth and resilience. As a lifelong Mary J. Blige fan, I was surprised by how profoundly this song spoke to my soul, offering comfort and solace during a challenging season. It brought self-empowerment, personal healing, and the desire to live a more meaningful and authentic life. Thank you, Mary J. Blige.

Part 1

LIL' SHAWNIE

Chapter 1

HEY, SHAWNIE!

> *"For I know the plans I have for you, declared the Lord, plans for welfare and not for evil, to give you a future and a hope."* —Jeremiah 29:11 (ESV)

Going to grandma's house on the weekend was one of my favorite memories as a little girl. What I didn't know then was that those memories would carry me through many life experiences that I would eventually face as an adult. Who would have thought those warm memories would comfort me in my times of loneliness and grief? Like most of you reading this book, I can recall many childhood memories that bring comfort to me. Wait ... let me first introduce you to this bundle of joy.

Anticipation filled the air as my loved ones eagerly awaited my arrival. I was their precious little one and already the apple of my father's eye, the joy of my mother's love, my grandmother's sweet delight, and my big brothers' cherished "chocolate angel." I was born 10 lbs and 21 ½ inches long on Monday, January 3rd, 1977, shortly after 2 PM, to the union of

Willie Joe Witt and Sharon Denise Ratliff-Witt. I was their firstborn together but Willie's third child.

My mother kept copious notes in my baby book, and just recently, I took the time to read through them and was amazed to learn so many things about baby me. As I read through the book, I felt the excitement that my mother once had when she birthed me; the excitement that I felt could have helped me in the younger parts of my life. The excitement that I often yearn for.

Let me share some highlights with you: I laughed when I was 1 week old; I turned over at one month old; my ears were pierced at two months; I sat up at four months; I crawled backward at five months; I was hospitalized at five months for two days due to pneumonia. I took my first step in my walker at six months; I walked at almost 12 months. A very ambitious, talkative, and independent me.

I learned I was christened at six months on the 3rd of July by Rev Stafford at Mt. Tabor Baptist church. I was blessed to have Charles and Luvenia Ballance as my godparents. I received my potty chair on September 28th; I sat down and took my first pee at 5 PM. Of course, I first learned to say "Da-da-da-da" at six months, and at seven months, I said "Mama," "Hi-hi!" and "Bye-bye." At almost four months old, I took my first flight—United Airlines Flight 896—to Birmingham, Alabama, where I would spend 10 days getting to know my father's family. Wow, my mother really documented everything. I am very thankful for these memories, as I don't recall much of that part of my life. Special thanks to my mother for recording this information.

In one of my baby books, my mother recorded everyone who came to see me. Wow, I was so popular at one week old. Later in the book, my mother wrote that I enjoyed ice, beer, and wine ... Um, OK! Mommy and Daddy, before I was even one-year-old? I also read that my favorite pet was

Michelle. I remember her. My favorite toy was an elephant and the telephone. How significant! OK, enough with doting on my first year of life.

I was a well-behaved girl with pigtails down my back, always tied in ribbons. But beneath my demure exterior, I wore matching Wonder Woman underwear. I talked all day and never quieted. I was a very inquisitive girl who loved to read and play with dolls and stuffed animals. I had an imagination out of this world. I could talk anyone out of anything that I wanted. Believe me, it's no secret that talking too much has been a challenge for me. My report cards from Del Amo Elementary School and Carnegie Junior High School stated, "Talks too much." A teacher once told me that she had never seen a black person who talked so much. I never forgot that comment. But talking too much would eventually lead to how I birthed my purpose out of pain because I survived my mess, and we all know that yesterday did not kill me.

According to Auntie Mona, my family has affectionately called me Shawnie since I was a baby. Only a handful of people address me as Shawnie. They are special, and I will always answer to that name. Auntie Mona gave me the name La Shawn (named after a friend of hers at the time of my birth), and Denise is the middle name I share with my mother.

La Shawn means "God is gracious," and Denise means "Dedicated to God." I stand proud to use my full name. People often ask me why I use my entire name. The reason is that I am proud to be La Shawn Denise Witt, as you can see. When you hear that name, you will know I am a woman of determination. I must admit here that if you know me well, I am adamant that you better spell La Shawn correctly. Yes,
La Shawn is two words. If I have had to correct you on my name, you already know. If you continue to misspell it, I just don't respond.

Oh, how I miss my grandmother so much! She was fondly called Ms. Josephine. She was simply my rock! A very sweet and kind lady who lived on 43rd Place off of Figueroa in the middle of the block. To be exact, 612 W. 43rd Place, Los Angeles, CA 90037. When I have moments, I drive down the block, park, and cry. I talk to her as if she were right here with me, listening. I find myself talking to others just as she did. That lady was something else. The memories of spending time with my grandmother have never left me.

Memories of my childhood are filled with laughter and playtime with our beloved family dogs: Tasha and Chanel, our Cocker Spaniels, and Ginger—a lively poodle mix. I cherished walking down 43rd Place to visit Cousin Ding-Ding. Afternoons were spent watering our lawn and sharing stories with Ms. Hogan, our friendly next-door neighbor. And what better way to cap off a sunny day than with an ice cream cone from Thrifty's? Three scoops of Cookies & Cream was our favorite ice cream order! My grandmother would sometimes send me down to Thrifty's to get the ice cream myself. I remember my long legs in shorts skipping down the street. With quarters and nickels clutched tightly in my hand, I felt unstoppable, ready to make what seemed like the most epic purchase of my life.

People nearby knew that I was Ms. Josephine's grandbaby. They would wave and say, "Hey, Shawnie!" 43rd place knew who I was. Even the lady behind the counter at Jack-in-the-Box at the corner knew who I was. Chicken strips and orange soda were a big treat for me. Now, I cannot stand to eat at that place. Writing this paragraph, I busted into an ugly cry. I miss that lady so, so much. Words cannot express how her death still hits, as if she left me yesterday. It's been 28 years. Whoever said you get over death shortly after obviously lied.

My grandma was the secretary at Paradise Baptist Church. Everybody loved her. I would go to work with her and spend hours immersed in her crossword puzzle books while she attended to her duties. I sometimes got a chance to sort the copies or carry things and put them away.

At eight years old, I loved working with my grandma. She was a servant and loved to give. She retired from the county of Los Angeles after many years of working there. She was a no-nonsense woman who wouldn't tolerate foolishness from anyone. Honestly, I don't even think I ever saw my grandmother get angry. Folks knew not to try her. She always said, "God don't like ugly, and He ain't too fond of pretty." As I write this chapter, I see so many parallels between us. If you met her today, she would say, "Boy, that Shawnie talks so much, but she is so smart and helpful; she makes me so proud." Yes, that was her. She could talk on the phone all day to Ding-Ding, Ms. Mingo, and V'essa, just to name a few. Everybody loved talking to her.

My grandma was a prayer warrior and sharpshooter who could dress herself off. Her wardrobe was a treasure trove of luxury: feathered hats, extravagant headpieces, tailored suits, dazzling diamonds, and designer labels like Anne Klein and Gucci—she had it all. She was neat and organized. Her clothes lined up in the closet by color, even as she got older. Today, I arrange my drawers just as she used to. She was also a phenomenal cook. Honestly, I think you'd struggle to beat her in a cooking competition—she was that good. I always said I was her favorite, but I'm everybody's favorite—the favorite daughter, sister, granddaughter, and niece. If you knew my grandma, you truly knew how much she loved me.

Most weekends with Grandma Josephine always included a trip to Nordstrom, Robinson's May, Bullock's, or somewhere fancy to get a dress and cute patent leather shoes for church on Sunday. If I were lucky, a matching purse would end up in the shopping bag. I saw myself excited for Sundays. Sunday School was the place to show off your new outfit. In my mind, I would be the best-dressed kid in Sunday School. Matching ribbons and balls on my long ponytails.

We would often catch the bus downtown if Auntie Mona (Mom's baby sister) couldn't take us. Auntie Mona had a white Nissan 280ZX. I always cherished lying down in the hatchback. Believe me, it was the spot to be! My grandmother never learned to drive, but we always made it to where we needed to be. As a matter of fact, Uncle Maurice (Mom's older brother) or my father would sometimes pick us up and take us to Fedco and a few other places I can't recall. All her children—Gregory (d), Maurice, Sharon, Anton, and Mona—made sure that if she needed to go somewhere, she got there with me (her Shawnie) in tow.

Sunday mornings, before service at Paradise Baptist Church, included breakfast with the best biscuits. My favorite was the Knott's Berry Farm apricot or strawberry jelly. I only wanted the Knott's brand; she couldn't get me to try anything else. I loved to sit in the kitchen and watch her cook. I just hated eating those peas, yuck! She made the best breakfast. I think my grandma was the only person to scramble eggs in bacon grease. I learned it from her and still do that to this day. I always wanted to stir, taste, or do whatever she would allow me to do. As a matter of fact, I was her cooking assistant. I'd sit there while she cooked. She always did one of four things while she cooked: dragged that house phone (213-234-7339) to the kitchen to talk to her buddies, did her crossword puzzles, read her Sunday school lesson or *Our Daily Bread*, or talked to herself—I would later learn she was praying. Little did I know that this experience would lay the groundwork for my future endeavor—Diva's Fabulous Fixins'.

As I cook for people during the holidays, it reminds me of being in the kitchen with my grandmother. As her little helper, I watched and learned as she cooked, and those moments remain etched in my memory. To this day, I still remember how she prepared food. I have done my best to write out recipes from my memory, and I prepared dishes over and over again until I got them right. I thank my grief therapist for helping me transform the pain of losing my grandmother into a meaningful connection that sustains me until we meet again. She helped me find solace in memories and recipes, keeping Grandma's legacy alive.

Memories of my grandmother's relentless prayer life remain sharp in my mind. She prayed all the time. I would hear her pray, and the things she prayed for seemed so general. I can remember her saying prayers that were quick and short. I would also listen to her pray; I don't think she ever knew I was paying attention. She would pray, "Lord, please fix it. Amen!" And that was it. I would later understand that one of the scriptures she quoted often was 1 Thessalonians 5:17, "Pray without ceasing." The Bible that sat on her nightstand has found a new home on my nightstand ever since she died in 1996. She had this very scripture circled with many stains on the page. As early as five years old, she instilled in me that prayer was the answer to everything. It took me over 30 years later to figure that out. I now know that I am called to be an intercessor. Without prayer, I don't think you would be reading my story. You will often find me out shopping and just praying out loud. You can see me walking through the airport, speaking in my heavenly language. I promise it keeps me sane—not too many things can keep me from knocking someone out these days.

During my childhood, I had to endure many difficult situations. I didn't know them to be difficult until I began experiencing certain issues in my late teens and early adulthood. As a child, I grew up in a two-parent family home with my brother, Kevin. I had the best life—caring parents, aunts, uncles, and grandparents who nurtured me. My father had two older sons, William(d) and Jon—affectionately known as Jo-Jo and Jonny. I didn't see them much as a child, but eventually, we grew closer in my teens. They would visit sometimes when their mother allowed them. Jonny would eventually come to live with us when I was in high school. I was the only girl ... you know, the favorite daughter and sister. I know it makes no sense, but listen, they all have me spoiled. What do you expect? (My brother Jo-Jo passed before the release of this book. He said he couldn't wait for my book to come out and promised to be the first one to purchase it.)

Growing up, I was very excited to have two big brothers. Unfortunately, the parentals had complications when we were young, but we got it together as adults. My younger brother Kevin remains my pride and joy. He really is the opposite of me, but we are two peas in a pod. As teenagers, we fought and hated each other. Now we're besties. I love my Kevin Anton (he will kill me for saying his middle name).

Christmas was lit. I felt like Santa outdid himself when he got to our house. I always left cookies for him because those Barbie gifts were a sight to see. Yes, I believed in Santa Claus until I was probably about 12. Please don't ask me why. I also believed in the tooth fairy. My parents will share with you that one year, I ran downstairs and told them I saw and heard Santa on a sleigh passing our house. I often wondered where that came from. The Easter Bunny left lots of money. I was the one known by my friends for devising a plan to help them pull their teeth out.

We had family gatherings and holiday parties at our house. Oh, those house parties that my father and mother hosted! If you were invited to 1454 E. 220th Street in Carson, you were sure to have a good time. Mom could cook too, but I am not sure if she could cook as well as Grandma. Those parties were fun—well, for the adults. I can remember being upstairs with my little brother, Kevin, hanging over the banister, peeking—when we should have been sleeping. People were booed up, kissing and dancing to the sounds of Johnnie Taylor, Marvin Gaye, and Johnny "Guitar" Watson (Mommy's favorites). They were also drinking, smoking cigarettes, and doing whatever else they pleased. You already know! I still remember my mom's words, "Shawnie, you and Kevin, go upstairs to your room!"

The Ratliffs, Butlers, and Witts knew how to host a function. Now, those of you who know me know that this is why I have always loved hosting events at my house. I got it from my family. (My family, friends, all of my aunts and uncles, when you read this, you will remember we could throw a party!!) One memory that sits with them is "nosey Shawnie." I was always in everybody's business. I laugh because this looks different today but not too far from the truth. They will tell you, "Shawnie talks too much, and Shawnie is very nosey." But one thing they can all say is, "If you want something done or need to know something, call Shawnie. She will get it done!"

We had family gatherings and holiday parties. In my mind, my parents had a great relationship, but my mom would eventually struggle with a drug addiction. I pray that my mother will one day write her own story. It has taken her a while to speak publicly about her past, but her testimony is one of the strongest testimonies out there. I am proud that she overcame her drug addiction almost 28 or so years ago. It was very difficult for my father to deal with. I can recall many family therapy sessions and visiting my mom at various drug rehabilitation centers. I watched my parents' marriage erode right in front of my eyes due to her addiction. I always begged Daddy not to leave Mommy. I would call Grandma and say, "Please, pray for Mommy and Daddy; they have to stay together." My mother tells her testimony best, but she doesn't know that I am so grateful that she is here today to walk in her purpose. (Fun fact: My mother still calls me "Boom Boom." At 47, why does she still call me that? Hopefully, she will finally stop calling me that when I get married. God! I can't imagine my husband hearing my mother call me that.)

I appreciate having Willie Joe as my father. He is my number one fan. He listens to me, my bold ideas, my rants, my desires, etc. However, he expects to give you his wise counsel and that you will listen. My father has always been a great example of what my husband should be. I do believe most daddy girls feel this way. I'm grateful to be his favorite and only daughter. I appreciate the sacrifices he continues to make even to this day, ensuring I am well taken care of.

My parents' divorce had a huge impact on me. No matter how many times my dad shuffled us to see the therapist, nothing helped. I would cry all the time; it really hurt me. This is the first time I have admitted to how that made me feel. I was very embarrassed to tell my friends that my father moved out. I would make up lies about how my father had to go and do police work and would be gone for a while. My father worked for the sheriff's department. He retired as a lieutenant. I remember calling my dad every day at work, and on the other end of the phone, I would hear, "Lt. Witt, your daughter is on the phone." I was so special to everyone.

Kevin and I lived with our mother when my parents first split up. I watched my mother battle depression, and life just stopped for her. My mother worked for the County of Los Angeles as well. She was a keypunch operator. She would eventually become a stay-at-home mom. She did her best and really tended to her two children, but eventually, her drug addiction would win. Above all, she was a good mother and did her best to provide a good home. Kevin and I had everything that we needed. We lacked nothing except a happy home with both our parents. Sleepovers were often at my house. Everyone loved coming to my house. We played games; we stayed up all night watching scary movies. Mom would cook big feasts. Those sleepovers were everything. You haven't been to a slumber party unless you came to the ones my parents allowed me to host at our family home.

Fast forward, in addition to drug abuse, my mother also struggled with mental health issues, which made her "check out" of life from time to time. I began having to care for my mother because I didn't want anyone to know that she was sick and had drug issues. While my friends spent quality time with their families, I finally realized that I no longer had two parents in the home. What would people think of me? I felt ashamed and embarrassed. I remember one incident when my mother had a nervous breakdown while I had friends over. I panicked and became terrified because I didn't know how to explain it to my friends, and I didn't know what they were going to think of me. People began talking about me at school and calling my mother crazy. I would run to the bathroom and cry. I knew my mom wasn't crazy; she just wasn't well. Although I did not fully understand what was wrong, I knew God was going to heal her because my grandmother told me so.

My mother was exposed to drugs in her earlier years. However, I can remember growing up, my mother always told me and my brother to stay away from drugs. In junior high school, I had friends who smoked marijuana. I was always scared when I saw them smoke; I saw firsthand how it destroyed my family. Today, I still fear drugs. Many of my friends and even students tease me because I always tell them I never did drugs. I got tricked into eating some gummy edibles. I will let my best friend Stephanie explain that story. Never again will I try that! I just couldn't allow myself to become involved with something that had torn my family apart. I equated drugs to making one crazy. I knew it just wasn't for me.

The divorce was so hard to understand. The days of my grandmother praying became useless. I was mad at God. Dad left, and that was it. My family was destroyed, and nothing would ever be the same. Shortly after, my mom's drug addiction got out of control. My mother always thought we didn't see her use drugs, and she would always deny being high. I saw my mother use them on several occasions. I also knew when she was under the influence. I would just look at my mom and repeat the prayer that I heard my grandmother say, "Lord, fix my mommy." My grandma would get on the floor and talk to God about my mother. So, I began to mimic her because I felt powerless and desperately wanted to help my mom. It was difficult to watch her struggle, but I was determined to save her.

I would call my father and tell him that my mom was high. I always blamed him for her drug use because he left her. I was a child, and that was how I processed everything happening. Then, there were days when I would blame myself for my mother's drug addiction. I would go to school and figure out how I could get an award or do things so that my teacher could call home to let my mother know that I had achieved something that would make her proud. Maybe with that call, my mother would stop the drugs. Sometimes, I would go to the park and hope for someone to kidnap me—maybe if I were kidnapped, it could get my mother's attention. I would even come up with plans to run away from home. I just knew I needed to do something to get her attention so that she would not do drugs. I attempted several times to run away but it never worked.

After a while, my father had had enough. He took us from my mom and raised us. I did not want to go live with my dad. Who was going to take care of my mommy? Who was going to save her? Who was going to get her out of the crack houses? In my mind, nobody could save my mother. I felt disgusted because I didn't feel that I had the power to save her. My father continued to help my mother by encouraging her to go to a drug rehabilitation center. I knew it wasn't going to work because she had been there before. I went through a season of hating my father. I once told him, "You said you love God, but you left Mommy."

When my parents finally got the divorce, my father moved out permanently, and my mother took on the job of raising us by herself. Her drug addiction got out of control, so my brother and I would go back and forth between my grandmother and my father. I experienced a lot of self-esteem issues, as I felt like I wasn't good enough because my mother wasn't present in my life. I began to withdraw from friendships and lie about my mother's whereabouts. This was the beginning of me creating another world with my lies and learning how to mask things and "show up" in whatever way protected me but hindered people from finding out the truth about my mom. I recall sneaking out of the house and walking the streets at night "to go save Mommy." There were a couple of nights I was on a quest to find my mother. I'd go to the crack houses that I knew on my street, desperately trying to save my mother. I don't think my father ever knew about this, but my grandmother did when she caught me attempting to leave her house one night. I didn't know where I was going, but I was determined to save my mom. I didn't care what it took. I knew my mother was out there somewhere. I hadn't seen her for weeks. She needed me to save her. I remember finding her passed out in the den one night. She looked disgusted and defeated, and it broke my heart. What happened to her? Why was I once the joy of her heart but could not make her stop the drugs? This was the point where I developed a false identity that caused me to carry around this heavy, false burden of being people's savior and trying to fix them or their situations.

My mom was in and out of drug rehabilitation centers because she knew the right thing to do, but there were some issues that had to be fixed in her life, just like all of us. At times, we could very well know that what we are doing is not right, but there's something in us—trauma, pain, the issues of life—that cripples us and causes us to always return to it.

The birth of my daughter, Morgan, was the event. I told my mother she could not touch Morgan until she was clean. I didn't want her around, as I felt she would hurt Morgan like she hurt me. I internalized it that way. It wasn't until later in life that God showed me that it wasn't about me. When I told my mother that she could not have a relationship with my daughter until she got off drugs, I meant that. I blamed her for leaving me all alone as a teenager. I blamed her for the pang of sadness I felt when I started my period without her support, a moment many girls share with their moms. It was her fault I no longer got to enjoy school clothing shopping experiences with her, a tradition I cherished. Everything was her fault, and I was determined to be the best mom I could be.

Today, we celebrate my mother's journey to recovery and her commitment to staying drug-free. God is so good! She is almost 28 or so years clean now—it changed her life and pivoted our relationship. My mother now counsels others; she now intercedes and ministers to God's people. My mother, like my grandmother, has a prophetic gift. As I grew in my faith, God revealed to me that my prophetic mantle was birthed from both my grandmother and mother. God is so good at how He does things.

My father is my best friend. I love to say I'm his favorite daughter, although I'm his only daughter! My father always saw the best in me, and our bond strengthened over time. When I was in high school, I strived to prove myself to my dad because I wanted my dad to always be proud of me and always be there, rooting me on, especially since my accomplishments did not change my mother's life. I had one more parent to get it right. I was scared that he would leave me like he left my mother.

When I had my daughter, my relationship with my daughter's father at the time was estranged. We had a rocky relationship and weren't together at the time I conceived. He was a very active dad when Morgan was born.

He immediately moved to Atlanta to accept a job offer and would soon marry. This made me nervous because I knew that Morgan's relationship with her dad would likely differ from the blessed one I shared with my dad. My father stepped up and was the best grandfather for Morgan, along with her uncle, Kevin. Their support helped me accept that I was now a mom, and that was my number-one priority.

As I transitioned from childhood to my teenage years, I journaled a lot in my diary. When I hit these pitfalls, I would journal, telling myself, "You aren't worth living." When people called my mom crazy, talked about me, or thought I was weird, I wrote in my diary, "I WANT TO DIE! I WANT TO DIE!" At 12, I vividly recall sitting on the floor, reading the label on a bottle of pills that I had found, contemplating taking them. I don't remember where I got the pills from. The bottle had only 7 pills left. That was my first suicide attempt. I really wanted to die but it did not work. I felt like when things didn't go my way, the best way to handle it was to die. I took that perspective with me my whole adult life. To be honest, I still struggle with the thought sometimes, even to this day. When I give my all to people, and they create distance or treat me a certain way that I am not familiar with, those discarded feelings come back. That was how I felt at 15—discarded. Mom was out there on drugs, and dad was raising me. At the time, my brother and I hated each other. Looking back, I can't help but wonder why we hated each other so much. Now, we are neighbors, and he and I are truly "ride or die." I remember calling my grandmother on the phone and telling her I didn't want to live anymore. At the time, I didn't quite know if she was in tune with what was happening, but I believed I would die that night. I just needed her to know I was not OK and wanted out of this life.

DECREE AND DECLARE

A PAGE FROM MY DIARY

"Thou shalt also decree a thing, and it shall be established unto thee: and the light shall shine upon thy ways" (Job 22:28, KJV).

- I am bold
- I am beautiful
- I am confident
- I am secure in myself
- I am talented
- I am gifted
- I am the one
- I love myself and everything about me
- I love the girl I see in the mirror
- I am a queen
- I make quick decisions
- I am fearless
- I take action daily

Declaring decrees, even unknowingly, sets a powerful intention for our lives. These decrees are more than just words; they are affirmations that shape our reality and guide our path forward. When we speak positive declarations, we align ourselves with a higher purpose and call forth the greatness within us. As I look back on those entries in my diary, I see now that each statement was a seed planted in fertile ground. Those seeds, nurtured over time, have blossomed into the experiences and achievements

I see today. The power of spoken word is real, and it begins with the courage to declare who we are and what we aspire to become.

PAUSE AND DECLARE

I invite you, dear reader, to take a moment right now and pause from reading this book. Reflect on the desires of your heart and the dreams you hold for your future. What words of affirmation can you declare over your life today? Write them down. These decrees are more than just statements; they are seeds of purpose, strength, and intention. As you continue with me on this journey, you will see how the decrees I made early in my life became anchors that steadied me when I was all over the place. Your words hold the same power. Start building your declarations now, and let them be the foundation for the greatness that awaits you.

1.) _____
2.) _____
3.) _____
4.) _____
5.) _____
6.) _____
7.) _____
8.) _____
9.) _____
10.) _____

Chapter 2

LOST! WHAT A LIFE!

> *"For I am the Lord your God who takes hold of your right hand and says to you. Do not fear; I will help you."* —Isaiah 41:13 (NIV)

I was still a teenager when I was raped. I had this guy I called my boyfriend—if that's what you want to call him. I was in the 10th grade at King/Drew Medical Magnet High School. I was a very smart kid who did her best to achieve everything, but when it came to boyfriends, I didn't fare as well. I was good to this guy. I would save money to buy him gifts so that he would visit me at school. He didn't go to school and was in and out of juvenile hall. He was always pressuring me about sex. I obviously knew what sex was but didn't understand the whole concept and what needed to happen. I certainly was not ready to have sex at 15. I knew it wasn't something I was ready for.

One day, I ditched school, and my boyfriend and I were together. I kept telling him, "No, I don't want to do this." He raped me. Yes, I finally wrote and believed this. He raped me! I didn't understand what had happened at the time. I just knew he tied my hands together and made me do all kinds of things to him. I cried for days and didn't tell anyone about the experience. When I finally did, some people blamed me for putting myself in that predicament. Every time I spoke to my boyfriend, he blamed me for it and said that I should not have let him do that to me. He called me all kinds of names and belittled me. It took years of therapy to finally understand that my traumatic experience was, in fact, called rape. I never wanted my name associated with the word rape.

From that experience, I got pregnant. I didn't know how to tell my family. I was only 15 and in the 10th grade. I remember carrying the baby until 6 months. I didn't know where to turn for help. I didn't know how I was going to have the baby. I didn't know what to do. Some of my family members realized I was getting chubby. So, finally, I told one of my aunts what happened, but I didn't tell her it was rape. I simply said, "I had sex with this guy and got pregnant." Shortly after telling my aunt, I got an abortion. That abortion killed me. I lived with the grief of making that decision. No, I wasn't ready for a baby. I certainly wasn't going to marry that boy. He definitely would never be someone I would want to be with. I hated him for what he did to me and how he made me feel.

Nightmares continued to haunt me, as I would see myself crying over a tiny grave or even a baby. I knew it was the enemy that continued to torment me about the abortion. At that time, I knew in my heart I could not mother a child. Remember, the father called me all kinds of names and made me feel as though I asked him to rape me. What would I tell our child? For many years, well into my 30s, I lived with the shame of knowing I took the blame for saying no. I took the blame for ending the life of a precious child.

I still battled with the guilt of not telling my dad. I knew my father would be so hurt upon realizing that I did not tell him. But I could not imagine embarrassing my father, who was in law enforcement and would later become a minister. What would people think or say? I just could not do it. Again, I was at a place where my mother was not in my life, and I continually blamed myself for her drug addiction and my parents' divorce. The thought of telling my father what happened crushed me. I was already embarrassed.

I wasn't ready to become a mom, but I felt like something was snatched from me. I literally felt something die on the inside of me. I have forgiven myself and continue to forgive myself because, of course, those thoughts of "What if …?" still try to visit me. At 38 years old, I decided to go public about being a rape survivor. I lived with this secret for over 23 years, and it was literally torture.

I would see him from time to time, and each time, he made me have sex with him. He told me that I owed him that, and if I didn't have sex with him, he would kill me. He was in and out of jail, but somehow, I continued to be there for him. Perhaps I believed that my life would be in jeopardy if I ignored him. He wrote to me from jail and asked me to send him pictures. I hated him and would try to ignore him as much as I could. But there was still this piece of me that cared about him.

About a year ago, I saw him pop up on my Facebook, and it didn't look like life changed much for him. I literally felt a rage come out of me like I could kill him. I had to go through a deliverance session, and forgiveness had to happen. That was the first time I realized I had not forgiven him for what he did to me.

Do you know how many years it took me to declare that I am a rape survivor? I would have nightmares for years. When I sought out a therapist to talk about the experience and began to embrace the reality of what happened, I was able to heal from being raped. As women, sometimes we berate ourselves by compulsively recounting the details of the moment and saying, "Well, I shouldn't have been there" or "Maybe if I had not dressed that way, it would not have happened." Irrespective of how you choose to look at it, it is still rape. You did not deserve to be overpowered and taken advantage of. Therapy helped me reach the conclusion that it was not my fault. When you say "No," it's no. No means no.

I believe this experience propelled me into a life of just sex. I eventually began dating different guys and became very sexual and promiscuous because I felt like in order to please them, I had to have sex with them. Thinking back on it, I never truly enjoyed those moments because I wasn't doing it for myself. It was to keep them. I didn't even understand what was going on with me and why I felt the need to abandon myself that way. This behavior also spilled over into me doing things for men, validating myself through men, and buying expensive things for men because I wanted to be needed and loved. Let me tell you, I purchased cars, name-brand items, and gifts from Gucci and Louis Vuitton; I went on vacations and hosted lavish birthday parties. You name it. If he was with me, he had it made.

I think back to those relationships, and I can see the impact and imprint of my experiences from childhood impressed upon my mind and how it shaped my reasoning and way of perceiving the world in such a way that I did not know how to love myself or how to receive God's love. I carried unresolved emotions from my relationship with my mother, where I took on roles that weren't mine—saving, protecting, and caring for her—while longing for nurturing and a mother's love, coupled with my struggle to prove myself to my dad, seeking validation to ensure his presence and love. I felt robbed. I felt like I had to get into these relationships because it was something else to make me feel good about myself. OK, I will circle back to this later in the book.

In my late 30s, on the cusp of 40 years old, I had a team of three therapists. Yes, you need a team! We got to the root of my issues: "What's behind the need to feel validated? What do you have to prove? Why are you in these self-sabotaging, self-abandoning cycles?" I needed to learn to love myself, accept my flaws, and break off shame and rejection. I had to get to the root of my dis-ease for life. Why was I so unhappy, so discontent in life? Why was I lying? Why did I put on a mask? What reason did I have to be afraid? I had to ask myself, "La Shawn, what is going on with you?" I had to deal with the lies and accept the truth, and it took therapy to help me find peace within myself and have a resolve about my life.

When you're searching for a sense of belonging, it produces the need for validation, which manifests in people-pleasing. Living with the relentless pressure to validate my place in people's lives is a draining, lonely, and suffocating experience. Trying to prove yourself to people will drive you crazy and have you engaging in unmentionable, irrational behaviors. I found myself going to great lengths to belong. I had to go through a deliverance process to be satisfied with God and God alone; on the other side of the process, I learned how to deal with myself, accept myself, and have peace with my life. I had to truly be at peace with myself and allow God to quiet me and put me in a state of ease and rest. I am here because God already had a seat at the table for me.

I remember sitting in my room as a child with a brush in my hand and with all my care bears lined up, and I would pretend to preach. I don't know what I was saying, but that memory always visits me because I know that was God showing me that He was going to use me to minister to people. My grandmother would always tell me that I was going to be a great household name one day. I would always be afraid to entertain such grandiose thoughts because I was afraid of people knowing about my life. I now know why I have such a desire to be transparent and tell my testimony; God was already preparing me as a child, standing in front of my stuffed animals. The funny thing is, I have always done that. Whenever I'm alone, I talk aloud to myself—preaching to myself, encouraging myself. I knew I needed to deal with rejection that caused me to behave in strange, toxic, self-abandoning ways.

Let me share something that God laid on my heart to share: You may think you're finished, that you've missed your destiny or made too big of a mistake, but the Scripture reminds us that God's plan doesn't end in defeat, mediocrity, addiction, or injustice. Your story ends in triumph. You may not understand everything that happens, but you can be confident in knowing that God sees the end from the beginning. Sometimes, He has to lead you backward to propel you forward. He has to dig deep to prepare you for the heights He's taking you to. He prunes so that you can bloom.

If you remain in faith, you will witness how everything works together for your good. If things are holding you back, seem out of place, or feel messy, don't be discouraged. God is saying, "You're right on schedule for victory. Your story isn't over—I'm still at work. What I started, I will bring to completion."

Proverbs 18:21 (AMP) says, "Death and life are in the power of the tongue, and those who love it and indulge it will eat its fruit and bear the consequences of their words." Did you know that the words you speak today are shaping the direction of your life? If you want to know what your life will look like in five years, listen to what you're saying about yourself today. "I'll never get well. I'll never break this addiction. I'll never recover from this setback." These are not just words; they are prophecies of your future. You can't proclaim defeat and expect victory. You can't proclaim sickness and expect health. You can't proclaim lack and expect abundance.

Pay attention to what you say about yourself, your family, your finances, and your health. You will become what you consistently declare. That's why getting in the habit of speaking victory over your life is crucial. Throughout the day, declare what God says about you: "I am blessed. I am strong. I am healthy. I am surrounded by favor. Something good is going to happen to me." The fruit of those words will be blessing, favor, and abundance. It's not enough to just think it; speak it.

THERE IS POWER IN WHAT YOU SPEAK

- I walk in faith consistently, for Jesus has taken away fear and doubt in my life. Fear will not rule me. Faith will! I speak words of life. Today, I cast all my cares on Christ. I choose to meditate on the promises and not the problem.
- I speak life today, for Jesus has destroyed the murmuring and complaining tongue in my life. My tongue will speak forth words of life today. I walk in total triumph in every situation, for Jesus has destroyed failure in my life.
- I am an overcomer and can do all things through Christ. I decree that Jesus is Lord of my spirit, body, and soul. He is Lord over my relationships, circumstances, finances, and ministry.
- Greater is He that is in me than he that is in the world.
- For with God, nothing shall be impossible!

Part 2
THE DESTRUCTION

Chapter 3

OUT OF CONTROL

> *"And after you have suffered a little while, the God of all grace, who has called you to his eternal glory in Christ, will himself restore, confirm, strengthen and establish you."*
> —1 Peter 5:10 (ESV)

As you can see, it all began in my teenage years. In my mind, life would go into disarray simply because of a circle of toxic dysfunction. It felt like I began each day by putting on a mask to conceal my true self, the scars of my childhood, and my uncertain future. My grandmother always said, "Don't look like what you're going through." But to me, it translated to: "Shawnie, just look good; play the part." Lord knows the burden of that facade almost destroyed me mentally and emotionally.

As I look back, I believe the masking started shortly after my abortion in the 10th grade. The years I cried over aborting that child tormented me. Lately, I've been reflecting on this question: "What would my life be like if I had chosen to carry and raise a child conceived through rape?" You will later learn that this wasn't the only abortion I had.

As a student in high school, I continued to excel in my classes and was part of many extra-curricular activities. I've always had my hand in everything. It makes sense today, doesn't it? Even at that time, I was very hard on myself. I always believed that I needed to be perfect in order to succeed in life. As I previously shared, I believed in my heart at that time that I was responsible for my parents' divorce, my mother's battle with drugs, and so many other things. I began telling myself that nothing was ever right for me. I prayed, but it always seemed like things would never pan out.

Earlier in the book, I shared phrases I memorized and recited daily. Although I didn't grasp their full impact then, these decrees would eventually become lifelines. At the time, I repeated them without conviction, often hearing my own inner doubts. The voices in my thoughts contradicted my words, revealing my unbelief. It seemed futile, but little did I know that those declarations would one day sustain me.

My self-prescribed therapy consisted of writing raw letters to God, pouring out my pain in phrases like: "Because You didn't answer my prayer, I feel like I don't want to live." Who was I fooling? These tantrums would go on for years. My grandmother always told me, "Take your problems to the Good Lord." But were they my problems? Or did I just internalize them to be? And why hasn't He solved them? What was the delay? The wait felt endless.

I would hear from my mother off and on. I always prayed for her but feared that I would one day not see her again. As mentioned earlier, for years, I blamed myself for my mom's sickness. You have no clue what it was like to always feel like you're going to receive bad news about your mother. Watching my friends interact and do things with their mothers was so painful. For years, I desperately yearned for that kind of attention. I really missed the moments with my mother. Running errands, shopping, and even listening to my mother gossip on the phone. Those were just some of the simplest things that I wanted. I just didn't feel loved, even though my father was always there. Not having both parents in the home always seemed to be the one thing everyone had, except me. Thank God for my relationship with my grandmother and aunt. It felt like they were there to help normalize things at the time. However, it just wasn't my mother.

I continued with my weekend visits pretty much through high school. It was like a vacation away from home and the problems that I conjured up in my mind. Some weekends, I was blessed to actually see my mom. It was different each time, but I recall hearing God say, "She is going to be OK." I remember my 9th-grade graduation; my mother showed up high. She looked very sad. I think it truly hurt her not to have her kids in her life. But at the time, her priority was masking her pain through drug use. I knew in my heart that one day, she would conquer her drug addiction.

One thing I struggled with was friendships. That validation and need for love popped up after I began to shut myself off from what may have turned out to be meaningful relationships. You have no clue how many years it took me to realize this would be a problem. Seeking validation should be a sin in itself. Playing the life of the party made me feel popular, but secretly, I craved meaningful connections—friendships that would endure beyond the music and laughter. I also knew some people just wanted a friendship with me to gain benefits. I am a giver and am always there to support. I'd frantically seek the spotlight, showering others with gifts and attention to keep them close. But in the next moment, the emptiness would settle in—my efforts felt hollow and unfulfilling. I would shift gears when my feelings got hurt. It was a space I would go into at the time; I didn't realize I was going into an unhealthy emotional space. A space that would be both helpful and detrimental to who I was, or so I thought. I learned not to express my feelings. It was easy to hold everything in, but it would eventually cause issues for me in the long run.

Lies after lies after lies! Whatever I had to do to hide what was going on, I would lie about it. Easy! That way, I could hide my feelings, get out of trouble, or distance myself from those who hurt me. I could easily create a narrative that would save me from having to share how I felt or what was bothering me. Besides, who really cared that I wasn't OK?

Every time I got extremely overwhelmed in life, I contemplated suicide as a way of escape. I literally would imagine myself dead. It would solve the issues or pay people back for hurting me. *If I could just die, this would all be over.* Yes, I thought this way at a very young age. Recently, I read through some of my journals. I cannot believe how many entries I read about wanting to take my life. I shared I was a pre-teenager when I first attempted suicide. Do you know why I felt that I needed to do that? I was trying to fit in with my friends at school and coping with my mother not being in my life.

One day, after school, I was walking home, and my friends were talking about going somewhere with both of their parents. One of my friends turned to me and said I wouldn't be able to go to the event because my mom was at the crazy house. I didn't know how to explain to my friends exactly what was going on with my mother. That same weekend, I was in my room; I got hold to another bottle of pills. Again, I assumed this was the correct method to successfully kill myself. I took all of those pills that night. I woke up so upset because my plan didn't work.

Being a child, you don't fully understand the information you're receiving, and I remember hearing that if you take too many pills, you will die. As I reflect on that time in my life, I realize that there was a lot of hurt and pain in that little girl, and she didn't know how to process it. You may not understand what it's like to not have what others have. My grandmother would always tell me to be thankful for what I had. But it just wasn't the same when interacting with friends your age.

After high school, I decided to attend Loyola Marymount University—one of the 46 colleges and universities that offered me admission. Yes, my father enrolled me in one of those college application programs at First AME, and I ended up applying to a wide range of schools—anywhere and everywhere. However, Howard, USC, and Pepperdine denied my applications. How dare I be denied when Uncle Gregory graduated from USC and Uncle Anton graduated from Pepperdine University! I am thankful that Howard University accepted Morgan and that she is a proud graduate.

I chose to attend LMU. I really wanted to go away, but I had a boyfriend at the time. I was in love, or so I thought. To this day, I regret not attending an HBCU. However, I attended one of the greatest universities in the entire world, Loyola Marymount University. I saw LMU as an opportunity for me to prove myself. I was the first grandchild in my mother's immediate family to attend college. It was the reality check that I really needed, or so I thought. There were many rewarding experiences that provided me with an opportunity to enjoy college.

It was during my sophomore year that I got pregnant with Morgan. I mean, obviously, I was doing something to get pregnant. I was 19, living in a college dorm. I'll never forget how I felt when I learned I was going to be a mother. I was conflicted about the earlier abortion that I had; Morgan's dad and I weren't together; my mother was still not there; and I was a college student, making $4.85 an hour, working multiple work-study assignments on campus.

How would this work? I was determined to show the world that I could persevere in life and be a young mother. I will never forget the day I told my father. He gave me a choice: either drop out of college and get a job or stay in school and fund my schooling. I figured it out. I decided to have my child and stay in school. I didn't realize this was the choice that would essentially change my life.

On the day Morgan came, February 10th, I was taking a Spanish midterm at school. Whoops, I had to go! She was coming that day. Everything happened so fast. She was born; I was a mom, and I was back at school two days later to finish my midterms. Yep, it happened that fast!

Motherhood as a college student hit differently. I worked multiple jobs; at one point, I had four jobs. I was an RA on campus. I worked in the IT department and in financial aid. I worked at a law firm as a legal secretary. I was literally in full hustle mode. I juggled multiple responsibilities: caring for my baby, working nighttime shifts as a phone sex operator, and squeezing in homework until 3 AM. Yes, I was a phone sex operator. I connected with some guy on campus. I don't believe he was a student. He was like, "Your voice is cute. Wanna make some money?" I replied, "Yes, I have a baby to support." My beautiful voice earned me about $300 every few weeks by engaging in phone conversations with older men with questionable intentions.

Everyone always says, "La Shawn talks so white" or "La Shawn talks so proper." That really is one of my pet peeves, by the way. Let's just say I talk like I got some sense. Anyway, the phone sex operator job was easy but not something I should have been doing. I answer the phone and read a script. They loved me! No, I don't remember a single fantasy I sold them because, at the time, most of those calls were scripted, though we were allowed to go off-script. Yes, I always went off-script. I would listen to the client say all of the things that made me want to puke. I felt uneasy, but the financial reward made it bearable—until payday, at least. I think only a few people knew about that job, and even now, the mere thought of it still fills me with embarrassment.

I'm grateful for some of my very close friends who helped with watching Morgan while I went to class. Liz, Alicia, Lisa, Tenecia, Monica, and many others who supported me along the way. My LMU sisters really blessed me. I had a community. Riding the bus at night, trying to make ends meet, was a lot, but I was determined to provide better for Morgan. She would never have the negative experiences that I had growing up. Most people thought I grew up privileged; little did they know that there were many voids I needed to fill. The commentary was always, "La Shawn has it all."

As I grew into adulthood, I often thought about the suicide attempts, and I would question why it never worked. Now, I just can't stop wondering why, in my pre-teen years, I would even want to do such a thing. But as time went on, I found myself contemplating a third suicide attempt. At the time, I was still grieving my mother not being in my life and my grandmother's death. My mother would pop in and out of my life as she was getting help. I knew she was away, getting help, but I still did not fully understand why I could not have her present in my life.

My daughter's father did not want to be in a relationship with me, and I was devastated. We weren't together when I conceived. You know, things happen—and it happened. As I think back, I wonder if I had the expectation of us being together because of our child. I tried the co-parenting route, and of course, that didn't end well. My advice to anyone in this situation is to be completely over him before you think you are able to work through those challenges. Later in the book, I will discuss the relationships and how I got "got" multiple times. The things we subject ourselves to for men.

I was convinced that no one would want me because I was a single mother, and my weight began to spiral out of control. So, once again, I decided to take a bottle of pills. I had just put my daughter to sleep; I grabbed the pills and gulped them with a large glass of wine. I fell asleep and had a dream where I saw myself running through flames; I saw everyone that had ever let me down. I got to the end of a tunnel and there was a beam of light. Then I woke up. So, of course, that suicide attempt did not work. I would literally cry for days, trying to figure out why in the world my suicide attempts were not working. When a person wants to go, why doesn't God just let them go?

After my third failed suicide attempt, I decided to seek counseling again, but I didn't stick to it because of the stigma associated with being a black woman going to counseling. All the questions and discussions seemed so standard that I felt it just wasn't for me. Although my father took us to a therapist when we were younger, I did not know how to appreciate it or commit to it in order to develop coping techniques. I still walked away, feeling empty and depleted because I did not understand the purpose, and I had not yet reached a point in life where I wanted help and knew how to be vocal about it. After surviving my second suicide attempt, I adopted a motto: "Don't look like what you've been through." I turned to retail therapy, using credit cards to fund a shopping spree of clothes, shoes, and accessories, desperate to conceal the feelings of rejection, abandonment, and shame. I did well to overcompensate in desperate attempts to convince people that I was okay, but of course, I knew the truth. That's when I began to lie and make up fantasies. I went to great lengths to cover myself. I did not know how to deal with my issues. It resulted in blaming myself for everything once again.

MY LAST CALL

In 2016, I attempted suicide for the fourth and final time. At that time, I thought I was in a relationship with a guy I wasn't in love with, but I was in love with the idea of being in love. Does that make sense? Of course, it doesn't. I would later find out he had moved on without bothering to inform me. So, he created this little family. That experience taught me that some relationships are better suited as friendships. You sometimes feel you have to force something, but if it doesn't work, just let it go.

During that time, my daughter, who was a student at Howard University, finally told me what I knew to be the case—that she was gay. My immediate response, shaped by my church upbringing, was, "Oh my God … what would people think?" I internalized my daughter's sexual orientation and found a way to make it about me. I also learned that there was an active investigation into some disability claims that I had filed. I would later learn that an employee at one of my previous employers had reported certain inaccurate information. I was in and out of relationships as well, so it's safe to say I felt like my world was crashing and burning. So, I found myself contemplating suicide once more, but this time, I knew I had to get it right.

I took a day off work to write letters to my mom, dad, brothers, and daughter. I apologized for being a horrible person and discussed in detail what was going on with me. The letters were laid out with gifts, copies of insurance policies (that would have no value, duh), and burial plans. I had even purchased the outfit I wanted to be laid to rest in.

I had taken a full bottle of pills after returning home from a meeting that afternoon; I took another full bottle after my evening bath. I then lay down and went to sleep. Before I finished the wine and went to sleep, I had attempted to slit my wrists. The site of blood and self-inflicted pain didn't work out well. I then mixed a few different types of alcohol and even added a cleaning solution. This was the attempt that would take me out. After taking my bath, I decided my last night would end with everything in order. I unlocked my doors, wore one of my beautiful pieces of lingerie, and made sure everything was in order. I combed my hair and put on lip gloss. In my mind, I wanted to be found beautiful. Yes, it was that detailed.

I remember feeling drowsy before I finished taking everything I had put together. I cried out to God, overwhelmed by life's struggles, and begged Him to ease my burden. I couldn't bear the thought of another day, and I pleaded with Him to make sure that Morgan was in good hands. At this time of my life, I knew I wasn't good for anyone. I recall praying to God, "I know I won't make it to heaven, but please know I tried. I did all I could." How do I remember that prayer? I rehearsed it in my mind multiple times before that day would come.

Finally, I had consumed all the pills and finished the concoctions I had prepared. At some point, I must have fallen asleep. Later that night, according to my medical report, I somehow ended up at a grocery store in Sherman Oaks at about 3:31 AM. Apparently, I had woken up and driven myself about 15–20 miles from my home to a grocery store. I would later learn that I walked through the store, stepped on a piece of glass, cut my foot because I was barefoot, and ended up on the freezer aisle. To this day, I still have the scar at the bottom of my foot to remind me of that horrific experience.

I vividly recall standing with my hands raised in surrender, shielding my face while tears streamed down. I fell to the ground and looked up; I saw a huge light, the same light I saw at the end of the tunnel in my dream. I saw a hand stretched out to me, and I saw my grandmother. Then I heard the voice of the Lord say, "Enough is enough! There is a greater call on your life!" The next thing I remember is waking up in the hospital. Of course, I was on suicide watch. How embarrassed I was when I realized where I was. At the hospital, a sorority sister immediately recognized me. Thank God my parents or my daughter were not contacted.

The hospital called my ex to notify him. To this day, I have no clue how and even why he was there. I had no identification of any sort. But somehow, someone from the hospital got his information and called him. He was certainly not the person I wanted there, but I swore to him never to tell my parents about the incident. I gave him instructions to call my job and report me ill.

While on suicide watch, I would talk to God and myself out loud. I remember the nurse saying, "Talking to yourself isn't going to get you out of here." I was decreeing healing over my life and calling out to God. I owed her a good cursing out—but you know that wouldn't end well. Nobody really understood why I needed to go. I knew why I needed to go. But I just didn't understand what was my purpose. If everything wasn't going to go how I envisioned it, why allow me to stay?

I remember someone came in to sit with me while I was hospitalized. Who was she? I cannot tell you. She played gospel music from her phone as I lay there and listened. I listened to that music and just cried. I am forever grateful for that angel. I have no clue who she was, but she saved my life. It was at that moment I felt God's presence. If you know who you are, I thank you.

I promised God that if He got me through that situation, I would live the way He wanted me to and commit myself to a life that would be pleasing to Him. I just needed help. I just needed strength to get through that season. I guess you can say that this final attempt was my "Damascus" moment. According to Acts 9: 1–5, Saul, driven by a murderous intent, was en route to Damascus to continue persecuting Christians. Suddenly, a radiant light from heaven enveloped him, and a voice pierced the air, "Saul, Saul, why do you persecute me?" Startled, Saul asked, "Lord, who are you?" The voice responded, "I am Jesus, whom you are persecuting." I believe God, and I had a full, similar conversation that night in the grocery store like this:

Jesus: "La Shawn! La Shawn! Enough! Enough is enough! Why are you persecuting me?"
La Shawn: "Lord ... is that You?"
Jesus: "I am Jesus, the one you are persecuting!"
La Shawn: "But ... I'm confused. I'm not doing anything to You! I'm trying to kill me! It's my fault! It's all my fault! I'm to blame!"
Jesus: "La Shawn! Enough is enough! Enough is enough! These lies must be exposed and cease their effect on you! You will know the truth, and the truth will set you free. Killing you is like killing me. Why should you have to die if I have died already? What problem will your death solve when my death has already solved all the problems of the world? And where were you when I put the sun and the moon in the sky? Were you here before the foundation of the world to make it be? Were you the one who spoke the world into existence? It is pride that is treating your pain as a puppet and causing you to believe that your death is a great sacrifice when I am the only lamb that is worthy. Enough of this demonic reasoning. Enough of this oppression and depression. Enough of this spiritual blindness and lowliness. Enough of going through life as an imposter. Enough is enough. Take my hand; your Prince of Peace is here."

I am the very image of God. The spitting image. In fact, we all are. So, He was right; I was killing Him. I am God's temple. I had spent my entire life being a god to myself and those around me. So, of course, if I'm god, then I'm responsible for all sin. If I'm god, I'm responsible for all the bad that happens. If I am god, I am the judge and just one. If I am god, I need to do something good, a great and ultimate sacrifice in order to compensate for all the wrongs done in my life. So, since I saw myself as a god, I came to the conclusion that the best wage for my pain was my physical death. Wait a minute; who told me that I was my own protector? Oh, the devil did when my mom abandoned me, when my classmates ridiculed me, when that young man raped me, when none of my relationships worked out, and so forth.

Being a god is too great of a job. It's too complex. I'm sure the Kingdom of God is so advanced that we could not even begin to fathom what it is like to be a god. The one thing about trying to be our own god, defender, protector, or judge is sin. Defending ourselves at times results in murder. Justice in our hands looks like slander. Protecting ourselves looks like lying, deceiving, intimidating, and feeling superior. "'Vengeance is mine,' says the Lord!" (Romans 12:19). We cannot handle vengeance; only a holy God can do that. We can redeem ourselves, avenge ourselves, and restore ourselves, but we are not responsible for ourselves. We have a daddy! His name is Abba! Abba Father loves us completely, fully, and unconditionally. His love has no lack and no bounds!

When you believe you are a son/daughter, then you will trust the God of your salvation! When you trust God, you won't feel the need to do it yourself. You won't feel the need to make things right. You have a perfect God who causes all things to work together for good! He's the only one perfect enough to turn all the junk of our lives into treasure. If I had known then what I know now, I would not have worked so hard to be my own shield and buckler when God is my fortress, my strong tower, and my place of safety; I would have known that when mother and father forsake me, God will lift me! The Bible clearly says that those who dwell in the shelter of the

Most High will rest in the shadow of the Almighty! The devil is the author of confusion and the father of lies. The devil takes advantage of our innocence and ignorance; he suggests certain decisions we should make in our imaginations. The devil knows that if he can convince you, he can kill you.

Suicide is not the way out. Did you hear me? I'll say it again. Suicide is not the way out. Suicide is not the answer. Suicide is not the ultimate act of selflessness, love, and atonement. Suicide is a lie. Suicide does not alleviate problems but, instead, creates a new burden for someone else to deal with. I can't imagine how life would be today for Morgan or my family had I not been here. How selfish of me to have thought that taking my life would solve issues! Why do we think that suicide is the answer?

The death of Jesus did not bring the world great sorrow and suffering. Instead, it brought reconciliation. Suicide births pain, sorrow, and suffering. Where there is no vision, there is death, and where there is no hope, the heart is sick. You need a vision for your life and a hope to see your way through life. Your beliefs shape your reality. Our lives are designed in such a way that whatever we believe, we inherently receive. Faith begins in the heart, where we truly believe, and is activated when we express it openly through our words. Why is that order important? Because you confess what you believe! I believed that I was to blame for my mother's addiction, her departure from my life, and my parents' divorce. I believed that I deserved to walk around ashamed of my daughter and the traumatic events of my life, and as a result, the only way out was to die. But the devil is a liar! And although the devil comes to steal, kill, and destroy, God has given me abundant life! I have a hope and a future, and so do you! You must write out a vision for your life. What does God say about you? Knowing your rights in Him is your powerful reminder to live boldly and freely. Your kids aren't your reason to keep going. Your ambition to buy your mom a house is not the reason. Your desire to give your wife/husband the world is not the reason. God says your life is good, and that's reason enough to keep living. Your life is good, pleasant, and full of purpose and hope.

You may be at an empty place. Perhaps you don't see how you could ever be happy again. I hope no one ever has to experience what I went through. Let me share one of my favorite stories. The Bible tells us that Naomi was heartbroken after the death of her husband and two sons. She was empty and bitter. But when Ruth (her daughter-in-law) fell in love and married Boaz, a son named Obed was born from that union. Naomi's life was renewed. She was so happy that she took care of Obed as her own. You know what was so special? Obed was David's grandfather, and Jesus came out of David's family line. Naomi couldn't see it, but through her heartbreak, she became instrumental in the birth of our Savior. If Naomi were here today, she would tell us to trust God. God has incredible plans in store for our future, beyond anything we could ever imagine. You may not understand the hardship right now, but trust God! It is all part of His plan. Keep believing, Keep living. Keep expecting His favor!

Sing Your Way Out

In 2002, Donald Lawrence released a song titled "The Best is Yet to Come." This song would really help me to keep pushing. The song ministers an inspirational and uplifting message that conveys a sense of hope, optimism, and faith in better days to come. This song was on constant repeat, and I couldn't help but sing and dance my heart out. Here is an excerpt from the lyrics:

> *There is a master plan in store for you*
> *If you just make it through*
> *God's gonna really blow your mind*
> *He's gonna make it worth your time*

For all of the trouble you've been through
The blessings double just for you

The best

Is yet

To come

The lyrics acknowledge that life may have its share of challenges, but it also emphasizes our potential to overcome those challenges and emerge stronger. This song conveys a sense of celebration and gratitude for the blessings that are already present in our lives and the anticipation of even greater blessings in the future. Overall, this song is a song of hope and assurance, reminding me to keep my faith, maintain a positive outlook, and trust that better days are on the horizon, especially because I have placed my trust in God.

Chapter 4

DEAL WITH YOU!

> "Above all else, guard your heart, for everything you do flows from it." —Proverbs 4:23 (NIV)

Are you still with me? After my last attempt at suicide, I had the opportunity to reach out and get help, but I believed that the best way to deal with it was to continue hiding. *Tell nobody nothing!* This space made me feel safe, as if I needed to protect myself from being hurt or judged. I lied often to hide the things that I was feeling. I mastered the art of masquerading, only to discover later that it wasn't an essential skill. People would ask me how I was doing and would say things like, "You look like you're carrying a lot," but my response was always, "Oh no! I'm doing great!" To even remotely think it was OK to share what I was dealing with was embarrassing and shameful. Oftentimes, I was battling depression, but you would never know.

I always had a level of comfort dating different men simply because they chose to date me. They were present in my life, and I believed for the time being that they would give me the love I deserved. I began excessive spending, purchasing things that I couldn't afford because it was easy to play a part. The men in my life were treated as kings. There was no limit on what I would spend on them. Cars, clothes, jewelry, vacations, parties, trips—just everything. Unfortunately, those things weren't reciprocated. By the time I thought I had fallen in love, I often wondered where the same lavish gifts were in return. I did everything under the sun to prove my love and that I was worthy to be kept forever. One of my exes brought flowers to me often. I can honestly say that was probably the best gift I ever got during that time in my life. I can recall the time I gave one of my exes $4,500.00 to spend on me for Christmas. It was my justification; well, at least he tried! I knew in my heart that wasn't the right thing to do, but it hurt me that I wasn't valued enough for these men to do for me as I had done for them. It wasn't until I started the therapy sessions that I learned that buying was far more than just gift-giving. It was a form of keeping them where they were and overcompensating them to stay in the relationship with me. I knew I was not happy, but I had a man, even if it was a piece of a man.

If you know me, you know I'm very big on birthdays. I celebrate the man in my life royally. I would always expect that in return, but it just didn't happen. On one particular birthday, I called an ex and asked him if he could take me out. There was no special man in my life that year. But I knew there was one ex I could always call. He told me he didn't have money. I asked him, "Could you at least take me out for ice cream?" He said, "I only have $27 and can't afford it." That night, I went to bed crying because I celebrated my birthday all alone. Do you mean to tell me I couldn't get all dolled up and taken out for ice cream? Year after year, I spent thousands to show my love and appreciation for the various men in my life. The year 2017 was the year that I knew I needed to love myself more than I had in the past. It was time to work on my healing. No more chasing men who didn't see my value or were only in the relationships to receive.

As a teenager, I had already begun feeling I was lacking that good man. I had friends who had boyfriends and seemed very happy. They would show up to drill team practice with flowers and candy. That was it for me. I developed a knack for "hood dudes." I was not attracted to men who were just plain or what we call the good guys. I needed dudes that were running the streets. Somehow, even today, my eyes turn to the men who have that street edge, tattoos and all.

I would then move on to another boyfriend who was in and out of juvenile hall. That was where it started—but he needed to be saved. Don't mind me. Anyway, my second boyfriend in high school showed me a whole other life. He was really about that life. I was Bonnie to his Clyde. He, too, started putting demands on me for sex. I was a preacher's kid; I was not supposed to be having sex. I had already been raped and was still trying to process that. Let's not forget the abortion. But I liked him a lot and loved telling all my friends about him. Sex happened. I often wonder where he is today. Well, I moved on from him to the next. Everything he wanted, he got, even when I didn't have enough allowance to make it happen.

I stole a shirt out of JcPenny's for my first boyfriend. It was a button-down gingham shirt. I couldn't afford the shirt, but I knew he had to have it. If I remember correctly, it had a price tag of $37. How embarrassing to be caught! Not much happened; I was lucky. My best friend and I got detained. Remember, my father was a lieutenant for the sheriff's department. "Really, La Shawn? Why?" my dad asked me. I told him I didn't know. Deep down inside, I just wanted my boyfriend to love me. Well, so much for that. He was a cheater, anyway. La Shawn scored again.

You know, back in the day, gifting men with the things they wanted was so important. I began to buy all kinds of things. As I think back, I am like,

"Damn! What was I thinking?" His relationship didn't last because he was always in trouble and in/out of jail. I snuck and accepted calls from him until my father caught on. One day, I decided to catch the bus to his house. I had to put together a box of things I wanted to get to him. I had planned to leave it with his mother. Well, let's just say he was home, and that visit didn't go well. The audacity to have some other girl over at his house! He called me for weeks, apologizing, but I was done. I can honestly say that was the first time I felt betrayed.

I was on the hunt again for bad boys. They had their challenges—challenges I wasn't quite ready for. Relationship after relationship continued for years. It was the same cycle over and over again. One thing these dudes can say is, "La Shawn showed me the life and took care of me," but in return, all I can say is that I was broken and just trying to find myself. How did I really get here?

Sex was another way for me to deal with rejection in these relationships. It was the answer to feeling accepted, loved, and needed. I knew what I was looking for. It was the love that came with having sex with your boyfriends. I had to have sex; that was the answer. It was a feeling that people always talked about. "You're going to fall in love, and the men will love you even more." That's all I heard. But as of today, I haven't found that—whatever it is. As I shared earlier, I had my first abortion in the 10th grade. So, yes, I was sexually active at the young age of 15. We all know that men love sex. It was one thing I knew I had to master. *If I could give good sex*—and that I did—*he would want to be with me*. Again, I thought I had found a way to receive the love I desperately sought, but I was wrong!

There was a time when I had multiple sex partners. I felt as though I wasn't being satisfied, so I would return to my ex. Yes, I was a cheater. The same person whose car windows I would shoot out was the man I cheated on. The audacity, right? Do you know how many years it took me to admit that? The day I shot those windows out, I knew I had lost it. I was lucky I didn't go to jail. But I was definitely scorned. Now, let me tell you; the car was in my name, and something about those windows shattering gave me that "Yeah, nigga" feeling. As I shot each bullet, my mind was racing through my past relationships, replaying every hurt and heartache. Eventually, my actions did nothing for me, absolutely nothing!

One relationship that I found to be very adventurous was the one that I carried on for years with a male exotic dancer. Most people knew my boyfriend was a well-known dancer from the local strip club in Los Angeles. Yes, The Right Track. In my mind, I had hit the jackpot. I knew in my heart that I was really in love. But that, my friends, was not the relationship I was mature enough to handle. It was a competition to outdo the women who had his attention. There were times I was in the club, throwing thousands. It was the thing to do. I prioritized keeping everything comfortable and in order, making sure he knew I was always ready to support him, no matter what. Again, I was broken and trying to find the love I desperately desired.

During this relationship, I got pregnant again, this time with twins. What?! I had always wanted twins, but the situation I found myself in was not ideal. Three children, two baby daddies; that was a hard no. Again, I went through the same type of guilt, but this time, I was harboring all these babies that never had a chance. Morgan was enough, and I already felt as though I wasn't providing her the balanced home she needed.

My relationship with the exotic stripper always made me feel undesirable. I always felt I didn't do it for him. As a male exotic dancer, he obviously had the attention of many women. I wanted that attention, but feeling undesirable had me in deep depression. I found the answer: plastic surgery.

In 2007, I was determined to make my then-boyfriend pay attention to me. I had gained a lot of weight due to depression again. I was connected to a celebrity plastic surgeon, Dr. Jan Adams. I recall my consultation with him was very intense. Not listening to any word he said, I literally yelled, "Just make me like Halle Berry." I remember the look on his face as he chuckled. I said, "My boyfriend thinks that I am overweight." Three weeks later, I returned to his practice to make my $48,000 payment for my upcoming surgery. I had a tummy tuck, a Brazilian butt lift, liposuction, breast reduction, and a breast lift. I will never forget that day. I lay on that table before they began to administer the anesthesia and dreamed about how my new body would look. I would finally get the attention I deserved.

After the surgery, my then-boyfriend (the exotic male dancer) wanted nothing to do with me. He would angrily tell me, "I told you not to do it." As you can imagine, that relationship ended shortly after that. While I worked to heal and recover, I was so mad that my ex resented me for having the surgery. I did my best to explain why I had it. In my mind, I thought I was doing something that would make me more desirable. As you can see, the cycle continued; I was in a war for approval, which always ended in failure. Was it that hard to be loved? Shortly after that relationship ended, I found myself in another relationship—just a few months later. As a matter of fact, several relationships.

I remember a time when I was involved in a sexual relationship with a man who lived with his girlfriend. I felt like I needed to be with him to feel like I belonged, to validate my worth and appearance. I craved someone to tell me I was attractive and to desire me sexually, and he did that. It didn't hurt that he was a church guy—we even attended the same church. We hooked up all the time, and he couldn't get enough of me. But even with all of that attention, I was never truly happy. I felt empty inside.

I found myself crying out to God, begging Him to take away the desire to fornicate. It wasn't just about wanting to be celibate—it was about making room for God in the places where I felt weak and vulnerable. I had tried sex, shopping, lying, hiding—all of these things to fill the void in me—and none of them worked. As cliché as it may sound, I reached a point where I was ready to try God because nothing else was working. But even then, I wasn't perfect. Just a few weeks later, I slipped up again.

I prayed for strength to abstain from sex, and I'm proud to say that after almost eleven years (and counting) of practicing abstinence, I'm in a much better place. God has truly freed me from being a slave to my flesh and filled my heart with His desires. The Bible tells us, "Delight yourself in the Lord, and He will give you the desires of your heart" (Psalm 37:4). To truly "delight" in the Lord means to find joy and deep pleasure in Him, to prioritize building a relationship with Him just like you would with anyone else—by spending time talking to Him and getting to know Him.

When I began confessing my struggles directly to God—without holding anything back, whether it was pride, overspending, or lying—I turned to Scripture to see what God had to say about those things. That was when I started genuinely delighting in Him. I immersed myself in His Word, meditating on it day and night, just as David did. I hid God's Word in my heart so that I wouldn't sin against Him. Through that process, God began to cleanse me, renew my heart, and fill me with a hunger and thirst for righteousness. But the turning point in my journey to abstinence came after a moment I will never forget.

I had reunited with an ex, and we spent Christmas together in sin, engaging in what I thought would bring me comfort—sex. But when it was over, I lay in bed, staring at the ceiling, and saw demons swirling above me. Horrified, I tried to wake my ex to show him what I was seeing, but he brushed it off, thinking I was just dreaming. He told me to relax and enjoy myself, but the truth was, I hated every moment of it. I felt disgusted with myself for falling back into that trap.

Those demons wouldn't go away, and I knew it was a sign that I needed deliverance. I jumped out of bed, got dressed, and left. As I drove home, I cried to God, "Whatever that was, I don't ever want to experience it again!" In my rearview mirror, I kept seeing flames following me. Then I heard God say, "Let me love you, daughter."

I ended up driving to the beach at 2 AM, where I cried out to God for hours. I didn't know where my life was headed, but I knew it wasn't in a good place. I made a promise to God that night: if He would heal me, I would commit to abstinence until marriage. I needed healing—spiritually, emotionally, and physically. A few days later, I wrote down every detail of what I had experienced, knowing I would need to remember it for the journey ahead.

The pursuit of sex led me down paths filled with emotional and mental abuse. Listen, I loved sex. I would do anything to have sex. I was so lost that I didn't even recognize myself anymore. My reckless behavior eventually caught up with me, and I contracted herpes. Yes, you heard that right. I had to live with that reality for years, all because I was chasing love in the wrong places and sleeping with people to fill the void of loneliness. But God performed a miracle in my life—He healed me from herpes in 2017.

To this day, my gynecologist still believes she misdiagnosed me, but I always tell her, "No, God healed me!" How could I ever return to having sex with someone who isn't my husband after such a miracle? It's a documented miracle, a testament to God's healing power. I truly believe this was all spiritual—a warning before it would manifest in the physical.

I'll be honest—I love sex, and I once thought I couldn't live without it. But the peace I've found in knowing that I no longer need to use sex as a way to seek validation or endure abuse is on a completely different level. Don't get me wrong; this journey hasn't been easy. But when I marry my kingdom purpose mate, trust me, he will be very happy! So, please keep him in your prayers now.

Choosing the path of abstinence has been one of the most empowering decisions of my life. It has given me a renewed sense of clarity, allowing me to look inward, remove distractions, and truly understand my own heart, desires, and purpose. Without the noise of external influences, my mind feels lighter, my focus is sharper, and I am more in tune with what God has called me to do.

Abstinence has also been a journey of breaking away from patterns and connections that kept me bound. I began to see clearly which relationships and habits were only adding weight to my spirit, holding me back from the life I was meant to live. By letting go of these unhealthy bonds, I've found a new freedom—one that is rooted in self-respect, strength, and a commitment to nurture only those connections that uplift and inspire me. But perhaps the most profound part of this journey has been the realignment of my relationship with God.

In choosing abstinence, I have felt God's presence in ways I couldn't before; my spirit feels more open, more in harmony with His guidance and love. This choice has placed me in a space of peace where I can hear His voice clearly, unfiltered by the noise of worldly distractions. It's as if I've been reset, brought back into His arms, and anchored in His grace.

Through abstinence, I've learned that true strength lies not in what we hold onto but in what we're willing to release to become the person we are meant to be. This journey has drawn me closer to God, given me a fresh perspective on life, and renewed my commitment to walk in purpose and alignment with His will.

This journey has taught me that real love doesn't come through temporary satisfaction or seeking approval from others but from knowing who I am in Christ. God's grace has brought me through the darkest moments, and His healing power has restored me in ways I could never have imagined. I'm no longer defined by my past, and I'm not willing to settle for anything less than what God has promised me.

So, as I continue to wait for my kingdom purpose mate, I rest in the assurance that God's timing is perfect. Until then, I'll keep praying, healing, and trusting that my story is a testament to His grace and love ... More to come on this topic.

A WORD FROM GOD

When you understand that God uses difficulties to prepare us, stretch our faith, and change us, you don't complain when things don't go your way. You realize it's serving a purpose. When you do the right thing when the wrong thing is happening, you're getting ready to carry the weight of glory. That's why God doesn't remove everything instantly. So, be patient.

CHAPTER 5

"MY MR. !"

> "Wait on the LORD: Be of good courage, and he shall strengthen thine heart: wait, I say, on the LORD."
> —Psalm 27:14 (NKJV)

God shifted me, and He did it quickly! You might be wondering, "How?" In 2017, He gave me an assignment—one that I initially resisted with everything in me. I threw tantrums, hated it, and questioned why I had to go through it. But here's the thing: as a kingdom-minded woman, balancing ministry, work, and faith can be challenging. I was honest with God and asked, "How do I live this life? How do I speak to women and share my story authentically?" The answer wasn't in my own strength but in the tools God gave me—surrounding myself with like-minded sisters who are walking the same path, developing a serious and active prayer life, fasting regularly, and staying rooted in His Word.

Sometimes, even close friends living different lifestyles can make it challenging, but you have to stay focused on the assignment. And let me tell you, when God performs a miracle in your life, the impact is profound. It changes you in ways that leave no room for doubt. It hits differently because it's not just about survival anymore—it's about thriving in His purpose and staying on course, no matter what.

    I fought with God during that time because as my light grew, I began to isolate myself from many friendships. Yet, despite my resistance, the instruction was clear: "Cover these women in prayer. Pray for their purpose to be fulfilled and for God to bring their God-ordained spouses." I couldn't help but ask, "Why am I praying for women to be married? God, what anointing do I have to carry out this assignment?" It didn't make sense to me at first. I wasn't a wife, and I had never been married. How was I supposed to cover these women in prayer for something I had no experience in? But that's when I realized I needed to study the role of a wife, not just through the lens of marriage, but through the heart of God. I needed to understand the spiritual significance of being a wife and how that role is intertwined with purpose, partnership, and prayer. God was equipping me to intercede for these women, even though I wasn't where they were. It wasn't about having the title; it was about having the heart for the assignment.

    God led me to study couples in the Bible. And honestly, that's where my mindset shifted. I began to find value in who I was and who God had created me to be. My worth was not in a man; it wasn't in some desperate relationship I created to be loved. They experienced the same issues we have. When we read the Bible or hear references, we tend to believe they didn't have the same needs. Studying Scripture taught me my role as a wife and God's expectations for me to fulfill the role in the kingdom-purpose relationship that He has for me. Ladies, know your worth! Men, recognize and value it!

There is a particular couple in the Bible, Priscilla and Aquila, whom I was led to study. There was not much about them. In the latter part of 2017, a prophetess ministered to me, and in that prophecy, she said God had told her to tell me to study this couple (Priscilla and Aquila), as my marriage would mirror theirs in today's world. It literally scared me, as I knew that God had led me to this couple some time ago. Over the years, I did my best to study them, but there wasn't much in the Bible that I could gather. At that time, it didn't make any sense to me ... but later, it would.

At the airport the next day, a woman approached me and said, "You will meet your husband in a different way." She told me where he was located. When she said it, I was like, "Ma'am, clearly you have the wrong person." Now, mind you, I had never received a marriage prophecy before. So, it didn't really make any sense. She said, "Your marriage will be an example to many, and the two of you will witness to many couples via your marriage, as you will encounter warfare before the promise. You both will be in ministry and the marketplace together." I literally looked at her, like, "Oh, OK." She said, "You will meet him audibly; it will be a different connection, but it will happen."

I wasn't much into prophecies because it was never something I wanted to hear. At that time, I was frequenting psychics. I had one psychic who was my "spiritual advisor." She lived in Brazil; we met regularly over WhatsApp for a short season. In addition, during my yearly visits to New Orleans, I would often see my favorite psychic. My quest was to just figure out where my husband was and why on earth we had not crossed paths. I spent thousands on psychics, only to hear what I already knew. Consulting psychics is a clear no- lesson learned! Yes, I had long-standing relationships with them but the spiritual warfare I faced was intense. True repentance and deliverance transformed my life. Just recently, God revealed that my obsession with psychics had bound me to attracting witches and darkness into my life.

Anyway, my call is to encourage and support women who are trusting God for their spouses. Some of you already know you're on my prayer list. Over the years, I've witnessed so many women being checked off the list while I've remained in spot number one. Little did I know that God had declared 2024 as the year of alignments within covenants, and I've witnessed the beautiful union of many couples I had prayed for.

A friend once told me about a guy she was seeing; despite feeling ready for a relationship, she struggled to fit into his life, unsure if he was the right one. I simply told her, "God showed me he is. I think you need to give this one to God." After I said it, I scared myself. I couldn't believe I'd spoken the words aloud. Yet, visions of their future marriage flashed before me, reassuring me that I was right. Later, she came back and admitted I was right. She confessed that her actions were driven by frustration, fear, and insecurity, worried she might never get married.

Over the years, I've prayed for many women who have since gotten married. I would dream of their spouses or receive impressions revealing 'the one' God had for them. Often, God gives me a word or something seemingly random to share with them, and it almost always relates to who they are going to marry. It was almost eerie at times because I kept thinking, "God, where's my man? Why am I getting words for others but not for myself?" And when I felt like God wasn't answering me, I'd throw a spiritual tantrum and tell God, "I should just go back to seeing my psychic besties—at least, they always have something to say."

There are many women who are called to marriage, yet they remain in a season of waiting, fearing their vision for a lifelong partnership may never come to pass. You feel it is time to release your inner Sarah and take bold control of your life. If that's you, lovely! I want to tell you what the Shulamite woman told her friends—and what I ended up saying to my friends too: "I charge you, O [daughter] of Jerusalem … Do not stir up nor awaken love until it pleases" (Song of Solomon 3:5).

You cannot make someone love you if they don't, and you can't make their heart feel something it refuses to feel. Anything else is simply manipulation and witchcraft. Isn't that what Satan does? In other words, you can't change people, and you can't make them step into a potential or vision that they don't see for themselves. You are not God! Even God respects our free will to either choose or refuse to be in fellowship with Him. So, as His child, you should extend that grace to others. As for this desire to prove your worth, you are already worthy. God has already justified and validated you through His grace, so you do not have to mold yourself to somebody else's expectations or jump through their hoops. Even God does not make us work for His love. He just loves, so anybody who makes you feel any differently is the unworthy one—unworthy of you and also unworthy to be your husband.

Listen, it's always tough to wait for something you desperately want to happen. Trust me, I know, even when you have received prophecies or confirmations from God. It's like death, literally. That is my testimony! I am a self-confessed control freak, so I don't wait very long for the things I want, either! But as Psalm 127:1 says, "Unless the Lord builds the house, they labor in vain who build it." You may have your ideas, blueprint, and timeline about how and when things are supposed to happen in your life, but as a child of God, you must have known by now that your life is not your own. Stop trying to run ahead of God while asking Him to bless the work of your hands, for all that is good and perfect comes from Him (not you). He is God, and the Bible says that God is love (1 John 4:8). So, it stands to reason that if and when it pleases Him, He will beautify your life with love in due time. Sisters, sit still and know that your kingdom-purpose partner is on the way!

Waiting can be hard, especially when that waiting is filled with uncertainty. God uses His perfect timing to shape us into who He wants us to be. I bet you hate waiting—and so do most people and me! Nobody likes to wait in this era of Amazon Prime and instant everything. Yet, no matter who you are, waiting is part of your life. I know because it's part of my life too. The real issue isn't the waiting itself but rather what we're waiting for and why. Why does God allow waiting in our lives? Why does God often seem so slow in answering the desires of our hearts?

The fact is that your waiting season is not the exception—it's the rule. We're all waiting for something. A quick scan of God's people and God's ways shows that God is a God who doesn't mind waiting. A thousand years in His eyes are like a day, and a day like a thousand years, as the Bible reminds us in Psalm 90:4 and 2 Peter 3:8. You can't rush God. You can't push God. You can't even manipulate God. See, in Hebrews 11:1, we're given a glimpse as to why: "Now faith is the substance of things hoped for, the evidence of things not seen." Waiting is about faith. It's about control—or, more specifically, yielding control of your life to God. Waiting is about trust. Abraham had to learn it and waited 25 years for his son of promise, Isaac. Joseph had to learn it in prison. Moses waited 40 years in the wilderness for his calling. David waited for Saul to settle down before he became king. The stories are too many to count, but rest assured: you're not the first person to wait, and more significantly, you're never alone in your waiting. While God may not be in a hurry, you can rest assured: He's always on time.

God allows us to wait for several reasons. The first reason is to reveal who we really are. When the pressure of life increases, the truth of who we are overflows. And nothing will reveal the real you like a season in the waiting. It shows what's in your heart. The second reason God allows us to spend time in the waiting is to slow or get rid of the self-sufficient you. We're all born with an intense desire to control our own lives. It's like we're born with a Ph.D. in doing it our way in our time. But when it comes to God's economy, obedience and yielding are the currencies that bring peace. The third reason God allows us to wait is that waiting grows the best version of you. It's in the waiting that God strips our independence and self-will and builds character and hope in our souls. It's in the waiting that we learn to be still and know that He is God. It's in the waiting that we finally wear down enough to say, "Yes, Lord, I'll do what You want. I surrender to You."

Back to me! I had to do better. I knew God had a call on my life, but I didn't want to embrace that call until I got the right man. Sorry, single folks, that isn't quite how it works. You fall in love with God first and allow Him to complete you before He presents you to your kingdom-purpose partner. Now, I will not lead you to believe that it's easy. It is not! While I have been abstinent for almost 11 years, I have grown so close to God. There are moments when I feel like I am being punished for all the wrong I've done. Can you imagine being a wedding planner, celebrating and planning love all the time? Or scrolling on social media and seeing God do it for everyone else? Well, that was me. But I know that God is preparing the perfect man for me. And, honey, let me tell you, he's perfect, and he is so worth the wait!

As a woman (or man) standing in faith for your future spouse, I encourage you to study the couples in the Bible. God will reveal the specific couple He wants you to focus on, and He will confirm it through His word. It will most certainly bless your life. Let me share what I've learned and the prayer points God has given me:

Let me share what I've learned and the prayer points God has given me:

1. **Abraham and Sarah:** Trust in God's timing, even when it seems like the promise is delayed. Pray for patience and faithfulness as you wait.
2. **Ruth and Boaz:** Pray for discernment in recognizing your spouse when they come and for grace to walk in humility, like Ruth, even in unexpected places.
3. **Priscilla and Aquila:** Pray for a partnership in purpose—a spouse with whom you can serve and build in God's kingdom. Marriage, Ministry and the Marketplace.
4. **Isaac and Rebekah:** Pray for the wisdom to seek God's direction, just as Rebekah was led to Isaac, trusting in His divine orchestration.

Let me tell you about Priscilla and how my study of her life has deeply impacted me. Priscilla represents a strong, capable woman who balanced managing her household, pursuing a trade, and being thoroughly involved in Christian ministry. She had a profound understanding of Scripture and was a skilled teacher, a respected leader in the early church, and known for her hospitality. Alongside her husband, Aquila, she contributed greatly to the spread of the gospel during the early years of the church. What's remarkable about Priscilla is that she didn't just support her husband—she worked alongside him as an equal partner in ministry. Together, they traveled, served, and even risked their lives for the gospel. Their relationship shows what a true partnership looks like: they were one in ministry, one in the marketplace, and one in their home. Studying Priscilla made me see a reflection of myself in her, which is why I say, "I am Priscilla!"

Now, let me share what I've learned and the prayer points God has given me as I prepare for my God-ordained marriage:

Priscilla and Aquila: Preparation for My God-ordained Marriage

Scripture References: Acts 18:2–3; Acts 18:18–19, 26; Romans 16:3–5; 1 Corinthians 16:19; 2 Timothy 4:19

Key Lessons:

- Priscilla and Aquila's names always appear together, indicating that they were never apart and always unified in their purpose.
- They endured hardships together, showing resilience and unwavering commitment to each other.
- They worked, traveled, and served the Lord together.
- Their home became a place for church gatherings, making them not just partners in marriage but in ministry and hospitality.
- They were risk-takers, willing to put their lives on the line for the gospel.
- Their marriage modeled the love of Christ for the church, exemplifying unity and spiritual strength.

As I began to reflect on the learning points from the passages, God gave me a specific assignment. He gave me prayer points to pray over my union. These were specific to the call that He has on my husband's life and mine.

Prayer Points:

1. **Commitment:** Pray that the Lord gives us the same unwavering commitment to one another as seen in Priscilla and Aquila's marriage.
2. **Unity in Purpose:** Ask for the Holy Spirit's guidance so that me and my spouse will function as a unified team in marriage, business, and ministry—two hearts becoming one.
3. **Growing Together in the Word:** Pray for a marriage where me and my spouse grow in our knowledge of God's Word and can teach and correct others with love and wisdom.

4. **Advancing the Kingdom:** Pray that me and my spouse will be relentless in advancing God's kingdom together, no matter the cost.
5. **Obedience to God's Calling:** Pray that me and my spouse will have the courage to follow God's leading together, wherever and whenever He calls.
6. **Marriage as a Ministry:** Pray that my marriage will be an example to those we minister to, demonstrating the love of Christ in all that we do.

This study of Priscilla has truly shaped my understanding of what it means to be in a God-ordained marriage, and I hope it helps someone else who is preparing for or standing in faith for their future spouse.

Many women often ask me, "How do you prepare to do what you do?" I am in no way the master at this thing. I don't want anyone to ever think it is easy. However, enjoying life as a single woman without a spouse can be a fulfilling and liberating experience. After many therapy sessions, I had to figure it out over time. Let me give you some tips that will help you:

- **Discover Personal Passions:** Use this time to explore your own interests and hobbies. Engage in activities that bring you joy and a sense of accomplishment, whether painting, dancing, writing, gardening, or any other creative or physical pursuit.
- **Cultivate Friendships:** Nurture existing friendships and seek to make new connections. Spending time with friends can offer companionship, support, and opportunities for fun outings or meaningful conversations.
- **Travel and Adventure:** Embrace the freedom to travel and explore new places. Solo travel can be incredibly enriching, allowing you to immerse yourself in different cultures, try new cuisines, and create lasting memories.

- **Personal Growth and Development:** Focus on your personal growth by setting and achieving goals. This could involve pursuing further education, learning a new skill, or working on self-improvement in areas that matter to you.
- **Physical Well-being:** Prioritize your health and well-being through regular exercise, a balanced diet, and self-care routines. Engaging in physical activities like jogging or meditation can promote both physical and mental wellness. I remain committed to fellowship and exercise by gathering with my sisters of Black Girl Run.
- **Volunteer and Give Back:** Contributing to your community through volunteering or participating in charitable activities can provide a sense of purpose and fulfillment. I exercise both of these through the social and professional organizations I am a member of.
- **Cultural and Social Activities:** Attend cultural events, concerts, art exhibitions, and other social gatherings to stay connected with your interests and meet new people. I absolutely love concerts. I am a huge fan of music.
- **Solo Adventures:** Don't hesitate to engage in activities by yourself, such as going to the movies, dining out, or taking day trips. Developing a sense of independence can boost your confidence and self-esteem. I traveled almost 8,000 miles across the world in July 2023 and 2024 to my favorite place, the Maldives. Do it, sis!
- **Journaling and Reflection:** Spend time reflecting on your thoughts and feelings through journaling. This practice can help you gain insights into your emotions, track your personal growth, and celebrate your achievements. I have so many journals, each labeled according to how I feel. I have found my own advice by reading some of my journals over the years.

- **Positive Mindset:** Cultivate a positive mindset by practicing gratitude and focusing on the things that bring you joy. Surround yourself with positivity and affirmations to maintain a healthy outlook on life.
- **Career and Personal Goals:** Dedicate time to your career aspirations and personal ambitions. Setting and achieving goals can provide a sense of accomplishment and purpose.
- **Therapeutic Outlets:** Engage in activities that provide emotional release and stress relief, such as practicing mindfulness, attending therapy or counseling, or participating in support groups.

Remember, enjoying life as a single individual is all about embracing your individuality, pursuing your passions, and creating a fulfilling and meaningful existence on your own terms. It's an opportunity to focus on self-discovery and personal growth, leading to a more empowered and satisfying life journey.

Most of us are very focused on the destination for our lives, on our dreams coming to pass, and on our problems turning around. But it's important that you learn to enjoy where you are today while you're on the way to where you're going. Life is not about the destination; it's about the journey—with all the bumps in the road, the disappointments, the things you don't understand. Too often, we rush through the day, trying to force our way through the challenges and setbacks to reach the destination when we should slow down and enjoy the journey. You're going to be frustrated living like that. You have to realize that God is ordering your steps. Often, the journey He leads us on is not comfortable, but all the difficulties, delays, and betrayals are a part of His plan to get us to our destiny. He will work all these things for your good. Stay in the present. Take it one day at a time. You don't have grace for tomorrow. You have grace for this present step.

In the words of Esther Crown, "I don't care how much a man tries to deny it ... Even if he didn't initially choose wisely ... a man of God, in God, recognizes his wife! He recognizes something in her that he hasn't seen in any other woman. Even if he isn't yet spiritually mature enough to pinpoint what it is, his spirit can't deny that there is something familiar about this woman! He can't deny her faith; he can't deny her anointing; he can't deny the connection! He recognizes himself in her, and this may be a bit scary if the man doesn't fully understand God's order concerning marriage. Some men just thought God taking a rib from man and making a helpmeet was a nice biblical story ... until he met her!" This quote beautifully captures the profound spiritual recognition that occurs when a man of God encounters the woman destined to be his wife.

Esther Crown's words emphasize that even if a man may not have made wise choices in the past, once he is in alignment with God, he can't help but recognize his wife's unique essence. There's something deeply familiar about her that speaks to his spirit—a connection he cannot deny, even if he isn't fully aware of its divine significance. Her faith, her anointing, and the sense of completeness he feels in her presence all point to something greater: the reflection of God's divine order for marriage.

The idea of the rib, often seen as a biblical metaphor, becomes a real experience when he meets her. It's not just a story anymore—it's God's design for the two to become one. This recognition can be overwhelming, especially if the man doesn't yet fully understand God's plan for marriage, but it's unmistakable. The connection goes beyond physical attraction or even emotional compatibility. It's spiritual—his spirit recognizes in her the helpmeet that God intended for him from the very beginning.

PROPHETIC DECLARATIONS
MARRIAGE DECREES

One night, God woke me up and instructed me to write these decrees. He told me to share them with a select group of women, and I have witnessed God's hand manifesting through these words. These decrees are powerful reminders of what God has in store for your future marriage.

I PROPHESY:

- Soon, it will be my turn. It will be my turn to have someone in my corner who loves me for who I am, not just for my gifts or achievements.
- It will soon be my turn for God to send someone who can handle my tenacity, drive, determination, boldness, and passion.
- It will soon be my turn for God to bring me someone to build with, serve with, do ministry with, and enjoy life together to the fullest.
- It will soon be my turn that, even though I may be surrounded by other amazing people, I will be the one they choose.
- It will soon be my turn to live a fulfilled life, enjoying intimacy and connection with my spouse. I declare that we will experience the joy of love, whether it's deep, meaningful moments or spontaneous fun!
- I'm just saying… it's my turn and my time. The 4th quarter is here, and God's alignment is upon me!

For My Future Spouse:

- My spouse will have a heart that desires to be in the Word daily, striving to live a life that pleases the Lord.
- My spouse will be reminded that God desires to bring them goodness and fulfill the desires of their heart. They will cling to God and find their fulfillment in Him.
- My spouse will lead us with Christ at the center, loving me as Christ loves the church—selflessly and sacrificially.
- My spouse will have the strength and courage to pursue their calling and purpose.
- My spouse will be surrounded by people who are godly influences, like-minded in their pursuit of Christ and in maintaining healthy relationships.
- My spouse will be plugged into a strong church community, with a support system of friends who encourage and pray for them.
- My spouse will flee from temptation and stand firm in God's truth, keeping their heart and mind pure.
- My spouse will take time to seek God, setting aside time to be alone in His presence.
- My spouse will honor God in how they conduct themselves, and I pray for God's protection over them wherever they go.
- My spouse will have the conviction and boldness to share their heart with clarity and confidence.
- My spouse will be a person after God's heart, willing to pray for and with me. They will embody wisdom, be financially wise, and have a strong work ethic.
- My spouse will bear the fruit of the Spirit, be a person of integrity, keep their word, and treat everyone with kindness and respect.

- My spouse will see me and treat me like their favor, understanding that I am the answer to prayers they didn't even know they were praying.
- My spouse will walk in their purpose, knowing exactly why God brought us together to fulfill His will.

Chapter 6

MOVE FORWARD!

> *"I will instruct you and teach you in the way you should go;*
> *I will counsel you with my loving eye on you."*
> —Psalm 32:8 (NIV)

How to: Move Forward!"

I destroyed many friendships due to my dishonesty about my struggles and covering up situations I didn't want to face, as lying seemed easier than confronting the truth. I didn't realize how powerful dishonesty was until I began to lose friends and hear rumors about me being a liar. There were so many nights when I wept because of my dishonesty and desire to be seen, helped, and rescued truly, but I didn't know how to escape the reasoning I had succumbed to. Here I was, lying to keep people from looking at me a certain way, when in truth, I feared to let people see me for who I really was and give them the opportunity to support me and be there for me. I wasn't sleeping at night. I would gain a lot of weight, join a weight loss program, and lose the weight—wash, rinse, repeat. Oh, and don't let there be a "man interest"; I can shed that weight overnight.

I knew there was a piece of me that I needed to connect with. After hearing God's voice that night in the grocery store after trying to kill myself, I knew I wanted to be better. I knew it was time for me to face my issues. I started seeing a Christian counselor and other types of therapists again who specialized in different things. Then, one day, I watched a YouTube video about finding yourself. Some of the points the speaker made reminded me of some things my grandmother would say. I always reflect on my grandmother's wisdom and laugh about how it all makes sense now. But I had a team of folks helping me. I selected a therapist at Kaiser. I was also seeing a grief counselor and another therapist. I needed everyone!

I knew it was time for me to buckle down and seek God. I began googling words that I knew I was dealing with—pride, lying, heartbreak, loneliness, suicide. I would write down scriptures pertaining to these words because it was important that I knew what God had to say about my life. I would post these scriptures on my wall and rehearse and quote them. I would often wake up in the middle of the night, sit on the floor Indian style, and meditate on the scriptures. I began to connect with God in a new way. Then, my prayer life increased. We'd have healing conversations. I would sit in the presence of God for hours. Over time, between therapy and spending intentional time with God, I began to heal and actually felt good about life. For the first time, I experienced a deep satisfaction that wasn't tied to material possessions or sex. It was a beautiful, peaceful sense of contentment that came from knowing God. I began to speak in faith. Instead of being pessimistic, I developed a faith language the more I spent time in prayer, and I began to believe for better and speak those things that were not as though they were.

One of the best things about having a relationship with God is being able to cast your cares on Him! You can be so honest without shame. I would cry out to God, "I'm lonely! I want a man!" or "I'm feeling very low right now and want to kill myself! I need You to help me!" I received supernatural strength just on the other side of crying out. In the presence of God, you receive an outpour, a filling that can't be explained. There is confidence in knowing that God is with you and for you. I now believe that I have something to say. I believe I have a story that will bring glory to Christ and that I no longer need to hide because I am a city on a hill that cannot be hidden! I am the light of the world! I am pressing toward the mark. I know you all are perfect and probably cannot relate, but it was a tough place to get to.

In counseling, I learned to take responsibility for my life and forgive myself. Forgiveness is essential to the prosperity of your life. It is not an easy feat. Hello! The cross was all about "Forgive them, Lord, for they know now what they do." That is the literal depiction of how painful forgiving can be, but it's also liberating. To forgive is to free yourself from guilt, shame, and bitterness and to free others from facing a death sentence that you're not God enough to say they deserve—because God is the only one holy enough to be a judge. We are not strong enough to be unforgiving. If so, it would not manifest physically in our bodies. Studies have shown that harboring unforgiveness can be attributed to high blood pressure, stress that leads to death, insomnia, anger, impulsivity, compulsivity, cardiovascular problems, chronic bodily pain, and more. I experienced all of this.

Our trauma and life experiences can not only pollute our hearts but also become trapped in our bodies, manifesting as sickness or pain. I had to say, "La Shawn, I forgive you for all the lies you told. I forgive you for sleeping with multiple men. I forgive you for hating and trying to kill yourself. I forgive you for thinking you weren't worth someone loving you for you. I forgive you for pleasing people at the expense of yourself. Lord, I repent for trying to be the god of my life as well as others who are close to me."

Then came My Sister's Keeper, the nonprofit that birthed the Refresh, Restore, Revive, and Renew Retreat, later rebranded as The Wonder Woman Conference. This initiative provided me with a platform to minister to women who, like me, weren't perfect and had made mistakes. However, we weren't afraid to dust ourselves off and continue on our path to pursue God wholeheartedly. As I grew in my faith and deepened my understanding of the Word, my desire for ministry flourished. I felt a strong calling to empower and inspire women, particularly in helping them turn their passions into multiple income streams.

The Wonder Woman Conference was birthed from a profound desire to empower women from all walks of life—those who strive to overcome their pasts, pursue their dreams, and embrace their identities as strong, capable individuals. This conference symbolizes strength, resilience, and the unique power women possess to effect change in their lives and communities. The name "Wonder Woman" embodies the qualities of bravery, determination, and the ability to juggle multiple responsibilities while remaining grounded in one's faith. It serves as a reminder that every woman has the potential to be extraordinary, even amid challenges. Through this conference, we aim to create a space where women can come together, share their stories, and inspire one another to pursue their passions unapologetically. The mission extends beyond inspiration; we are committed to providing tangible resources and strategies for women to turn their passions into multiple income streams.

The Wonder Woman Conference is not just an event; it's a movement aimed at transforming lives, fostering community, and equipping women with the tools they need to thrive. By focusing on healing, wholeness, and wealth-building, we encourage women to rise as leaders in their families, businesses, and communities. The conference serves as a platform for collaboration, networking, and mentorship, ensuring that every woman leaves feeling empowered and equipped to make her mark in the world. Ultimately, The Wonder Woman Conference is about celebrating each woman's unique journey and reinforcing the belief that, together, we can achieve greatness. This conference would become more than just an inspirational gathering; it would serve as a transformative platform to help women build wealth and become whole, healed individuals. This journey ultimately led to the establishment of Charity House and Rahab's Daughters, further extending my mission to uplift and support women in their personal and financial growth.

I love talking with women, praying with them, and being that light for them by courageously sharing my testimony. I believe I have a breaker anointing on my life to free women who are oppressed, empowering them to live the purposeful life God has for them. I knew that writing this book would provide the opportunity for my readers to recognize their worth and boldly affirm, "I am better than this!"—no matter what "this" represents to you. I am praying for you! Forgive yourself, I beg of you! Go to counseling; find support groups; write letters to yourself! You are not defined by your circumstances, the choices you've made, or the harmful experiences that have shaped your life. You are so much more than these things; your true worth and potential extend far beyond.

Through letter-writing and prayer, I found solace. I'd write, pray until I felt freedom, and then ceremoniously burn the letters, letting go of the pain. Sometimes, you have to do practical, concrete things to demonstrate faith. Well, writing letters was my act of faith—giving my problems to God, casting my cares on Him, and trusting that He hears me. I released my burdens, confident that I wouldn't pick them up again. Setting the letters on fire symbolized receiving beauty for ashes.

LA SHAWN DECREE AND DECLARE

- Your Word tells me not to worry about anything but, instead, to pray about everything. It says, "Tell God what you need and thank Him for all He has done."
- God, Your Word says it is not good that my husband (wife) should be alone. You said, "I will make him(her) a helper comparable to him(her)." You have created me for my Husband (Wife). Your Word also says that at the right time, You will make it happen.
- Angels will shift, move, and set things up to prepare things for me. Please send angelic help to me. Set me up for victory.
- God, You said You will give me what I need.
- Thank You for the increase, advancement, and acceleration.
- Father, Your anointing is on me today. It breaks the yokes off the oppressed. Your Word is alive in me today! Revelation knowledge flows out of me today. I operate in the gifts of the Spirit as the Spirit wills in me today.
- I walk in safety and supernatural protection every day. No weapon that the enemy forms against me today shall prosper. I walk in financial abundance. God supplies all of my needs—not half of them, but all of them.
- I walk in faith consistently, for Jesus has freed me from fear and doubt. Fear will not rule me; faith will! I speak words of life. Today, I cast all my cares on Christ. I choose to meditate on the promises and not the problem.

SCRIPTURES TO SUPPORT THE JOURNEY

- "When I am afraid, I put my trust in you. In God, whose word I praise, in God I trust; I shall not be afraid. What can flesh do to me?"—Psalm 56:3–4
- "Therefore, I tell you, whatever you ask in prayer, believe that you have received it, and it will be yours."—Mark 11:24
- "But I have trusted in your steadfast love; my heart shall rejoice in your salvation."—Psalm 13:5
- "You keep him in perfect peace whose mind is stayed on you, because he trusts in you. Trust in the Lord forever, for the Lord God is an everlasting rock."—Isaiah 26:3–4
- "Blessed is the man who makes the Lord his trust, who does not turn to the proud, to those who go astray after a lie!"—Psalm 40:4
- "Trust in the Lord with all your heart, and do not lean on your own understanding. In all your ways acknowledge him, and he will make straight your paths."—Proverbs 3:5–6
- "For I know the plans I have for you, declares the Lord, plans for welfare and not for evil, to give you a future and a hope."—Jeremiah 29:11
- "There is no fear in love, but perfect love casts out fear. For fear has to do with punishment, and whoever fears has not been perfected in love."—1 John 4:18
- "Commit your way to the Lord; trust in him, and he will act."—Psalm 37:5

Chapter 7

"IF IT DON'T MAKE CENTS, IT DON'T MAKE SENSE!"

> "But remember the Lord your God, for it is he who gives you the ability to produce wealth."
> —Deuteronomy 8:18 (NIV)

Here we are, at a heartfelt and transparent chapter in my journey, where I'm ready to share my story of overcoming struggles with money management—a topic that once felt overwhelming and intimidating. Like many, I faced my share of financial struggles, often feeling lost in a sea of bills and responsibilities. However, through introspection and perseverance, I discovered valuable principles that not only helped me regain control over my finances but also transformed my relationship with money. In these pages, I aim to candidly reflect on my experiences and the lessons I've learned, hoping to empower you to embrace your own financial journey with confidence and clarity. Together, we can navigate the complexities of money management and build a brighter, more secure future.

My journey with money began in college. Like many young adults, I was excited about the newfound freedom that came with being financially independent. I can still remember the Lair Patio at Loyola Marymount University—a bustling area filled with students, where companies set up tables offering the latest "opportunities" to apply for credit cards. They made it seem so easy and enticing. All I had to do was fill out an application, and within weeks, I'd have another shiny new credit card waiting for me in the mail.

By the time I was a sophomore in college, I had accumulated 33 credit cards. Yes, 33! Many were store cards from retailers I couldn't even pronounce, let alone afford. I wasn't just buying books or covering tuition; I was living beyond my means, spending money on things I didn't need and could barely justify. And the worst part? I thought it was all harmless. I felt invincible, as if those little pieces of plastic were a passport to a better life.

The Allure of Credit: A False Sense of Wealth
At first, credit felt like free money. I remember the rush of excitement whenever I swiped my card to make a purchase—whether it was clothes, electronics, or even meals out with friends. Each swipe felt like a mini victory, like I was getting away with something. The adrenaline rush was real. Every time I swiped that card, I wasn't thinking about how I'd pay back. I was only focused on what I could get in that moment.

I bought extravagant clothes, shoes, and Gucci bags I didn't need, thinking they would somehow enhance my status or make me feel more confident. I remember buying a pair of shoes that cost more than my entire meal plan for the semester. I didn't even wear them that often—they just sat in my closet, a symbol of my reckless spending.

Then there were the electronics. I once maxed out two credit cards to buy the latest stereo system for my dorm room. It wasn't even something I needed—just another impulse purchase driven by the thrill of spending. The stereo made me feel good for about two weeks, but that high quickly faded when the bills started rolling in.

The Emotional Rollercoaster of Debt

As the number of credit cards in my wallet grew, so did my debt. Eventually, the weight of it all became unbearable. Maxing out cards became a constant cycle—paying the minimum balance just to stay afloat, then charging more and digging myself deeper into a hole. The things I bought no longer gave me joy; they became reminders of the financial mess I had created for myself.

I remember sitting in my dorm room, surrounded by clothes and gadgets, but feeling completely empty. I had all this stuff, but it did nothing to fill the void. If anything, the constant pressure of making payments and avoiding collection calls only made the anxiety worse.

A Personal Anecdote: The Emotional Impact of My Spending
One of my most vivid memories is from my junior year of college. I was planning to attend a friend's birthday dinner at an upscale restaurant. Of course, I didn't have the money to cover the cost, but that didn't stop me. I bought a new outfit, complete with a designer purse and shoes, just for that one night. I wanted to impress my friends, but deep down, I knew I was living a lie.

The night itself was enjoyable—I felt glamorous and confident—but the next day, reality set in. I received yet another credit card bill, and it was the straw that broke the camel's back. My balance had reached a point where even the minimum payments seemed impossible. I sat on my bed, staring at the bill, overwhelmed by a sinking feeling of dread. How did I get here? How had I allowed myself to get so out of control?

The Wake-Up Call

It wasn't long after that night that I hit rock bottom, financially speaking. The credit card companies started calling, and there was no more pretending that everything was fine. The purchases I had made in an attempt to impress others or fill some emotional void had backfired. Instead of feeling empowered, I felt trapped. I had allowed my desire for material things to cloud my judgment, and now I was paying the price—literally and emotionally.

Reflection: Reckless Spending and Emotional Purchasing

Looking back, I realize that my spending habits weren't just about wanting nice things. They were driven by deeper emotional needs—needs for validation, acceptance, and self-worth. Each credit card swipe was a temporary band-aid for feelings of inadequacy, stress, or insecurity.

I know I'm not alone in this. So many of us fall into the trap of emotional spending, using money as a way to cope with the pressures and challenges of life. But the reality is that no amount of spending can fill the void inside. Instead, it creates more problems—financial stress, emotional anxiety, and a never-ending cycle of debt.

Reflection for Readers: Evaluating Your Own Spending Habits

I encourage you to take a moment and reflect on your own spending habits. Are there times when you find yourself shopping or spending money to cope with stress, loneliness, or the need for approval? What patterns of reckless spending have you noticed in your own life? Here are a few questions to consider:

- What motivates your spending? Do you buy things to feel better or impress others rather than out of necessity?
- Have you ever made a purchase that you later regretted, financially or emotionally?
- How do your spending habits impact your overall well-being—emotionally, mentally, and financially?

Take some time to reflect on these questions and evaluate whether your spending aligns with your values and long-term financial goals. Remember, it's never too late to break free from the cycle of emotional purchasing and start making smarter financial decisions. Listen, if you good, you good!

Fresh Start: Learning Financial Responsibility

One significant turning point in my financial journey came during my college years when I found myself drowning in debt. My carefree spending had caught up with me, and the weight of those maxed-out credit cards was becoming unbearable. Despite my outward appearance of confidence and independence, internally, I was overwhelmed by the reality of my financial situation. I knew drastic change was necessary, so I swallowed my pride and turned to my father for help. I was so embarrassed to tell him the amount of debt I had racked up. It wasn't just from tuition or books but from years of reckless spending—new clothes, meals out, gadgets, and everything in between.

At the time, I couldn't bring myself to admit that my spending wasn't out of necessity but a way to mask the emotional pain I was dealing with. I had used shopping as a form of escapism, hoping that new things would somehow fill the void I felt inside.

When I finally sat down to tell my dad about my financial situation, I felt I had failed. I expected him to be angry, to lecture me about my irresponsibility. But instead, he listened calmly. He didn't judge me, and to my surprise, he agreed to help me. My dad paid off the majority of my debt—a staggering amount—and with that gesture, he gave me a fresh start.

Personal Anecdote: The Emotional Impact of My Dad's Generosity
I'll never forget the mix of emotions I felt the day my dad bailed me out. On one hand, I was deeply relieved that the suffocating weight of debt was lifted. But on the other hand, I was ashamed. I realized that I had put my father in a position where he had to step in and fix my mistakes. His generosity wasn't just a gift—it was a lesson. I knew this wasn't just a financial transaction; it was a reflection of his belief in me and his hope that I would learn from this. His act of kindness forced me to take a long, hard look at my relationship with money. Up until that point, I had treated money as something fleeting, a tool for instant gratification, not something to be managed or respected.

My dad's help made me realize how much responsibility I had to take for my financial actions, not just for myself but for those who cared about me. This experience marked a shift in how I viewed money. I realized that money was not just about what I could buy or achieve in the short term—it was about long-term security, legacy, and responsibility. My dad sacrificed his hard-earned money to clear my slate, and I knew I had to do better.

Reflection: The Ripple Effect of Our Financial Decisions
It's easy to think of our financial decisions as isolated—something that affects only us. But the truth is, our financial choices can have a ripple effect on the people who love and care for us. I never considered how my debt might impact my father—not just financially but emotionally. He had worked so hard to provide for me and give me opportunities, and here I was, throwing money away on things that didn't matter.

I was fortunate that my father was in a position to help me, but not everyone has that safety net. And even if they do, is it fair to expect others to clean up our financial messes? My experience made me realize that every financial decision I make is part of the legacy I'm building—not just for myself but for those who come after me. Whether we realize it or not, we are all leaving behind a financial legacy.

Take a moment to think about how your financial decisions today are impacting the people in your life. Have your spending habits ever caused stress for someone else? Have you had to rely on family or friends to help you out of a financial bind? How did that make you feel?

More importantly, consider the legacy you want to leave behind. Financial responsibility isn't just about saving money or paying off debt; it's about building something sustainable that you can pass on to future generations. What kind of financial example do you want to set for your children, family, or community? The choices we make today will echo in the lives of those we care about.

Now is the time to shift your mindset about money. Let your financial decisions be guided not just by your immediate desires but by the long-term impact they will have on the people you love and the legacy you leave behind.

Things Were Fine for A While

After my father paid off my debt, I made a conscious effort to live within my means. I created a budget, cut back on unnecessary spending, and told myself I'd never end up in that position again. For a brief period, it felt like I had turned over a new leaf. I had a handle on my finances and was beginning to build a healthier relationship with money. But as time went on, old habits began to resurface. Slowly, I started to fall back into the same dangerous patterns.

My spending would spiral out of control, often triggered by moments of stress or emotional lows. I would buy things I didn't need just to make myself feel better, and before I knew it, I was back to racking up credit card debt and taking out personal loans with no savings to fall back on. It became a vicious cycle—moments of control followed by periods of financial chaos. No matter how hard I tried, I couldn't seem to break free from the emotional pull of spending, and each time I thought I had a handle on it, the weight of financial mismanagement would creep back in. It felt like I was constantly starting over, never able to move forward.

Desperation's Detour: Lessons from the Wrong Turns

When people accuse me of anything illegal or unethical involving money today, I can say with absolute certainty that it's completely false. I am terrified of crossing any legal or ethical lines, even when it comes to something as minor as taxes. I don't play with anything that could jeopardize my integrity or freedom. That fear stems from a time in my life when desperation led me down a path I never thought I'd take.

During one of the lowest points in my life, bills were piling up, and every day felt like a losing battle against survival. In an attempt to make ends meet, I got involved with some old friends in using stolen credit cards and writing bad checks. At the time, it felt like the only way out—a quick fix to solve immediate problems. I justified it by telling myself I didn't have a choice, but deep down, I knew it wasn't right.

What I didn't realize was that every swipe of a stolen card and every signature on a fraudulent check wasn't just a financial misstep—it was a step away from my integrity, my values, and the person I wanted to be. Instead of bringing relief, these choices brought more stress, guilt, and a gnawing feeling that I was headed down a destructive path.

Looking back, I see how those moments of desperation became pivotal lessons in my life. They taught me the high cost of shortcuts and the importance of aligning my actions with the values I aspire to live by. More importantly, they showed me how God's grace can redeem even the worst of decisions. I was eventually able to find my way back—not just financially, but spiritually and emotionally.

Today, I am intentional about maintaining integrity in all areas of my life. I've seen what happens when desperation clouds judgment, and I refuse to walk that road again. My past mistakes are a reminder of the importance of honesty, accountability, and doing things the right way, no matter how challenging life gets.

Learning the Hard Way: Spending Money on Men

In my quest for love and validation, I mistakenly believed that money could buy affection, loyalty, and commitment. Looking back, I can see just how misguided that belief was. I mentioned earlier I often found myself spending large sums of money on men—whether it was taking them out to expensive dinners, buying extravagant gifts, or covering costs that weren't my responsibility—all in the hope that these material offerings would secure their love and devotion. Deep down, I was trying to use money as a way to prove my worth and loyalty, as if each purchase would somehow solidify the relationship.

One relationship stands out in particular. I remember being in a relationship with a man who I thought, at the time, was "the one." He wasn't in the best financial shape, and I wanted to help. I'd take him out to dinner, pay for our weekend trips, and even help cover some of his bills when he struggled. I bought him clothes, tech gadgets, and gifts for no reason at all—other than wanting to show him how much I cared. I thought that by giving him these things, I was proving my loyalty and commitment, but in reality, I was using my money to keep him attached. I thought, *If I do this for him, he'll see how much I care and love me in return.*

At first, it felt good to give. I told myself it was part of building a relationship, but over time, it became clear that the affection I was trying to buy was shallow and conditional. He didn't reciprocate the same level of effort, financially or emotionally. The relationship ended up being one-sided, and the more I gave, the less I seemed to get in return. I remember a particularly low point when I spent a significant amount of money planning a surprise weekend getaway for the two of us, only for him to cancel at the last minute without a real explanation. I felt humiliated, not just by his actions, but by the realization that I had been using money to prove myself to him—only to be left feeling emptier and more insecure than before.

Overextending Myself for Love

Looking back, I realize just how much I sacrificed in an attempt to prove my love and loyalty to the wrong people. I've gotten apartments in my name for men, purchased cars for them, and even helped provide for their children in an attempt to build relationships with the kids. I thought that going above and beyond would solidify my place in their lives and hearts. I was constantly overextending myself, trying to fill a void or earn affection through material acts. I've done it all—and paid the emotional and financial price for it.

At the time, I believed these sacrifices showed my dedication and value in the relationship. But the truth was, I was giving from a place of insecurity, trying to find worth in being needed. I poured into these situations hoping they would see my heart and reciprocate, but instead, I often found myself drained—emotionally, financially, and spiritually.

It took hitting rock bottom to realize that love isn't something we can buy or prove through self-sacrifice. Real love honors, uplifts, and reciprocates; it doesn't demand you to lose yourself to keep it. The relationships I was trying to build with their children were rooted in a desire for connection, but I now understand that real connection starts with honoring my own worth first.

Personal Anecdote: The Emotional Toll of Buying Love
Over time, these types of relationships took a huge toll on my finances and my emotional well-being. Each time I overspent or made another extravagant gesture, I dug deeper into debt and emotional turmoil. It wasn't just the money I was losing—I was losing pieces of myself too. Every unreciprocated gift, every time I pulled out my wallet hoping for love in return, chipped away at my self-esteem. I started associating my worth with how much I could give materially, as if my value as a woman was tied to how much I was willing to sacrifice financially.

I would lie awake at night, knowing deep down that I was being used but too afraid to confront it. I feared that if I stopped spending or giving, he would leave—and in many cases, that's exactly what happened. The men didn't stay because I had given them so much; they stayed as long as it was convenient for them. When the money ran out or I started to question the dynamic, they were gone. I learned the hard way that you can't buy loyalty or love, no matter how much money you spend or how many gifts you give.

Reflection: Evaluating the Motivations Behind Spending
For those reading this, I encourage you to take a step back and evaluate your own relationships. Are you spending money in an attempt to seek validation or to prove your worth? Do you find yourself leveraging financial gifts as a way to keep someone attached to you? What are the underlying motivations behind your spending habits?

It's easy to fall into the trap of thinking that giving financially equates to giving love. But the truth is, when we rely on money to keep someone in our lives, we ultimately set ourselves up for disappointment. Ask yourself: "Is this person truly invested in me, or are they simply benefiting from what I'm providing financially?" It's a tough question—but one that can lead to important realizations about the relationship dynamics.

The Illusion of Worth

It took me time—and many painful lessons— to realize that true worth cannot be bought or sold. My attempts to impress men through spending money only left me feeling emptier than before. I was trying to prove my loyalty, love, and value through material things, but I wasn't getting the validation or commitment I sought. Instead, I was left feeling used and unappreciated.

I had to learn that my worth wasn't tied to how much I could give financially and that love isn't something you earn by paying for it. It's something that should be freely given and reciprocated. When I stopped using money as a tool for validation, I started to see myself differently. I no longer needed to impress anyone with lavish gifts or expensive gestures. I realized that my value wasn't determined by what I could give but by who I was—a woman worthy of love, respect, and mutual effort.

Personal Reflection: Learning to Value Myself Beyond Money
As I began to heal from these experiences, I reflected on why I had allowed myself to fall into this pattern in the first place. I realized that I was seeking external validation because I hadn't fully embraced my own self-worth. I thought that by spending money on others, they would see how much I cared, but I was really just trying to fill a void within myself. Once I

recognized this, I knew I needed to change—not just my spending habits but my entire approach to relationships.

I started to focus on building my own self-esteem, independent of what I could give to others. I worked on cultivating a sense of inner worth and learning to love myself without needing external approval or financial validation. The journey wasn't easy, but it was necessary. Over time, I realized that the right people would love and respect me for who I was, not for what I could offer them financially.

Scriptural Reference: 1 Peter 3:3-4
This lesson brought me back to 1 Peter 3:3-4, which says, "Your beauty should not come from outward adornment, such as elaborate hairstyles and the wearing of gold jewelry or fine clothes. Rather, it should be that of your inner self, the unfading beauty of a gentle and quiet spirit, which is of great worth in God's sight." This verse helped shift my perspective on worth and beauty. I realized that what makes a person truly valuable isn't the material things they can provide but the inner beauty of their character, their kindness, and their spirit.

By focusing on building a strong inner self—one grounded in confidence, faith, and self-respect—I started to attract healthier, more genuine relationships. I no longer felt the need to "buy" someone's affection or prove my loyalty through financial sacrifices. Instead, I valued myself enough to know that I deserved love and respect just as I was.

Reflection for Readers: Breaking the Cycle of Emotional Spending
For anyone who has found themselves in a similar situation, I encourage you to take a moment to reflect on how you may be using money in your relationships. Are you trying to prove your worth through financial means? Do you feel like you have to spend in order to keep someone in your life?

Remember, your worth is not tied to what you can give. It's tied to who you are. True love, loyalty, and commitment can't be bought. They come from a place of mutual respect, trust, and genuine connection. Don't let emotional spending become a crutch in your relationships. Instead, focus on building healthy, balanced dynamics where your value is recognized beyond what you can offer materially. Learn to appreciate the beauty within yourself and surround yourself with people who see and value that beauty too.

The Wake-Up Call: Filing for Bankruptcy

By 2018, my financial situation had spiraled completely out of control again. The brief moments of stability I had managed to create were long gone, replaced by an overwhelming mountain of debt that I couldn't escape. Personal loans, credit cards, unpaid bills—it all became too much to handle. Again, I was way over my head, struggling to make even the minimum payments each month, and I had no idea how I would get through this storm. On top of that, I was faced with the enormous responsibility of keeping my daughter at Howard University, one of the top priorities in my life at the time. It felt like I was drowning in quicksand—no matter how hard I tried to pull myself out, I was sinking deeper into debt, anxiety, and uncertainty.

The collection calls became a constant source of stress. Every time my phone rang, my heart would race with panic. There were days I would avoid answering the phone altogether because I couldn't bear the thought of hearing yet another creditor on the other end demanding money I didn't have. I was exhausted. The pressure of it all weighed heavily on me—not just the financial aspect but the shame, the fear of failure, and the uncertainty of what would happen next. I was terrified that I wouldn't be able to keep my daughter in school. I couldn't let her down, but I had no idea how I was going to continue paying tuition or manage the rest of my life at the same time.

Personal Anecdote: The Decision to File for Bankruptcy
Filing for bankruptcy felt like the only option left, but it was a decision I agonized over. It wasn't something I wanted to do. In fact, I had avoided it for as long as I could because it felt like admitting defeat—like I had failed not just myself but my family. When I finally made the decision, I remember sitting in my living room, staring at the paperwork. I felt numb. How did it come to this? How had I lost control so completely that I couldn't see a way out? I remember breaking down in tears, thinking about my daughter and the example I was setting for her. Would she see me as a failure? Would she think I had given up?

The process itself was draining, emotionally and mentally. I felt like I was baring all my mistakes and missteps to the world. It was a public declaration of my failure to manage my finances, and the shame weighed heavily on me. I had to disclose every detail of my financial situation—every debt, every missed payment, every loan—and it felt like standing naked in front of a crowd. Filing for bankruptcy meant acknowledging that I couldn't fix this on my own, and that was a hard pill to swallow. I had always prided myself on being independent and able to take care of things, but now I was admitting that I had lost control. But what hit me the hardest was the fear of how it would impact my daughter's future. Would I be able to keep her at Howard University? The tuition was steep, and I had already taken out loans to cover it. I feared that filing for bankruptcy would mean pulling her out of school, derailing her dreams and her path to success. That thought alone kept me up at night. In those moments, I prayed harder than ever, asking God to show me a way through the mess I had created.

Scriptural Reference: Proverbs 22:7

As I struggled through this painful experience, one verse kept coming back to me: Proverbs 22:7, which says, "The borrower is slave to the lender." It's a stark reminder of the reality of living in debt and the bondage it creates. That verse resonated deeply with me because that's exactly how I felt—enslaved by my debt. I was living paycheck to paycheck, not for myself or my family but to satisfy the demands of creditors. My life wasn't my own anymore. Every decision I made was influenced by how much I owed, how little I had, and how deep in the hole I was.

Debt creates a cycle of bondage, one that consumes not just your finances but your peace of mind. It seeps into every area of your life—your relationships, health, and spirit. I wasn't living; I was merely surviving, shackled to the burden of debt. And that's the lesson I took from Proverbs 22:7—debt is a form of slavery, one that keeps you from moving forward and living in the freedom God intends for you.

The bankruptcy process was my wake-up call. It forced me to confront the fact that I had allowed myself to become enslaved by my spending habits, desire for material things, and failure to be a responsible steward of the resources God had given me. I had to acknowledge that I had been living outside God's plan for my finances. God wants us to be wise stewards of our resources, not slaves to debt.

Reflection: The Burden of Debt and the Path to Freedom

Filing for bankruptcy wasn't the end of the story—it was the beginning of a long process of rebuilding, not just financially but emotionally and spiritually. It was a humbling experience, one that made me re-evaluate my relationship with money and the priorities in my life. I realized that my financial habits weren't just about poor budgeting—they were tied to deeper issues, like using spending to mask emotional pain and seeking validation through material possessions. But through that experience, I learned the importance of humility, asking for help, and trusting that God can guide us even when we feel lost.

The bankruptcy wasn't just a financial reset; it was a spiritual reset. It forced me to let go of the shame and start focusing on what truly mattered—my daughter's future, my personal growth, and my relationship with God. While it was an incredibly difficult chapter in my life, it also taught me that financial freedom isn't just about having money—it's about being free from the chains of debt, the anxiety of owing more than you can repay, and the stress of living beyond your means. It's about learning to live within God's plan for your life, trusting Him to provide, and being a responsible steward of what He has given you.

How It All Changed: Biblical Principles of Stewardship

Understanding the biblical principles of stewardship became pivotal in reshaping my approach to money. For years, I had been reckless with my finances, trying to control my life through material things while neglecting one of the most important financial principles found in the Bible: tithing. I wasn't consistent in my tithing, and that inconsistency was reflected in the way I handled the rest of my finances. Tithing—giving 10% of my income back to God—was a principle I learned growing up, but I hadn't prioritized it. The truth is, I hadn't trusted God enough to believe that by giving Him a portion of what He blessed me with, He would continue to provide for all my needs. It wasn't until I hit rock bottom financially, especially after filing for bankruptcy, that I started to reflect on the importance of doing things God's way when it came to money.

The Bible speaks clearly about tithing, not just as a command but as a form of trust and faith in God's provision. In Malachi 3:10, God says,

"'Bring the whole tithe into the storehouse, that there may be food in my house. Test me in this,' says the Lord Almighty, 'and see if I will not throw open the floodgates of heaven and pour out so much blessing that there will not be room enough to store it.'" That verse challenged me. God was asking me to trust Him with my finances, to put Him first by giving back a portion of what He had already given me, and to watch how He would bless me in return.

When I finally got serious about tithing, something shifted—not just in my finances but in my mindset. I began to understand that the money I had wasn't truly mine—it was God's, and I was merely a steward of it. I was responsible for managing it wisely and using it not just for my benefit but for His kingdom. Tithing was about more than just giving money to the church; it was about trusting God's provision and aligning my financial priorities with His.

Scriptural Reference: The Importance of Faithfulness
One of the key scriptures that guided me in this process of financial transformation is Luke 16:10–11, which says, "Whoever can be trusted with very little can also be trusted with much, and whoever is dishonest with very little will also be dishonest with much. So if you have not been trustworthy in handling worldly wealth, who will trust you with true riches?" This passage convicted me because it made me realize that if I couldn't be trusted with the money I had—even the little I thought I had—then how could I expect God to trust me with more? This verse taught me that faithfulness in managing worldly wealth was a prerequisite for receiving greater blessings—not just financial but spiritual and emotional as well. It shifted my mindset from thinking about what I could get to focusing on better managing what I already had. I had to stop viewing money as the answer to my problems and start seeing it as a tool for fulfilling God's purpose in my life.

Tithing and Giving to the Poor

In addition to tithing, the Bible also speaks about giving to the poor and those in need, especially when paired with spiritual disciplines like fasting. Isaiah 58:6-7 says, "Is not this the kind of fasting I have chosen: to loose the chains of injustice and untie the cords of the yoke, to set the oppressed free and break every yoke? Is it not to share your food with the hungry and to provide the poor wanderer with shelter—when you see the naked, to clothe them, and not to turn away from your own flesh and blood?" This verse expanded my understanding of stewardship.

Stewardship isn't just about giving to the church—it's also about using the resources God gives us to help those in need. When I combined tithing with intentional acts of generosity—whether it was giving to a local charity, helping someone in need, or supporting a cause that aligned with my values—I felt like I was living out the true essence of biblical stewardship. It wasn't about hoarding money for myself but using what I had to bless others.

Practical Application: Applying Biblical Principles to Financial Management

It took time, but once I committed to applying these biblical principles of stewardship, I started to see real change in my financial life. Here are some practical steps I took and that I encourage readers to consider as they seek to align their financial management with biblical teachings:

- **Start with Tithing Consistently**: This was the game-changer for me. I started giving 10% of my income to my church, even when it seemed like I couldn't afford to. It was an act of faith, and God honored that faith. If you've never tithed before, start now. It might feel uncomfortable at first, but trust that God will provide for you in ways you can't even imagine.

- **Create a Budget**: After I committed to tithing, I knew I needed to get serious about managing the rest of my money. I created a budget that prioritized my needs, savings, and giving. I listed all my expenses, separated wants from needs, and ensured I was living within my means. A budget isn't about restricting your freedom—it's about giving you control over your finances.

- **Set Financial Goals**: Once my budget was in place, I set both short-term and long-term financial goals. These included paying off debt, building an emergency fund, saving for the future, and continuing to give generously. Having specific goals in mind helped me stay on track and gave me something to work toward.

- **Prioritize Saving and Generosity**: Saving and giving go hand in hand in biblical stewardship. I made it a point to prioritize savings for emergencies and future opportunities that would allow me to continue giving. I also set aside a portion of my budget for acts of generosity, whether it was giving to charity or helping someone in need. It's important to remember that money is not meant to be hoarded; it's meant to be used for God's purposes.

- **Track Your Progress and Adjust as Needed**: I regularly reviewed my finances to ensure I stayed on track with my budget and goals. I adjusted when necessary, but I always kept my focus on faithfulness—faithfulness to tithing, saving, and giving.

Reflection for Readers

As you reflect on your own financial situation, I encourage you to think about how these biblical principles of stewardship might apply to your life. Are you consistently tithing? Are you prioritizing savings and giving? Do you have a plan for managing your resources wisely, or are you living paycheck to paycheck with no clear direction?

God has given each of us the ability to produce wealth, but with that ability comes the responsibility to manage it faithfully. Trusting Him with your finances by tithing, saving, and giving generously is not just about financial gain—it's about living in alignment with His will and purpose for your life.

Transforming My Mindset: From Scarcity to Abundance

Our mindset plays a profound role in shaping our relationship with money. For many of us, financial struggles can be deeply rooted in our thoughts, emotions, and beliefs. By transforming our mindset, we can break free from the limitations of a scarcity mentality and unlock a more abundant, prosperous life. In this section, we'll explore how shifting our perspective on money can have a profound impact on our financial well-being, and provide practical tools for budgeting and saving that can help us achieve our goals.

Shifting My Perspective on Money

For a long time, I operated from a scarcity mindset when it came to money. I viewed money as something that was always in short supply, something I had to hold onto tightly because I was afraid it would run out. My financial decisions were driven by fear—fear of not having enough, fear of losing what little I had, fear of being unable to provide for myself and my family. This mindset led me to make poor decisions. I was constantly either spending out of impulse or hoarding whatever I had, never feeling secure. But something shifted in me as I began to reflect more deeply on my faith and the principles of stewardship.

The change happened gradually, but the biggest turning point came after my bankruptcy. I remember feeling like I had lost everything, and in many ways, I had. I hit rock bottom, financially and emotionally, but in that low moment, I realized that my scarcity mindset had gotten me nowhere. I had been chasing after money, fearful of losing it, but it never brought me peace or security. I knew that if I wanted to rebuild my life, I had to change the way I viewed money—and more importantly, I had to trust God with my finances.

One day, as I was reflecting on scripture, I came across Philippians 4:19, which says, "And my God will meet all your needs according to the riches of his glory in Christ Jesus." That verse hit me like a lightning bolt. God had always provided for me, even in the darkest times, yet I had spent so much of my life believing that there was never enough. In that moment, I realized that I had been living with a scarcity mindset, believing that resources were limited and that I had to struggle to keep what I had. But God's provision is abundant. His blessings are limitless, and He gives freely to those who trust in Him.

That shift in perspective—from scarcity to abundance—was a game-changer. Once I embraced the belief that God's resources are endless, I stopped fearing money and started seeing it as a tool for growth and blessing. I began making better financial decisions because I wasn't operating out of fear. Instead of hoarding what I had, I started intentionally using my money, focusing on long-term goals and giving back to others.

Personal Anecdote: A Shift Toward Abundance
This shift in mindset wasn't immediate, but I can pinpoint a specific moment when I knew things had truly changed. Shortly after my bankruptcy, I was faced with a decision that tested my newfound belief in abundance. I had just started rebuilding my financial life and was slowly getting back on my feet. I had a small savings account, something I had struggled to accumulate, but then an opportunity arose to help a friend in dire need. Normally, I would have hesitated. My old scarcity mindset would

have kicked in, making me fearful of giving up any of my hard-earned savings. But this time was different. I remembered that verse in Philippians and trusted that God would continue to provide for me. I gave my friend the money and did it with a full heart, knowing there would always be enough. That act of generosity strengthened my faith and opened the door to even more financial blessings in my life. It was a powerful reminder that when we operate from a place of abundance, we allow God to work through us, and He will always meet our needs.

Reflection: Shifting from Scarcity to Abundance
I encourage you to take a moment and reflect on your own beliefs about money. Are you operating from a scarcity mindset—constantly worrying about not having enough, holding onto money out of fear, or spending impulsively because you feel deprived? Or are you embracing a mindset of abundance, trusting that there will always be enough, that God will provide for your needs, and that your financial decisions are guided by wisdom rather than fear?

If you find yourself stuck in a scarcity mindset, know that you can shift your perspective. It starts with trusting that God's provision is more than enough for you. Begin to view money as a tool for growth, not something to be feared or hoarded. Understand that abundance is not just about having more—it's about being at peace with what you have and using it in ways that align with your values and purpose.

Practical Strategies for Abundance

Shifting to an abundance mindset is important, but it's equally crucial to put that mindset into practice through intentional financial decisions. Here are some practical strategies that helped me shift from scarcity to abundance in a tangible way:

Budgeting and Saving

The foundation of financial abundance is good stewardship, which starts with creating a budget. For years, I had no real plan for my money, which contributed to my financial struggles. I spent impulsively and saved very little, always feeling like I was behind. However, once I shifted my mindset to one of abundance, I realized that having a plan for my money was an act of faith and responsibility.

Creating a budget doesn't have to be restrictive; it's about being intentional with your resources. A budget allows you to see where your money is going and helps you align your spending with your values and goals. It's also an important tool for setting aside money for the future—whether for emergencies, retirement, or other long-term goals. Here are a few practical tips for budgeting and saving:

- **Track Your Income and Expenses**: The first step in creating a budget is to track your income and expenses. Write down everything you earn and everything you spend for at least a month. This will give you a clear picture of where your money is going.
- **Separate Wants from Needs**: Once you have a clear understanding of your expenses, categorize them into "wants" and "needs." This will help you prioritize your spending and cut back on unnecessary expenses.
- **Set Clear Financial Goals**: Having specific financial goals can keep you motivated and focused. Whether it's building an emergency fund, paying off debt, or saving for a big purchase, write down your goals and work them into your budget.
- **Save Consistently**: Make saving a non-negotiable part of your budget. Even if it's a small amount, set aside money each month for your savings. Over time, it will grow, and you'll have peace of mind knowing you're prepared for the future.

Generosity: The Key to True Abundance

One of the most powerful lessons I learned in shifting from scarcity to abundance is the importance of generosity. Whether through tithing, charitable donations, or helping others in need, giving back is a key component of financial abundance. The Bible speaks frequently about the blessings that come from giving, and I've found that to be true in my own life.

Generosity not only blesses others but also shifts your focus away from fear and toward faith. When you give, you acknowledge that your resources are not just for you but for the greater good. You trust that God will continue to provide for you as you pour into others.

Here are a few ways to incorporate generosity into your financial plan:

- **Tithe Consistently**: As I mentioned earlier, tithing is a biblical principle that reflects your trust in God's provision. Give 10% of your income back to God and watch how He blesses you in return.
- **Give to Charities and Causes**: Find organizations or causes that align with your values and give regularly. Whether it's a local food bank, a global mission, or a cause close to your heart, giving is a tangible way to share the abundance you've been given.
- **Help Others in Need**: Be open to opportunities to help those around you. Whether it's giving a meal to a friend in need or helping someone financially through a difficult time, acts of kindness and generosity lead to a more fulfilling life.

Reflection for Readers

As you begin to shift your mindset from scarcity to abundance, consider how you can put these strategies into practice in your own life. Create a budget, set financial goals, and prioritize saving for the future. But most importantly, make generosity a central part of your financial journey. When you give freely, you're not only aligning with God's purpose but also embracing the truth that there is always enough—and in that, true abundance is found.

Setting Financial Goals for the Future

Achieving financial stability and success requires more than just managing our day-to-day expenses. It demands a clear vision for our financial future and a strategic plan to get there. By establishing well-defined financial goals, we can break free from the cycle of financial stress and uncertainty, and instead, build a brighter, more secure future for ourselves and our loved ones. In this section, we'll delve into the importance of goal-setting in achieving financial success, and provide practical guidance on how to stay committed to your financial objectives.

The Importance of Goal Setting

One of the most transformative things I did to regain control over my finances was learning how to set clear financial goals. I had been drifting aimlessly for so long, trying to stay afloat in a sea of debt and bad financial habits. Without a plan, I was just reacting to situations as they came instead of proactively managing my money. However, once I understood the importance of having specific goals for my financial future, I shifted from a mindset of survival to one of growth and purpose.

I vividly remember the moment I realized that I couldn't continue living without a financial plan. It was after I had filed for bankruptcy, and I was starting from scratch in many ways. My previous pattern of reckless spending and emotional purchases had left me with nothing to show for it. I had hit rock bottom, financially and emotionally, and it was clear that something had to change. I needed a strategy to avoid falling into the same traps and build a better financial future for myself and my daughter.

The first financial goal I set was simple: create an emergency fund. At the time, it felt impossible. I was barely making ends meet, and the idea of putting money aside for emergencies seemed like a luxury I couldn't afford. But I knew I had to start somewhere. So, I made it a goal to save $1,000 in an emergency fund, even if it took me months to do it. With that goal in mind, I started cutting unnecessary expenses and making small sacrifices. It wasn't easy, but I stayed focused and eventually reached my first milestone. That $1,000 may not have seemed like much in the grand scheme of things, but it was proof that I could set a goal and achieve it. More importantly, it gave me peace of mind knowing I had a cushion for unexpected expenses, which had always been a source of stress.

Once I saw that I could achieve one goal, I set more—like paying off specific debts, saving for my daughter's education, and even planning for future investments. Setting these goals gave me direction and purpose. I wasn't just trying to stay out of debt anymore—I was actively building toward a future that aligned with my values and my vision for a financially stable life.

Personal Anecdote: The Power of Small Steps

Each financial goal I set was like a small victory, a step toward regaining control over my finances. There was a point when I realized that setting financial goals wasn't just about the money—it was about reclaiming my sense of control, confidence, and peace of mind. For example, once I started saving for my emergency fund, I noticed how my mindset began to shift. I no longer felt as powerless in the face of unexpected expenses because I had a plan.

I also remember setting a goal to pay off one of my credit cards within a year. It wasn't the biggest balance, but the thought of eliminating one source of debt motivated me to stick with it. Every month, I put extra money toward that card, and slowly but surely, I saw the balance decrease. The day

I paid it off, I felt an overwhelming sense of accomplishment—not just because I was reducing my debt but because I had proven to myself that I could stay committed to a goal and see it through.

Setting financial goals helped me realize that my financial journey wasn't just about fixing past mistakes but about creating a better future. It gave me hope that I could change my relationship with money, one goal at a time.

Practical Application: How to Set Financial Goals

If you're ready to take control of your finances and set meaningful goals, here's a step-by-step guide to help you get started:

1. **Assess Your Current Financial Situation**: Before you can set goals, you need to know where you stand. Take a good look at your income, expenses, debts, and savings. Write everything down so you have a clear picture of your financial health.
2. **Define Your Priorities**: What matters most to you? Is it paying off debt, saving for a home, building an emergency fund, or investing for the future? Your goals should align with your values and long-term vision.
3. **Set Specific and Measurable Goals**: Avoid vague goals like "I want to save money" or "I want to pay off debt." Instead, set clear, measurable goals like "I want to save $5,000 for a down payment in the next 12 months" or "I want to pay off $3,000 in credit card debt by the end of the year." Be specific about the amount and timeframe.
4. **Break Down Large Goals into Smaller Steps**: Big goals can feel overwhelming, so break them down into smaller, manageable steps. For example, if you want to save $1,200 in a year, set a monthly goal of saving $100. This makes the process less daunting and gives you small wins along the way.

5. **Create a Budget That Aligns with Your Goals**: A budget is a powerful tool that can help you allocate money toward your goals. Look at your expenses and see where you can cut back or reallocate funds to make room for savings, debt repayment, or other financial priorities.
6. **Track Your Progress**: Regularly review your goals and track your progress. Celebrate your achievements, no matter how small, and adjust your goals as needed. This keeps you motivated and ensures that you stay on track.

Staying Committed to Your Financial Goals

Setting financial goals is the first step, but staying committed is where the real work begins. Life has a way of throwing unexpected challenges our way, and it can be easy to lose sight of our goals when things get tough. That's why accountability and perseverance are so crucial to achieving long-term success.

One of the things that helped me stay committed to my goals was finding accountability—both within myself and through others. When I started this journey, I would share my goals with a close friend, someone I trusted to hold me accountable. She would check in with me regularly to see how I was doing, offer encouragement, and help me stay focused. Knowing that someone else was rooting for me and holding me accountable made all the difference.

Accountability: The Key to Consistency

Accountability is one of the most important aspects of staying committed to your financial goals. Whether it's a friend, family member, financial advisor, or even an online community, having someone to check in with can keep you motivated and on track. Here are a few ways to incorporate accountability into your financial journey:

- **Find an Accountability Partner**: Choose someone you trust to share your financial goals with. This person should be someone who will encourage you, offer advice when needed, and hold you accountable if you start to slip.
- **Join a Financial Support Group**: There are many online communities and local groups that focus on financial accountability and support. Being part of a group can provide motivation, advice, and shared experiences as you work toward your goals.
- **Set Regular Check-Ins**: Schedule regular check-ins with your accountability partner or group. Whether weekly, bi-weekly, or monthly, these check-ins allow you to reflect on your progress, make adjustments, and stay focused on your goals.

Reflection: Celebrating Progress and Adjusting Goals

As you work toward your financial goals, it's important to celebrate your progress, no matter how small. Each milestone you reach is a step closer to financial freedom, and acknowledging your achievements helps build momentum.

Take time to reflect on how far you've come. Did you manage to pay off a credit card? Did you reach your first savings goal? Maybe you stuck to your budget for an entire month or made a significant dent in your debt. These are wins worth celebrating. But staying committed also means being flexible and willing to adjust your goals as needed. Life is unpredictable, and sometimes our goals need to evolve. Don't be discouraged if you encounter unexpected challenges—like a job loss, medical expense, or other financial hardship. Instead, re-evaluate your goals and make adjustments that reflect your current situation. The key is to keep moving forward, even if it means taking smaller steps for a while.

Reflection for Readers

As you set and pursue your financial goals, remember that the journey is just as important as the destination. Stay committed, seek accountability, and celebrate your progress along the way. Your financial goals are more than just numbers on a spreadsheet—they represent your future, your peace of mind, and the legacy you want to leave behind. Keep going, even when it's difficult, and know that each step brings you closer to the financial freedom and stability you deserve.

A Journey of Growth and Learning

In conclusion, my journey with money has been one of growth, learning, and transformation. Through the trials and tribulations, I have learned invaluable lessons about stewardship, self-worth, and the importance of a positive mindset. It's been a rollercoaster ride, and like any good rollercoaster, it has had its share of ups, downs, and unexpected twists. There were moments when I threw my hands up in the air, screaming in delight, and other times when I clung to the safety bar, terrified of what lay ahead. And let me tell you, it hasn't always been pretty. I've had those "What on earth was I thinking?!" moments, like that time I thought it would be a great idea to buy my then-boyfriend a brand-new gaming console to impress him—only to discover that he had no interest in gaming. Spoiler alert: the console ended up collecting dust while my bank account collected fees from the interest on my credit card debt. But I digress!

This journey has taught me that life is about learning from our mistakes and making the most of the lessons we encounter along the way. I wanted to share these financial principles that worked for me because nobody taught me how to navigate the choppy waters of personal finance. I had to figure it out through trial and error (mostly error, let's be honest). If my experiences can help even one person avoid the pitfalls I stumbled into, then it's all been worth it.

As you reflect on your financial journey, I encourage you to embrace the lessons you learned from your experiences. Remember that every setback can lead to a comeback and that God's promises are a source of strength and guidance. I learned that in my lowest moments, I was being guided toward a better future. That's a truth I hold onto, especially when my bank account doesn't seem to reflect my hard work!

Now, I'll let you in on a little secret: I am a builder of multiple streams. You know that scripture about making money from multiple streams? Yeah, that's my jam! Diversifying your income is not just a financial strategy; it's a way to ensure that you're not putting all your eggs in one basket. I've learned the hard way that when one stream dries up, you better have a few more flowing to keep you afloat.

As a purpose producer, my mission is to help people like you tap into those multiple income streams. There is wealth out there, and it's our job to go out and grab it! There are opportunities everywhere, whether it's through starting a side hustle, investing wisely, or simply being intentional with how you manage your money. The key is to look for them—and, more importantly, to believe that you deserve them.

So, let this mantra ring in your ears as you navigate your finances: "If it don't make cents, it don't make sense!" Use it as a reminder to approach your finances with wisdom, intention, and faith. We live in a world of financial complexity, but that doesn't mean we must be overwhelmed. Together, we can learn to steward our resources wisely while creating a life filled with purpose, abundance, and joy.

Now, let's get real for a second. Financial freedom is a journey, not a destination. Whether you're knee-deep in debt or just starting to save, it's important to remember that it's never too late to start. Life is unpredictable, and so is our financial journey. One day, you might find yourself dreaming of a beach vacation; the next, you're budgeting for emergency car repairs. Grab your running shoes and get ready for the adventure! With a little faith, a sprinkle of humor, and a solid plan, you'll be well on your way to building the life you desire and deserve. And here's the bottom line: financial success isn't just about how much you earn but how well you manage what you have. It's about setting goals, being disciplined, and knowing that you can create a legacy of financial stability and generosity for yourself and future generations. So, let's ditch the scarcity mindset and embrace abundance! There is wealth out there, just waiting for us to claim it.

Thank you for joining me on this journey. Here's to your future—a future filled with wealth, purpose, and laughter. Because if we can't laugh at ourselves during this wild ride called life, then what's the point? And remember, when it comes to your finances, "If it don't make cents, it don't make sense!" So, let's make cents and live a life of abundance together!

WEALTH WISDOM AFFIRMATIONS

I want to encourage you to repeat these powerful financial affirmations daily, write them down, or even incorporate them into your journaling practices. This can help foster a positive mindset toward your finances and reinforce your commitment to achieving financial wellness:

1. I am worthy of financial abundance and prosperity.
2. I attract wealth and opportunities effortlessly.
3. I manage my money wisely and make informed financial decisions.
4. I am in control of my financial future and take proactive steps to secure it.
5. Every dollar I spend and save is an investment in my future.
6. I release any limiting beliefs about money and embrace a mindset of abundance.
7. I am open to receiving unexpected income and financial blessings.
8. I create multiple streams of income that align with my passions and purpose.
9. I am grateful for my financial resources and use them to enrich my life and the lives of others.
10. I learn and grow from my financial experiences, turning challenges into opportunities.
11. I am confident in my ability to achieve my financial goals and dreams.

12. I deserve to live a life of financial freedom and security.
13. I make decisions that support my financial well-being and future.
14. I attract positive energy around money and create a healthy relationship with it.
15. I celebrate my financial progress, no matter how small.

Chapter 8

LOVING MY DAUGHTER OUT LOUD:
A MOTHER'S JOURNEY

> *"Start children off on the way they should go,
> and even when they are old they will not turn from it."*
> —Proverbs 22:6 (NIV)

Becoming a mother at a young age is a journey filled with both challenges and immeasurable joy. I was just twenty years old when I welcomed my beautiful daughter, Morgan, into the world. From the moment I held her in my arms, I knew my life had changed forever. Morgan was my blessing, my purpose, and my greatest joy. I often reflect on how our bond has been a guiding light in my life, illuminating the path through even the darkest times.

Embracing the Role of Motherhood

I won't sugarcoat it—becoming a mother so young was not easy. There were sleepless nights, moments of uncertainty, and times when I doubted my ability to provide for my daughter. But I knew deep down that I had been entrusted with a precious life. In those early days, I learned the importance of embracing motherhood wholeheartedly. I promised myself that I would love Morgan out loud, celebrating her every achievement and embracing her unique personality.

From the beginning, I chose to raise Morgan with intention. I wanted her to know she was loved unconditionally, no matter the circumstances. I sacrificed countless things to give her the world, wanting her to have experiences I didn't have growing up. I attended her karate practices, juggling my work schedule to make it to tournaments. Let's be real; some of those tournaments felt like Olympic events. I cheered her on as she practiced her kicks while secretly hoping she wouldn't accidentally karate-chop me in the process. And oh, how I followed her journey in basketball! I was the mom in the stands, enthusiastically shouting out her name while trying to look cool (but probably failing miserably). I thought she would go on to play ball in college, and I was ready to be her biggest fan on the sidelines. But then, plot twist—she discovered DJing! One day, I walked into her room and heard beats that sounded like they were straight from a club in Ibiza. I had to admit, I was impressed. My little girl had morphed into a full-blown entrepreneur, just like her mother—or, shall we say, a hustler?

Growing Together: A Journey of Mutual Love

What's beautiful about our relationship is how we grew together. Morgan is not just my daughter; she's a reflection of me. She's smart, full of personality, and charismatic. I often joke that she's like a little me but with better hair and a flair for DJing. As she navigated her childhood, I found myself evolving as a mother. She allowed me to love her freely and openly, teaching me that love is not only about giving but also about receiving. Through her innocence and joy, I learned to embrace the love that was available to me—not just as a mother but as a woman deserving of joy and fulfillment.

Morgan was my mirror, reflecting my hopes, dreams, and even my struggles. As I guided her, she taught me to be patient, resilient, and strong. Each day brought new opportunities for growth. Whether we were tackling homework together or sharing stories about our day, I cherished the moments we spent side by side. I realized that motherhood wasn't just about nurturing; it was also about learning from one another.

Raising a Strong, Independent Young Woman

As Morgan grew, I focused on instilling values that would guide her through life. I wanted her to be strong, independent, and confident in who she was. I always encouraged her to pursue her passions, to speak her mind, and to stand up for herself. I believed that by doing this, I was giving her the tools she would need to navigate the complexities of the world.

Education was always a priority in our household. I worked hard to ensure that Morgan had access to quality education and growth opportunities. When she expressed interest in attending Howard University, I was all in. I understood that this was a significant step in her life, and I was determined to support her every step of the way. Watching her graduate (virtually) from Howard was one of the proudest moments of my life. I felt like I had not only raised a daughter but also a force to be reckoned with.

Morgan's journey has been a testament to the power of love, resilience, and determination. I've always believed that when we nurture our children's dreams, we give them the wings to soar. I encouraged her to embrace who she is and to trust her instincts. I wanted her to feel empowered to pursue her own path, no matter where it led.

The Role of Her Father

I always wanted Morgan to have her father in her life, and I believe that family dynamics shape a child's identity. However, as she got older, their relationship wasn't what I had envisioned. My relationship with her father was complex, and I found myself compensating for not raising her in a two-parent home. I went into overdrive, pouring everything I had into being the best mother possible, sometimes to the point of exhaustion.

I worked hard to create a sense of stability and security for Morgan, trying to fill the void that was left by her father's absence. I remember trying to be both parents, encouraging her, supporting her, and making sure she felt loved and valued. But no matter how much I tried to bridge that gap, I knew there were things I couldn't give her, and that was tough to reconcile. I wanted her to have a father figure in her life, and I struggled with navigating those feelings while being her biggest cheerleader. Today, they have reconciled, and I am happy they are good!

The Joy of Motherhood

Through it all, Morgan has brought so much joy into my life. Her laughter, spirit, and unwavering determination are constant reminders of the beauty of motherhood. We've shared our dreams, fears, and hopes for the future in countless moments. I cherish our late-night talks, the times we dance in the living room, and our shared laughter over inside jokes. These are the moments that fill my heart with gratitude. But it hasn't always been easy. Although she declines my requests for TikTok trends.

When Morgan went away to college, I lost my grip on the day-to-day. The house felt emptier, and I often found myself feeling disconnected. The reality of her being away hit me hard, and I went into a bit of a depression. I struggled with the idea of her becoming more independent, and I missed the closeness we had built over the years. I worried whether I had prepared her adequately to face the world alone. However, I realized that my love for her—loving her loudly—was the most important thing I could do. I began to send her encouraging texts and surprise care packages, reminding her that I was still her biggest supporter, no matter the distance. I learned that even when we're apart, love doesn't diminish; it transforms.

Morgan, remember when I would fly to DC for the weekend to come clean your place and stock your kitchen up? Can I get "Mom of the Year"? LOL.

Encouragement for Other Mothers

To every mother reading this, I want to encourage you: love your children out loud. Let them know every day how much they mean to you. Celebrate their uniqueness and support their dreams, no matter where they lead. We have a powerful role in shaping our children's lives and self-esteem. When they know they are loved unconditionally, they can embrace their true selves without fear of judgment.

Our children are a reflection of us, and when we love them boldly, we create a ripple effect that can influence their lives and those around them. Teach them to stand tall, be proud of who they are, and face the world confidently.

A Future Full of Promise

Morgan has been called to a greater purpose, and I am excited to see where her journey takes her. I believe she will make a difference in the world, just as I have always encouraged her to do. As her mother, I will continue to support her, cheering her on as she navigates the challenges and triumphs of life.

In closing, I want to remind you that motherhood is not just a role; it's a privilege. It is a sacred bond that brings profound joy and fulfillment. I am grateful for every moment I have shared with Morgan and look forward to many more. Together, we are navigating this journey, creating a legacy of love, support, and resilience that will inspire future generations.

As I reflect on my journey as a mother, I realize that Morgan has changed my life and given me a purpose beyond myself. She has taught me about love, strength, and the importance of embracing life's challenges. I am proud to be her mother and will continue to love her out loud—today, tomorrow, and always.

Part 3
MY RECKONING

Chapter 9

STRIPPED TO RISE:
MY 'JOB SEASON' OF FAITH, FAILURE, AND REDEMPTION

> *"When you pass through the waters, I will be with you; and when you pass through the rivers, they will not sweep over you. When you walk through the fire, you will not be burned; the flames will not set you ablaze."*
> —Isaiah 43:2 (NIV)

The year 2023 started with high hopes and promises of an amazing year. I had spent the latter part of 2022 setting goals, praying fervently, and preparing for the new season. I prayed with expectation, fully believing I would witness those prayers unfold. However, it's one thing to pray for God's guidance and another to truly listen and follow His plan. After Wonder Woman 2023, I went on a reflective walk, thinking about what the next year might look like. I had been immersed in the testimonies and replays from the conference, and during my prayer time, I boldly declared to God that I was ready to step into new dimensions. I remember His response clearly: "It will take work." And with conviction, I replied, "God, I am ready to do Your will." But are we ever truly ready when we make such declarations?

As 2023 unfolded, my life took an unexpected turn, entering what I now refer to as my "Job season." I was confused and heartbroken, struggling to understand why God allowed me to endure such profound losses. When things we value slip away, we often see them as negative, but this season redefined my understanding of the phrase, "God's rejection is His protection."

God led me into a period of isolation, where it felt like it was just Him and me. In isolation, He chooses His people, drawing them closer and protecting them. I felt like I was so alone, and everything was falling out of place. If you've been feeling lost and confused, you might be going through an isolation period. This time, it was different. However, it taught me to be thankful because I was able to work on myself, build a deeper relationship with God, and learn how to trust in God completely.

As much as we want to control our lives, God has other plans and knows what's best for us. Divine timing is perfect timing. Once I grasped this, I stopped forcing certain situations in my life and learned to trust the path He had for me. This season of isolation taught me to let go, detach, and stay present. It wasn't until near the end of the season that I fully understood what was happening. I had prayed for elevation but didn't realize the journey would involve such deep internal transformation.

The Reckoning: You Lost

In May, I ran for a position that I had been praying for over many years. I believed it was my time, that God had opened this door for me. I campaigned with everything I had—praying, preparing, and believing. But when I didn't win, it felt like my heart had been ripped out. After the election, I sat in my car for over an hour, crying out to God, asking why He allowed me to fail. I distinctly heard Him say, "I am building resilience." But at that moment, resilience felt like a hollow consolation. How could losing an election be about resilience? I was so hurt that I stopped praying and withdrew from my time with God.

As weeks passed, I began to reflect on what was next. I had poured so much into this one desire, only to have it slip away. I wrestled with whether I had misunderstood God's direction, but deep down, I knew that even in defeat, God was working something out in me. I pressed forward, deciding to move on and redirect my efforts. Although I wasn't a sore loser, the loss cut deep because I value what I give, and this felt like an enormous defeat.

The Felony Case

Earlier in the book, I mentioned a felony case from over a decade ago. Sixteen years ago, I committed disability fraud. I continued receiving checks, even though I had returned to work and falsified signatures on forms. At the time, I was under immense financial pressure and justified it as something small—something many around me were doing. But eventually, someone reported me to the Department of Insurance, and the fallout was swift. In 2017, I was charged with nine felony counts.

Panic set in when I learned about the charges. How was I supposed to explain this to people? I called my father, and I could hear the disappointment in his voice. I had forgotten all about what I had done until it came back to haunt me. I appeared in court monthly for the next two years, listening to the DA and my public defender debate my fate. All I could think the entire time was, "How did I get here?"

In 2019, I received my sentence: 300 hours of community service and restitution for the disability benefits I had taken. I was lucky. I found a place called SHARE! to serve my community hours, working with adults struggling with addiction, mental illness, and homelessness. At first, I balked at the idea of cleaning bathrooms. I had a housekeeper—what was I doing scrubbing toilets? But soon, God began to humble me. As time went on, I built relationships and even found myself witnessing to others, praying with them, and talking about God. What I thought would be a humiliating experience turned into a powerful season of growth. In the end, I completed 500 hours instead of 300, and my life was profoundly impacted.

By 2021, my case was closed, the charges were reduced to a misdemeanor, and my record was expunged. I could finally move on, knowing that God had used this season to teach me humility and that my story would become a testimony one day.

The Credential Revocation

In 2022, I received a letter from the Commission on Teacher Credentialing stating that my teaching credentials would be revoked due to my felony case. I was shocked and devastated. My case had nothing to do with my ability to teach or lead in education. I followed their instructions and appealed the decision, but it was a long, drawn-out process involving multiple appeals and over $60,000 in legal fees. Despite praying and having people intercede on my behalf, the commission argued that I lacked integrity because I didn't disclose the charges when I renewed my credentials in 2017. The truth was, I didn't even understand the legal process at the time. It was that simple. I went through several rounds of administrative hearings, and each time, they ruled to revoke my credentials.

Fast forward to 2023, I went to court, feeling confident after a season of fasting and prayer. I had built an exemplary career in education, and I believed God would not allow my career to end this way. However, the judge denied my request to restore my credentials. His words were devastating, and I left the courtroom feeling like my entire career had been ripped away. We had one more shot to reinstate my credentials. I fasted and prayed for an entire month leading up to the hearing. Convinced, there was no way that this decision would stand. My attorney was convinced we would get the decision reversed.

I drove to court for the second hearing. I had literally been in my house for the past few weeks, on my knees, praying about this. I remember hearing a sermon where the pastor said, "Walk confidently as if God already did it." As I walked into court, I knew I would be on my way to work shortly. The judge came out and, again, read all of my character letters, reviewing the transcripts from court; it just went on and on. He left and returned to his chambers. I prayed the entire time he was gone. He came back and began to speak. He started off by speaking about my exemplary, well-noted career. He apparently had been searching me online because he referenced so many things he read about me, and he continued to compliment me. I smiled, as I knew he was going to temporarily restore my credentials while we awaited trial. But the words that would follow were chilling. He denied the request, leaving me stunned. "Are you kidding me?" was all I could muster. He concluded with a surprisingly encouraging statement: "You have all these degrees, experiences, connections, etc. You will definitely make an impact in your next endeavor." I bit my tongue, wanting to retort, "WTH did you just say?"

I stepped outside to consult my attorney and shared with him the research I'd done on similar cases where individuals had committed more severe offenses without facing credential revocation. What in God's name was I going to do? I had spent the last 20+ years in education and had no idea what I would do. My attorney did his best to encourage me, but I was so distraught I couldn't hear him.

As I drove home, I cried and kept screaming, "God, why?" I recall walking into the house, feeling exhausted, and collapsing onto the couch for a much-needed nap. Then I had a dream—a dream of an earthquake. I woke up, got on my knees, and cried out to God. God said, "Have faith." What in the world did that mean?

Friendship Lost

Shortly after, I faced another heartbreaking loss—the end of a friendship I deeply valued. This person had been, someone I held in high esteem. We spent a considerable amount of time together through business ventures, ministry, travel and shared experiences. However, beneath the surface of what I thought was a genuine connection, there was betrayal that I couldn't have imagined. I later discovered that this person had been speaking horribly about behind my back. Yet, to my face, they played the role of a supportive friend. The sting of those revelations cut deeper than words can describe.

You might think this sounds like the typical fallout of a friendship. But it was far from typical when you consider that this person wasn't just a friend—they actively helped me with the vision to grow my business and strategized with me to become my best self. At the same time, they greatly benefited from my resources, ideas, and connections. I poured into this friendship, believing in its mutual value and purpose, but looking back, it's clear that I gave far more than I received. That's what made the betrayal so much harder to process. How could someone who seemed so invested in my growth harbor such animosity toward me?

This is when I began to understand the concept of seasonal relationships. Some people are placed in your life as destiny helpers, but their purpose is only for a short time. They're there to assist you during a particular season, but they're not meant to walk the entire journey with you.

While their exit may feel devastating, it's often part of God's plan to protect and reposition you for what's next.

The relationship ultimately fell apart, fueled by misunderstandings and outside interference. When this friend told me, "God said to end our friendship," I was blindsided. How could God say one thing to them and something different to me? This loss sent me into a dark place, and I struggled with anger and confusion. I stopped praying and drifted away from my spiritual practices. One day, God woke me up and simply said, "Stay in position." Though I didn't fully understand at the time, those words would anchor me in the storms that followed.

I was in the grocery store, minding my business. I was literally smelling the strawberries to make sure they were not rotten. Out of nowhere, a woman walked up to me and said, "Ma'am, I hear the Holy Spirit saying to tell you to stay in position!" Whoa! I looked at her as if I had seen a ghost. She looked at me and said, "I guess that means something. Have a good day!" I drove home in tears and didn't quite understand. I just kept yelling out, "God, I feel like You're stripping things that I love away from me, and I don't understand why."

Midway through the summer of 2023, God called me to a fast. I had no interest in fasting, praying, or reading scriptures—nothing resonated with me. I was drowning in anger and disappointment. I was fighting the urge to fast because I was very upset. I had had enough of God; I wanted nothing else to do with my relationship with Him. I shut down. I was exhausted by what felt like relentless trials and public embarrassment. My life had become a spectacle, and I couldn't see how anything good could come from it. I told myself I had had enough of God and shut down completely.

I didn't just resist the fast; I resisted anything that might bring healing. I was angry—not just with life, but with God. I didn't understand why He would allow me to endure so much pain, so much humiliation, all while I was trying to live for Him. I questioned everything: my faith, my purpose, even my worth. The thought of seeking Him, the very one I felt had allowed this suffering, seemed unbearable.

But despite my resistance, the pull to fast grew stronger. I couldn't escape it. It was as though God's call was gently but persistently tugging at my heart. Reluctantly, I gave in. I started the fast, though my spirit was still hardened. I didn't dive in with joy or expectation—I started with doubt and bitterness. But even in my reluctant obedience, God began to move.

Through the quiet moments of fasting, the walls I had built around my heart started to crumble. I didn't realize how much hurt I had buried beneath my anger. As the days went on, I found myself crying out to Him, not with eloquent prayers but with raw, unfiltered pain. "God, where were You when I needed You? Why did You let this happen?" And in the stillness, He met me there.

It wasn't an overnight transformation, but slowly, I began to feel His presence again. The pain of public embarrassment didn't magically disappear, but it began to lose its power over me. God showed me that while the world might ridicule and reject me, He never would. He reminded me that my worth was not defined by the opinions of others or the setbacks I had faced.

Through the fast, God didn't just heal the surface wounds—He went deeper. He taught me to release the bitterness, to trust Him with my pain, and to believe that He was still working all things together for my good. What started as a reluctant act of obedience became a turning point in my journey of healing and restoration.

The fast reminded me that even when I feel abandoned, God is still there, waiting for me to turn back to Him. And when I do, He doesn't meet me with condemnation; He meets me with grace, love, and a path forward.

Pitfall: The Reunion Revelation

I had been looking forward to our family reunion in Dallas. Family reunions have always been a source of joy, a time to reconnect and celebrate with the people I love. But this trip took an unexpected turn, one that exposed some raw emotions and left me shaken.

Upon arriving, I found myself in an argument with one of my favorite cousins over what seemed like a small misunderstanding. Normally, I would have brushed it off, but I was on day 16 of my 40-day fast, and my emotions were running high. I was irritable, easily triggered, and full of unexpressed frustrations I didn't even know I was carrying. Two days later, the tension escalated, and what started as a verbal dispute turned into a physical altercation.

My father saw me in a moment I'm not proud of—cursing, yelling, and acting completely irrational. I was deeply embarrassed, but what cut me the most was when my daughter, Morgan, pulled me aside. "Mom, your behavior is unacceptable. I'm embarrassed," she said. She told me that people had been recording me, and she was mortified to see me acting so out of character. Morgan had never witnessed me like that, and it broke her heart—and mine.

Looking back, I'm not proud of how I handled myself. My brother Jo-Jo confronted me afterward and gave me some tough love. At first, I was defensive. I thought, *Doesn't anyone see I have reasons to be upset?* But I was truly mad at everyone—my family, my circumstances, and myself.

I withdrew from the family for the rest of the trip. I was hurt and confused. The combination of losing a friendship, the looming revocation of my credentials, my health challenges, and the emotional intensity of fasting had overwhelmed me. It felt like too much, all at once.

That Sunday, I decided to attend The Potter's House, seeking spiritual guidance. Pastor Sarah Jakes Roberts preached on the matters of the heart, and it felt like God was speaking directly to me. "Your heart matters," I heard her say. At that moment, I realized that I had allowed unresolved issues to fester in my heart, and they were pouring out in ways that were hurting not just me but the people around me. (I want to take a moment to publicly apologize to my family for my behavior. I love you all deeply, and I assure you, I will never let that happen again.)

I left the family reunion still angry and confused, unsure of what had triggered such a reaction. Was it my emotions from fasting? The grief of a lost friendship? The uncertainty about my credentials and career? Maybe it was all of the above. What I knew for sure was that I needed space and time to regroup.

Health: A Journey Through Healing and Faith

Like Job, I endured a season of physical challenges that tested my faith and resilience. It began with an embarrassing and relentless skin issue—my entire body was covered in painful rashes, and my feet were so inflamed with fissures that walking became nearly impossible. For almost a year, dermatologists struggled to pinpoint the cause, insisting it was eczema. But deep down, I knew there was more to it. My legs were covered in patches that looked bruised, and my right hand was marked with a large, scaly patch that would bleed.

One night, in the midst of my frustration, I awoke to a clear message from God: "Make a doctor's appointment." It was a simple directive, but I knew I had to follow it. I made the appointment and confidently shared my self-diagnosis of plaque psoriasis. The doctor was initially skeptical, but my diagnosis was confirmed after referring me to a specialist. However, that wasn't the end of my health journey. The blood tests revealed there were deeper issues at play.

Years ago, I had experienced severe gastrointestinal symptoms—vomiting in my sleep, bowel irritation, and unexplained fatigue. I had brushed it off, self-diagnosing through Google, and carried on, as I've always been the one to take care of others. The idea of burdening my loved ones with my health struggles was simply not an option. The problem had returned. Doctors had suspected cancer in my small intestine after multiple tests and biopsies at the time, but I decided to keep the news to myself—I didn't want the added stress of people worrying. Miraculously, the results were inconclusive, and it seemed like God had granted me another chance.

As I delved deeper into the underlying issues hinted at by my psoriasis diagnosis, new tests revealed a disturbing possibility—cancer cells might be present. Without medical insurance since losing my job, I faced delays in getting the necessary treatment. Navigating the complex healthcare system while applying for Medi-Cal was both humbling and terrifying, a daunting test of patience and resilience. Despite everything, I wasn't in physical pain; instead, it was the emotional and mental weight that was hardest to bear. I was determined to keep this battle to myself, to spare my daughter and father from the worry. It was a long and challenging journey, but I am now healed form the cancerous mass cells in my small intestine.

During this period, my panic attacks escalated. Manic episodes became a regular part of my life, triggered by the overwhelming stress. My blood pressure averaged around 140/90, and I was in and out of the hospital, battling episodes of anxiety and depression. For nearly three months, I went off the grid, struggling through a dark season of isolation, convinced that death was near. It felt as though God was preparing to call me home.

To add to my struggles, the medications I was taking began to affect my eyesight. I didn't realize how badly my vision had deteriorated until I found myself nearly blind at times. One day, while driving, I accidentally tapped another car because I couldn't see clearly. Thankfully, no one was hurt, but it was a wake-up call. My doctor temporarily suspended my driving privileges to keep me safe. But through it all, God's grace sustained me.

After multiple medical procedures and a renewed focus on my health, things began to improve. As of today, I've lost over 100 pounds, and my blood pressure has stabilized. I'm eating healthier, prioritizing self-care, and slowly but surely reclaiming my life. This journey has taught me that healing is not just physical—it's spiritual, emotional, and deeply personal. I learned to lean on God more than ever before, trusting Him to guide me through the darkest valleys. I'm still a work in progress, but I'm grateful for the strength to keep moving forward one step at a time.

Pitfall: Finding Peace in Solitude

Almost 8,000 miles away from everything, I needed to be alone—alone with my thoughts, my feelings, and most importantly, with God. After everything that had happened—the loss of my brother, the family tension, my internal struggles—I reached a breaking point. I couldn't stay where I was any longer. I woke up one morning and decided, "I'm taking myself to the Maldives."

Now, if you know anything about the Maldives, you know it's not cheap, especially for a last-minute trip. But I didn't care. I started looking at my points, credits, and every incentive I could gather. It didn't matter what it cost; I needed to get away. I needed space to breathe, heal, and reconnect with God. And just like that, the trip was booked for the end of July.

The Maldives became more than a vacation; it became a sanctuary. Every morning, I met God at the ocean. I would sit by the water, praying and pouring out my heart to Him. Several times a day, I would stop whatever

I was doing to talk to God. I spent the evenings at the ocean, watching the sun set into the horizon, feeling His presence like never before.

I remember asking God, "Why is my life in such disarray? Why does everything feel like a stumbling block?" I had been living in a way that I thought was pleasing to Him, yet I felt like my world was falling apart. But in those moments by the water, something began to shift.

There's no way to fully explain the level of peace I received during that trip. I could feel God; I could hear Him. It was as if He met me there, in the stillness of the ocean waves. One day, I cried for hours. I couldn't stop. It felt like a deep, hidden pain was being lifted out of me piece by piece. And as the tears fell, so did my burdens.

By the time I was preparing to travel home, I knew something had changed within me. I knew that everything would be okay despite everything I was facing. God had given me a new sense of peace—one that surpassed all understanding.

Pitfall: The Unexpected Goodbye

It was a Sunday morning in August, and I had just returned from traveling overseas. While watching a virtual church service, I received a call from my nephew that would change everything. His voice trembled as he delivered the devastating news: my brother had suffered a heart attack. But as I listened, something didn't click—my mind couldn't register what he was saying. My brother was gone.

I had just seen him laughing and full of life two weeks prior at the family reunion in Dallas. We had spoken only a few days before. How could this be possible? I called my father, who was at church, to deliver the devastating news. There are no words to describe the pain of having to tell your father that his firstborn son has passed. I could hear the pain in his voice, and it mirrored my own.

In the midst of my grief, guilt crept in. I replayed our last conversations in my head. During that family reunion, after my argument with our cousin, my brother came to my hotel room to check on me. He knew I was hurting, dealing with the weight of my personal struggles. I poured out my heartbreaks to him, but he shifted the conversation, sharing something that didn't fully register with me at the time. He spoke about what he wanted when his time came, what he wished for in death. I remember thinking, *Why is he talking like this? He's healthy, strong, a man of faith—he's not going anywhere.* But now, looking back, I believe he knew. He was preparing me in his own way. He told me he was proud of me, loved me, and that despite everything we had faced growing up, he was grateful for the strong bond we shared. I didn't want to hear any of it at the time; I was too wrapped up in my own pain to recognize that he was saying goodbye. I remember he said "You are my sister and will always be my little sister. My sweetheart!"

My brother had always been my protector, my rock. In college, he would send me letters and money for groceries, always looking out for me. One time, he even surprised me by showing up at career day at the school where I was teaching. He told my students, "My sister is a rock star, and I'm proud of her." I would laugh it off, thinking he was just being sweet. But after his death, I realized how much he truly meant it. He was always there, always proud, always willing to help.

After my brother passed, I learned even more about him through the stories shared by his friends, colleagues, and others who knew him. What touched me most was hearing how much love he had for me. He had spoken about me to so many people, and that gave me comfort.

However, another layer of pain emerged, one I hadn't anticipated. When it came time to plan his celebration of life, I was determined to honor the wishes he had shared with me. However, that didn't happen. His mother took control of the process, and I was left out. It felt like a betrayal—not just to me but to him. This was my brother, and I had promised to ensure his wishes were fulfilled. To be shut out of that process was devastating.

I wrestled with that hurt, feeling defeated and powerless. It felt like yet another loss on top of his death. But I had to release it. I prayed for God to heal my heart and to help me let go of the pain that came from being excluded from honoring my brother's final wishes. It's not a weight I can carry forever. That's something she will have to reconcile with while I focus on healing.

Fighting Spiritual Warfare: A Battle for My Voice and Home

During this intense season of my life, I could feel God preparing me to step into a greater calling—to speak to the masses, pray boldly, and teach scripture. I was recording daily videos, praying live in front of others, and sharing God's Word, even though I often battled feelings of inadequacy. It was a stretch for me, but I knew it was part of my divine assignment.

However, strange things began to happen. My voice would suddenly disappear without warning. I had no underlying illness, nor was I shouting, yet my voice would inexplicably become hoarse, reducing me to a whisper. I went to the doctor, who told me my vocal cords were strained, but there was no clear reason why. I followed their advice to rest my voice, yet the issue kept recurring. It was baffling, and I sensed something deeper was going on.

Around this same time, I began experiencing what I now recognize as spiritual warfare. At first, I didn't understand it, but looking back, I realize God was teaching me the power of serious intercession. The signs started appearing in my home. I began noticing strange bugs—unlike anything I had ever seen before. I complained to my leasing office, and they sent an exterminator multiple times, yet they found no evidence of an infestation. I would sit in my living room and see these bugs crawling around, seemingly out of nowhere. Determined to figure it out, I took photos and did a Google image search, discovering they were sewer roaches.

For anyone who knows me, you know I do not do bugs. The presence of these pests became more frequent and unnerving. I remember watching a YouTube video about how insects can sometimes be a manifestation of spiritual warfare. At first, I brushed it off, thinking it was just another conspiracy theory. Then, one night, I was jolted awake by the feeling of something crawling on me—it was one of those roaches. I leaped out of bed, frantically killing it, and immediately stripped my bed, throwing out my sheets, pillows, and everything I could think of. That's when I heard God's whisper: "This is warfare."

I began to pray fervently, seeking understanding. The deeper I studied, the more I realized that what I was experiencing was more than just a physical issue—it was a spiritual attack. It became clear to me that these bugs were a manifestation of a monitoring spirit, something or someone trying to disturb my peace and hinder my calling.

Despite multiple visits from exterminators, there was never any evidence of bugs in my home. One exterminator even used a special light to search for droppings or signs of an infestation but found nothing. It was frustrating and isolating; I started to wonder if I was losing my mind. I even went as far as capturing one of the bugs in a Ziploc bag and taking it to my leasing office, desperate to prove that I wasn't imagining things.

In my search for answers, I came across a book by Kevin Ewing about spiritual warfare prayers. I decided to dive deep into those prayers, and as I did, the bugs started to disappear. At first, I thought it was my DIY remedies working, but I knew deep down it was the power of prayer driving these spirits away—but it didn't end there.

One day, as I was getting ready for a gala, I was sitting on my bed, putting on lotion, when I leaned back to grab a handbag. To my horror, I saw three lizards crawling on my pillow. I was paralyzed with fear. All I remember was collapsing to the floor, gasping for breath. Morgan was home, and I screamed for her in a panic. Somehow, she managed to trap the lizards in my bedroom and frantically called my father, brother, and friends, but no one was available to help. Eventually, I reached the after-hours maintenance guy, who came and removed the lizards. This happened in October, and it was so traumatizing that I didn't return to sleeping in my room until January.

I began having recurring and unsettling dreams about the friend who had ended their friendship with me. In these dreams, it felt as though this person was trying to harm me- sometime even attempting to strangle me. The experience was so vivid that I would wake up with bruises on my neck, as if the attacks were real. It wasn't just in my dreams: I could even sense their presence in my home, a feeling so strong it left me terrified. The fear became overwhelming, and I would even stay awake all night just to avoid falling asleep and facing those attacks again. I came to the realization that this person was tied to witchcraft by their associations with witches and that these attacks were being spiritually sent to me. It became clear that what I was experiencing wasn't just in my mind- it was spiritual warfare. Monitoring spirits had taken over, the dreams, the physical sensations, and the overwhelming fear were all manifestations of these dark forces trying to harm me.

In the midst of all this, something incredible happened. As I fought these battles, I was drawn even closer to God. I spent countless hours praying and writing out warfare prayers, knowing in my spirit that there were forces assigned to take me out. But instead of breaking me, these experiences built something powerful within me. This was the season where everything changed. I realized that God was using these battles to prepare me for a new level of spiritual maturity and authority. I learned the true meaning of intercession and how to stand firm in the face of spiritual attacks. I emerged from this season stronger, more prayerful, and ready to step fully into my calling.

As I look at that season of my life, I know exactly what God was doing in me. Humility! God knew exactly what to do to get me to work on these matters of the heart. It was over; I could move on with life, and the lessons learned from that would one day become a testimony.

As I carried on with fasting and prayer, God revealed the presence of idols in my life. As I studied scripture, I came to understand that if you've lost many friends recently, it may be because their energy no longer aligns with yours. Your frequency has shifted, and God has heard the conversations of those around you. In His wisdom, He has separated you from individuals who do not have good intentions. This separation may be a sign that you've outgrown those friendships, as your evolving goals and purpose have left you with little common ground.

If you've been on countless dates without success, it may be God's intention for you to be alone right now. He is teaching you to love yourself and build a relationship with Him. This period is about shifting from chasing after relationships to attracting the right one. It doesn't matter if you're approaching 30 and longing for marriage and children; what truly matters is divine timing. If you find yourself in a waiting period, focus on living your life and becoming the best version of yourself. Trust that you will eventually attract the right person, as God often removes people from your life to make way for those who are meant to be part of your journey.

Growing up, I often felt different, as if I didn't fit in. This feeling is purposeful. You are meant to stand out because God has chosen you to fulfill a unique purpose in this lifetime. This season of isolation provides you with the time and space to discover that purpose. Have you ever contemplated why you were born in this time and place? Perhaps you are meant to be a teacher, a healer, or something even greater. God gives each of us a purpose, and there is a reason for our existence on this earth.

God protects His chosen people through isolation. Once you recognize this, you will stop forcing certain situations to unfold in your life. You'll develop greater faith and trust in your path. This journey of isolation has taught me to let go, detach, and be present in the moment.

Conclusion: A Path to Purpose

Reflecting on the tumultuous journey of 2023, I realize that every trial, every heartbreak, and every moment of spiritual warfare was not in vain. This chapter serves as a testament to the resilience that has been forged in the fires of adversity. It was a year of reckoning, but more importantly, it was a year of transformation—a transformation that put me firmly on the path to my true purpose.

Life has a way of taking us through valleys that seem insurmountable, testing our faith and resolve. I learned that in those dark moments, when the world feels heavy and burdensome, we are often being stripped away from distractions, from the idols we unknowingly cling to. Just as gold is refined in fire, I, too, was being refined—purified for the journey ahead.

The losses I experienced—the death of my brother, the revocation of my credentials, the betrayal of friendships—each represented a heavy weight that I carried. But through this pain, I found clarity. I was reminded that purpose often arises from the ashes of our struggles. In my grief, I discovered a deeper understanding of love, loyalty, and the importance of honoring those we lose. I committed myself to preserving my brother's legacy, which illuminated my path forward, reminding me that my purpose is intertwined with the love and memories we share.

Furthermore, the isolation I felt during this season became a sanctuary for reflection and growth. I learned to embrace solitude as a necessary step toward self-discovery. In those quiet moments, I could hear God's whispers, guiding me toward my true calling. Each encounter with spiritual warfare taught me that I possess the strength to confront challenges head-on. I am not just a survivor but a warrior equipped with divine purpose.

As I navigated through this storm, I also recognized the power of community and support. The friendships that remained were my lifelines, reminding me that I am not alone in this journey. God has placed destiny helpers along my path—those who inspire, uplift, and walk with me through the trials. I learned to cherish those connections and to release the ones that no longer served my growth.

This chapter has become the draw—the hook that invites readers into my world, allowing you to see the struggles that led to my triumphs. It is a reminder that we all have a story worth telling, a narrative shaped by the highs and lows of life. For anyone reading this, I hope you can find solace in your struggles and see them as stepping stones toward your own purpose.

I stand here today, renewed and ready to embrace the future. My journey through pain has paved the way for purpose, and I am excited about what lies ahead. I have learned that my experiences—both the light and the dark—are essential in shaping the person I am becoming. As I continue to walk this path, I carry with me the lessons learned, the love shared, and the resilience built.

So, as we close this chapter, I urge you to embrace your own journey. No matter how daunting the path may seem, remember that every setback is merely a setup for a comeback. Trust the process, lean into your faith, and recognize that you are equipped to rise above. Your purpose is waiting for you, and it is often found on the other side of the storms you endure.

Let us move forward together, boldly stepping into the light of our true calling. The world is waiting for your unique contributions, voice, and story. Stand tall, embrace your resilience, and know that the best is yet to come.

Chapter 10

FROM TRUMPS TO TRIUMPH:
FINDING YOUR PURPOSE IN THE JOURNEY

> *"And we know that in all things God works for the good of those who love Him, who have been called according to His purpose."*
> —Romans 8:28 *(NIV)*

Looking back on my life, I see a woman who faced battles most wouldn't survive. I've been through trials that felt like they would break me. I've faced disappointment, heartbreak, and moments when I didn't know how to go on. These moments—these trumps—could have been the end of me, but they weren't. They were the beginning of my purpose.

Purpose is a word that gets thrown around often, but truly discovering it isn't easy. It requires walking through some of the darkest moments in your life and coming out on the other side—not just alive but transformed. Purpose doesn't come when everything is going well; it comes when you realize that every hardship, challenge, and moment of doubt was a stepping stone on the path God designed for you.

For years, I wondered what my purpose was. I searched for it in titles, relationships, careers, and achievements. I thought if I reached a certain level of success, I would know my purpose. I didn't realize my purpose was already within me, waiting to be revealed through the very obstacles I faced.

The Early Struggles: When Pain Feels Like the End

Growing up, I saw pain up close. I witnessed addiction tear apart my family, and for a long time, I blamed myself for not being able to fix everything. I was young, naive, and felt powerless. I carried the weight of responsibility far too early, thinking that if I could do enough, be enough, I could fix the brokenness around me. But I couldn't. I wasn't meant to.

In my teenage years, I faced challenges that tested me in ways I wasn't ready for. I was dealing with relationships that left me feeling used and abandoned. When I was raped, I didn't even understand what had happened at first. It took years of therapy to come to terms with it and to realize that what happened to me was not my fault. The trauma from that experience stayed with me, and I thought it would define me forever. For years, I held onto the shame of that experience, feeling like it was a secret I had to keep buried. But here's the thing about pain—it has a way of forcing you to confront the truth about yourself. It breaks you open, and in that breaking, something new has room to grow. That pain, as much as I didn't understand it at the time, was preparing me. It was a fire that burned away the parts of me that were too afraid to stand in my truth, too afraid to speak up, too afraid to be who I was called to be.

Discovering Purpose in the Midst of the Storm

For years, I wondered why I had to go through all of this. Why did God allow these things to happen? Why did I have to face heartbreak, loss, and betrayal? And then, one day, it hit me—my purpose was birthed in those moments. The very things that were designed to break me were the things that built me. They were shaping me into the woman I was always meant to be.

I began to understand that my purpose wasn't found in my successes or achievements but in the ways I survived. My purpose wasn't in the titles I earned but in how I used my experiences to uplift and empower others. My purpose was in my pain, and it was through my healing that I would help others heal too.

God didn't allow me to go through all of this for nothing. He was preparing me for something greater. Every setback, every tear, every sleepless night had a purpose. And that purpose was tied to my calling—to help other women who, like me, have faced their own battles and need someone to tell them they can survive too.

The Turning Point: Aligning with God's Plan

There was a pivotal moment in my life when everything changed. I remember it clearly. I was sitting alone, feeling defeated, questioning why I had to endure so much hardship. I was angry with God. I asked Him, "Why me? Why this pain? What am I supposed to do with all of this?" And in that moment, I felt a deep sense of peace wash over me, as if God was saying, "This is not the end. Your story is not over. This is only the beginning." It was in that moment that I realized something important: I was not in control of my life, but God was. He had a plan for me, and all the things I had been through were leading me toward that plan. My job was to trust Him, to surrender my pain, and to allow Him to turn my brokenness into something beautiful. This was the turning point. I stopped fighting against the challenges and started asking, "What can I learn from this? How can I grow from this? What is this moment trying to teach me about my purpose?" Slowly, the pieces began to come together.

I realized that God had called me to be a light for others—to show them that no matter what they've been through, they can still find their purpose. I was called to be an example of resilience, strength, and faith. I was called to empower women to rise from their own trumps and step into the fullness of who they were created to be.

Lessons Learned Along the Way

I've learned a few key lessons on this journey toward purpose. These lessons have not only transformed my life but have become the foundation for how I help others discover their purpose:

1. **Your pain has a purpose.** The struggles you face are not random. They are refining you. Every hardship is preparing you for something greater. It's shaping you, molding you, and building within you the strength you need to walk in your purpose.
2. **God's timing is perfect.** For years, I wondered why I wasn't seeing the success I wanted or why I wasn't where I thought I should be. I questioned God's timing and even doubted my own ability. But looking back, I realize that His timing was perfect. Every delay, every detour, was necessary for my growth. God's timing is not our timing, and we have to trust that He knows what He's doing.
3. **Your purpose is bigger than you.** Discovering your purpose isn't just about you. It's about the people you're called to serve. It's about using your gifts, talents, and experiences to make a difference in the

lives of others. When I began to see my purpose as something bigger than myself, everything changed. I realized that my story wasn't just for me—it was for every woman who needed to hear it.
4. **Embrace the process.** Finding your purpose is not a destination; it's a journey. It's a process that requires patience, faith, and resilience. There will be ups and downs, but every step of the journey is leading you closer to who you're meant to be. Embrace the process, even when it's difficult, because you grow in the process.

Walking in Purpose

Walking in purpose is not a one-time decision; it's a daily choice. Every day, I choose to live in alignment with my purpose. I choose to use my story to empower others. I choose to stand in my truth, even when it's uncomfortable. I choose to trust that God's plan for my life is far greater than anything I could have imagined.

One of the most powerful things I've learned about purpose is that it's not about perfection. You don't have to have it all together to walk in your purpose. You don't have to have all the answers. You just have to be willing to show up, to be present, and to be open to what God is doing in your life.

Purpose is about using everything you've been through—the good, the bad, and the ugly—to make a difference in the world. It's about turning your pain into power and your struggles into strength. It's about knowing that your life has meaning, even in the midst of chaos.

Helping Others Find Their Purpose

As I began to walk in my purpose, I realized that part of my calling was to help others find theirs. I started mentoring women, speaking at conferences, and sharing my story with anyone who would listen. I wanted people to know that they are not defined by their past or their pain. I wanted them to know that they have a purpose, and it's bigger than anything they could imagine.

Helping others discover their purpose has become one of the greatest joys of my life. It's what keeps me going, even on the hard days. When I see someone's, eyes light up because they finally understand why they've been through what they've been through, I know that I am walking in alignment with my calling.

Helping Others Find Their Purpose: Lighting the Way

When I began to step into my purpose, I realized something profound: my journey was never just about me. It was always about the women I would touch, the lives I would help change, and the people who needed someone to light the way for them. My story, filled with challenges and triumphs, was the vehicle through which I could help others find their own path to purpose.

Helping others find their purpose is not just about giving advice or sharing my experiences; it's about creating space for others to explore who they truly are. Too often, we become defined by our circumstances—whether it's the trauma we've faced, the expectations of others, or the roles we've been assigned. But purpose requires us to break free from those definitions, to peel back the layers, and to discover the core of who we are meant to be.

Guiding with Empathy and Experience

The first step in helping others find their purpose is to meet them where they are. I often think back to my own journey and remember how isolated I felt when I was struggling to understand my place in the world. I didn't need someone to tell me what to do; I needed someone to walk alongside me, to listen without judgment, and to remind me that I wasn't alone.

When I mentor women, I lead with empathy. I listen deeply because I know how powerful it is to have someone truly hear your story without trying to fix it right away. Sometimes, all we need is someone to acknowledge our pain and remind us that it's okay not to have all the answers right now.

From my own experiences, I've learned that purpose doesn't reveal itself all at once. It unfolds over time, often in ways we can't predict. My role as a guide is to provide a safe space for exploration, to help women ask the right questions, and to encourage them to trust the process—even when the path ahead feels uncertain.

Empowering Women Through Their Stories

One of the most powerful tools I use in helping others find their purpose is storytelling. Sharing my journey—both the highs and the lows—has opened doors for others to see the possibilities in their own lives. I tell women that their stories, like mine, hold the keys to unlocking their purpose. Each experience, no matter how painful or confusing, is a chapter in a bigger narrative that is still being written.

I encourage women to reclaim their stories, to own the parts that feel messy or unresolved. There is power in naming your pain, facing it, and transforming it into something that fuels your growth. I remind them that their greatest challenges often contain the seeds of their greatest triumphs.

Through workshops, speaking engagements, and one-on-one coaching, I help women dig deep into their lives to find the lessons they've been carrying. We talk about the moments that shaped them—the moments that tried to break them—and, together, we look for the purpose that was born in those moments. When they start to see how their struggles are connected to their strengths, something shifts. They begin to see that their pain wasn't wasted; it was preparation.

Creating a Vision for the Future

Helping others find their purpose isn't just about looking back; it's also about creating a vision for the future. Once someone begins to understand the significance of their experiences, the next step is helping them translate that understanding into action. Purpose isn't static; it's something you live out, something that grows and evolves as you do.

I work with women to help them identify what lights them up, what they feel called to do, and what values they want to embody moving forward. Purpose isn't just about career goals or accomplishments; it's about living a life that feels aligned with who you are at your core.

In our sessions, we craft purpose statements, vision boards, and personal mission plans. We set intentions, not just for what they want to achieve but for who they want to be in the process. I remind them that purpose is a lifelong journey. It's not about arriving at a destination; it's about continuously growing, learning, and evolving.

Nurturing Confidence and Resilience

One of the biggest barriers to finding purpose is the fear of inadequacy. I see it time and again in the women I work with. They doubt whether they are capable of living out their dreams. They wonder if their past disqualifies them from walking in their purpose. My job is to nurture their confidence and remind them that they are more than enough.

I emphasize resilience—because the path to purpose is rarely smooth. There will be setbacks, failures, and moments of doubt. But those are not signs that you're off track; they are opportunities to refine your purpose, to deepen your understanding of who you are and what you're called to do.

I encourage women to embrace their imperfections and to see failure as a part of the journey, not the end of it. Just as I have had to navigate my own doubts and insecurities, I help others see that their worth isn't tied to their mistakes or past. They are worthy of living a life of purpose simply because they are.

Connecting to Something Greater

Ultimately, finding your purpose means connecting to something greater than yourself. For me, that something is God. My faith has been the foundation of my purpose, and I encourage others to seek out that connection—whether through faith, community, or personal reflection. I help women understand that purpose is about service, about using your gifts to impact the world around you.

When you discover your purpose, it's not just about personal fulfillment. It's about the lives you will touch, the people you will inspire, and the legacy you will leave behind. I help women see that their purpose is not just about them but about the ripple effect they will create in their families, communities, and beyond.

Watching the Transformation

There is nothing more fulfilling than watching someone step into their purpose. It's a transformation that starts quietly, often with a simple shift in mindset, and blossoms into something powerful. I've seen women go from feeling lost and unsure of themselves to becoming leaders in their communities, entrepreneurs, mentors, and changemakers.

The transformation is not just in what they do but how they see themselves. They walk taller, speak with more conviction, and carry a sense of peace and confidence that comes from knowing they are living in alignment with who they are meant to be. That transformation is the greatest reward of all.

Part 4

MY PURPOSE DEFINED

Embracing My Purpose: The Journey to Becoming the Global Strategist

Finding one's purpose is a journey—often filled with moments of clarity, doubt, discovery, and transformation. For me, the path to purpose was long and winding, filled with lessons learned through both triumphs and trials. Today, as the CEO and visionary behind The Global Strategist, LLC, I can look back at my journey and see how everything I've experienced has led me to this point.

My story is one of perseverance, resilience, and alignment. It's about learning to trust God's plan for my life, even when I couldn't see the full picture. It's about discovering my strengths, embracing my gifts, and bringing together every aspect of who I am to create an empire that reflects not only my skills but also my purpose.

1. The Search for Purpose: How My Journey Began

Like many people, I spent years searching for my purpose, trying to understand where I fit in this world and how I could use my talents to make a meaningful impact. I was always drawn to leadership and had a passion for empowering others, but I didn't yet have a clear vision of how those passions would come together.

As I navigated my career, I ventured into different fields—event planning, corporate consulting, leadership coaching, and even travel management. Each experience added a new layer of understanding, but it wasn't until I took a step back and looked at the big picture that I realized how each piece of my journey was building toward something much greater.

I began to see how everything was connected: the leadership skills I honed, the relationships I built, the challenges I faced, and the lessons I learned. These experiences were not isolated events but threads in a larger tapestry, leading me to The Global Strategist—the role I was always meant to play.

2. The Revelation: Discovering My Calling as The Global Strategist

The turning point came when I realized that my purpose was bigger than any one business or career path. It was about strategic empowerment, a concept that perfectly combined my love for leadership, my passion for transformation, and my desire to see people reach their full potential. I was called not just to lead but to strategically empower others to lead themselves.

This revelation came after years of searching, reflecting, and asking God for guidance. I remember moments of doubt when I wondered if I was truly on the right path. But in those moments of reflection, God revealed to me that The Global Strategist was not just a title—it was my purpose. I was called to create a platform where individuals, businesses, and communities could come to be empowered, find their voice, and thrive.

I embraced this calling fully, knowing that my work wasn't just about me. It was about the lives I would touch, the leaders I would help mold, and the organizations I would transform. I knew I had to step into my role as The Global Strategist with confidence and clarity.

3. Folding My Businesses Together: Aligning with Purpose

Once I embraced this calling, everything began to fall into place. I had built multiple businesses over the years—each one reflecting a part of who I was and what I cared about. But now, I saw that they weren't separate entities; they were all interconnected, working together to serve a higher purpose.

I folded Divine Diva Events, Fabulous Divas + Gents Travel, and my transformational coaching services under the umbrella of The Global Strategist, LLC, creating a cohesive empire that was aligned with my mission. Each business serves a different aspect of my purpose, but together, they form a powerful platform for empowerment and transformation.

A. Divine Diva Events

My love for event planning was always about more than just creating beautiful spaces. It was about creating experiences that brought people together, celebrated milestones, and reflected the essence of those involved. Divine Diva Events has always reflected my desire to serve others, make their dreams come true, and execute flawless, meaningful events.

As part of The Global Strategist, LLC, this business now extends beyond weddings and corporate events. It's about creating transformational experiences that inspire, empower, and bring people together in ways that leave a lasting impact.

B. Fabulous Divas + Gents Travel

Travel has always been a passion of mine, not just for the experiences it brings but for the ways it broadens perspectives and builds connections. Through Fabulous Divas + Gents, I've helped people explore the world, but more importantly, I've helped them step outside of their comfort zones and see life from a new perspective.

As part of The Global Strategist, LLC, Fabulous Divas + Gents has evolved into a division that provides luxurious and personalized travel experiences and creates opportunities for personal and professional growth. We curate trips that bring leaders together, foster collaboration, and spark creativity—aligning perfectly with my mission to empower and inspire.

C. Transformational Coaching and Leadership Development

At the heart of The Global Strategist, LLC, is my work in leadership development and transformational coaching. This is where I truly feel I am fulfilling my calling—helping others see their potential, embrace their leadership, and create lasting change in their lives and organizations.

Through one-on-one coaching, workshops, and leadership training, I work with individuals and organizations to help them overcome obstacles, unlock their strengths, and confidently step into their leadership roles. I teach them to think strategically, act boldly, and navigate the complexities of leadership with grace and wisdom.

4. The Purpose Behind the Empire: Empowering Through Strategy
The Global Strategist, LLC, is more than a business—it's the manifestation of my purpose. Every service we offer, every client we work with, and every event we create is part of a larger mission to empower others through strategy and leadership.

A. Strategic Empowerment
My purpose is centered around strategic empowerment—the belief that anyone can be empowered to lead and achieve greatness with the right tools, mindset, and guidance. This philosophy guides everything I do within The Global Strategist, LLC. It's about giving people the strategies they need to succeed in business, leadership, or personal growth.

I teach my clients that success is not just about talent or luck; it's about having a plan, being intentional, and making strategic decisions that align with their goals. Whether I'm working with an executive leader, a budding entrepreneur, or a woman looking to take control of her life, the goal is the same: to empower them to think and act strategically.

B. Serving Through Leadership
Another cornerstone of my purpose is servant leadership—the idea that true leadership is about serving others, guiding them toward their own success, and empowering them to reach their potential. This is the ethos that drives The Global Strategist, LLC. Everything I do is rooted in the desire to serve, whether through coaching, consulting, or event planning.

I've built my empire on the belief that leadership isn't about being in charge—it's about taking responsibility for the growth and success of others. Through my work, I aim to inspire and equip the next generation of leaders to do the same.

5. The Global Strategist: Living in Alignment with My Purpose
Finding my purpose and building The Global Strategist, LLC, has been a journey of alignment—aligning my gifts, passions, and businesses with the mission that God has given me. It hasn't always been easy, and there were times when I questioned whether I was on the right path. But through it all, I've learned to trust the process and embrace the calling that has been placed on my life.

Today, as The Global Strategist, I am living out my purpose. I'm not just running businesses; I'm building an empire that reflects my passion for leadership, empowerment, and transformation. I'm helping others discover their purpose, embrace their potential, and lead lives of impact and significance.

This journey has taught me that purpose is not a destination—it's a process. It's something you discover, embrace, and live out each day. As I continue to grow and expand The Global Strategist, LLC, I know that my purpose will continue to evolve, guiding me toward even greater impact and influence.

Conclusion: Purpose Drives Everything

In the end, purpose is what drives everything I do. The Global Strategist, LLC, is not just a company—it's a reflection of my mission to empower, inspire, and lead. It's the platform through which I serve others and help them reach their highest potential.

I have folded all of my businesses—Divine Diva Events, Fabulous Divas + Gents, and my coaching and consulting services—into one cohesive empire that serves a singular purpose: strategic empowerment. This empire is built on a foundation of leadership, service, and transformation, and I am honored to be at the helm of it as The Global Strategist.

I encourage everyone reading this to seek their purpose, embrace it fully, and let it guide every decision, every business, and every relationship. When you live in alignment with your purpose, you create something far greater than success—you create a legacy.

As I reflect on the tapestry of my life and the winding journey that led me to become The Global Strategist, I realize that every moment, every challenge, and every triumph has played a vital role in shaping my purpose. Finding one's purpose is not a linear path; it is often a complex journey filled with moments of clarity, doubt, discovery, and transformation. Yet, through it all, one thing has remained constant: purpose drives everything I do.

The experiences I have shared in this section serve as powerful reminders that purpose is not just an abstract concept; it is a force that fuels passion, ignites resilience, and inspires action. The challenges I faced—the heartache, the losses, and the betrayals—have all contributed to a deeper understanding of living with intention and clarity. Each trial has taught me invaluable lessons about perseverance, faith, and the importance of staying true to my calling.

Today, as the CEO and visionary behind The Global Strategist, LLC, I firmly believe that my purpose extends beyond my own success. It is about creating a legacy that empowers others to discover their potential and embrace their unique gifts. Every service we offer, every event we create, and every individual we work with reflects my mission to uplift and inspire.

The Power of Empowerment

The Global Strategist, LLC, is not just a business; it is the manifestation of my purpose. Through strategic empowerment, I aim to equip individuals, organizations, and communities with the tools they need to thrive. I firmly believe that everyone can lead and achieve greatness. It is my passion to help others unlock that potential, guiding them on their journey to becoming the best versions of themselves.

As I continue to navigate the ever-changing landscape of life and business, I am committed to serving as a catalyst for transformation. I want to encourage others to step into their power, embrace their purpose, and lead with authenticity. This is not merely a professional ambition but a calling that resonates deeply within my soul.

Living in Alignment with My Purpose

Finding my purpose has been a journey of alignment—aligning my gifts, passions, and businesses with the mission that God has entrusted to me. I have learned that living in alignment means being open to growth, embracing change, and staying true to my values, even when the road gets rocky. It requires courage to let go of what no longer serves me and to embrace new opportunities that align with my vision.

In this ever-evolving landscape, I recognize that my purpose will continue to unfold and deepen. I am excited about the journey ahead, knowing that as I grow and expand The Global Strategist, LLC, I will have the opportunity to impact even more lives. My purpose is a living entity, constantly evolving and expanding, guiding me toward greater influence and significance.

Chapter 11

"YOU ARE MORE THAN A CONQUEROR!"

> "No, in all these things we are more than conquerors through him who loved us."
> —Roman 8:3 (NIV)

Imagine the song "Survivor" by Destiny's Child, but with one powerful twist—replace the word "survivor" with "conqueror." I am more than a conqueror through Christ Jesus. You are more than a conqueror through Christ Jesus! It is not easy to change the course of how you've operated and processed life. It takes courage to change and be made new. When you survive, you continue to live on after a tragedy.

I am a rape survivor! I am a suicide survivor! I lived on! And I didn't live because I changed my mind! I lived on because God would not let me die. If you've made it this far in the book, then you know what I'm talking about. What's the acronym nowadays? IYKYK—If You Know, You Know!

Ha-ha! God would not allow me to kill myself. Three suicide attempts! I am here only by the grace of God, and not of my own self, so I can never boast! The outlook I have on life is only a credit to God. He knocked at the door of my heart, and I am so thankful that I answered it.

Whew! Okay, now let's continue. To conquer means to overcome with power. Now, I rest in the power of God to overthrow the devils of rejection and abandonment. I am conquering (getting the upper hand, gaining insight and intel, as to launch an offensive attack) the shame of my past and the guilt of my sins by constantly reminding myself that I am God's daughter, and I do not depend on the favor of men but of God. (By rehearsing the Word, you're sharpening your sword—the sword of the spirit.) I declare and decree that I will no longer prioritize pleasing others at my own expense. I will no longer say "Yes" when I need to say "No." I will no longer say "No" when I need to say "Yes." And when I've decided on something, I will let my yes be yes and my no be no. I no longer feel the need to overexert myself to "belong" since God assures me that I don't have to fear being alone or separate myself from His plans for me. He has already adopted me. He chose me so that I could choose me. He loved me first, and I love Him back! I am more than a conqueror through Christ Jesus, and so are you. Hallelujah!

It amazes me how I am just beginning to learn the power of the word "No" because, as someone who consistently sought to please others, I must admit that I was predisposed to saying only "Yes." However, the wisdom of these words has been etched into my heart recently, revealing that saying "No" to both the good and the bad allows me to say "Yes" to the best. Do you know that the most powerful refusal (or denial) in Scripture occurred in the Garden of Gethsemane? "… My Father! If it is possible, let this cup of suffering be taken away from me. Yet I want your will to be done, not mine" (Matthew 26:39, NLT). The Father answered Jesus' request with a "NO" so that He could say "YES" to our salvation. Just wow!

I encourage you all to use your words today and harness the power of your "No." You may need to say "No" to someone who negatively impacts your life or takes advantage of you. Having good boundaries is both wise and godly. Saying "No" to a bad relationship allows you to have margins and to invest in your best relationships. Maybe you need to say "No" to something that's monopolizing your time and has become an idol in your life. When I need direction, I fast and abstain from food, dedicating that time to prayer and connection with God, fostering spiritual growth and a deeper relationship. Maybe you need to say "No" regarding somewhere you thought you needed to be so that you can spend time with God. Saying "No" to a lesser priority can allow you to say "Yes" to your highest priority—God.

My friends, know that God has equipped you with an unexpected and miraculous word: No. Say this word to evil, discouragement, bad priority, idolatry, the wrong kind of anger, and selfishness. In saying "No," God can help you say "Yes" to His goodness, encouragement, the best priorities, choosing Him, joy, and selflessness. Prioritize self-care and confidently move forward with your "No."

Prayer is essential. I know it can be a struggle to maintain an active prayer life. I'm committed to a deeper level of prayer than ever before. My daily routine includes prayer at 2 AM, followed by a prayer call at 3 AM, and additional prayer time at 5 AM. This is the only way I can avoid areas that I have had to endure and come out from. The devil knows how to set traps for you. The devil knows the right thing to say in your hearing; he sends intimidating, desirable, and intrusive thoughts.

When I am moving forward, actively working out my deliverance in a certain area, the devil still presents himself at the right opportunity to tempt me. So, I am always intentional about praying. Yes, we make intercession for others and must also intercede for ourselves! Even when you don't know what to pray, pray in tongues. The Holy Spirit will guide your prayers. Interceding for yourself involves regularly casting your cares on God, confessing your sins, and thanking Him for His blessings and provisions.

When you hear a sermon or teaching on "pride" or find yourself discussing it, take a moment to reflect. Get alone with God and humbly pray, "Lord, search me and know my heart. Test me and know my anxious thoughts. Point out anything in me that offends You and lead me along the path of everlasting life. God, Your Word says You hate the proud but give grace to the humble. God, Your Word says You detest the proud, and the proud will surely be punished. God, Your Word says You hate pride and arrogance! God, Habakkuk 2:4 says, 'Look at the proud! They trust in themselves, and their lives are crooked. But the righteous will live by their faithfulness to God.' God, wherever there is pride in me, deal with me. Set me free from this yoke of slavery so that I may trust in You!" And so forth.

During your alone time with God, allow Him to transform you, helping you confront and love yourself so that you may be consumed by His perfect love, unhindered by worldly attachments. It is a daily walk. Pray every day! While we sleep, the devil seizes opportunities and plots against us. Start each new day with prayer to stay vigilant and gain spiritual advantage. It doesn't mean you won't face challenges, but learn how to still make time for prayer in spite of challenges. It is training our nature to hunger and thirst for righteousness like we wake up with our stomachs growling for natural food. It is training our nature to treat the Bible as we would a shower, washing ourselves clean by renewing our minds in the Word of God. It is training our nature to find recess in prayer like we find recess in drinking, smoking, overeating, binge-watching television shows, sleeping, etc. Our flesh is so used to doing what it wants to do, so we must get in the habit of taking off the old man and putting on the new man. Pray, read your Word, and fast because some things only come out by prayer and fasting!

I enjoy looking up scriptures and journaling them. As I write and meditate on Scripture, I rehearse and hide it in my heart. Treating God's Word like honey, I experience its healing power and gain a divine perspective on life. I write down scriptures and place them strategically around my home, including my bathroom, so I can easily see and reflect on them throughout the day. When reading Scripture, take time to tell God, "God, it is Your Spirit that guides me in all truth, and You said that I will know the truth, and the truth will set me free. Open my eyes to see You. I am Your sheep, and I will follow Your voice only in Jesus' name. As I draw near to You, God, draw near to me and reveal Yourself to me." God doesn't desire to be hidden from us. The seek isn't about toiling but rather seeking Him out "in spirit and truth." This means being honest with Him about our life circumstances, struggles, and emotions. When we do, we'll find Him and see Him clearly.

Journaling, for me, has become another place of safety. If I had a diary, I'd probably have a lock on it—that's how serious I am about getting my thoughts out and releasing my emotions in a safe place instead of finding comfort in sex or money. I have learned to curb my appetite, if you will. If I am feeling lonely and want to have sex, I curb my appetite with prayer and journaling. When dieting, curb your appetite by keeping healthy snacks on hand and avoiding temptations like a Snickers bar, especially when determination keeps you committed to moving forward. At times, it can take us a minute to get to the place of "No, I'm serious. I really need to stop doing this! Lord, please help me—this is ruining my life!" But once you get there, you must put certain disciplines in place in order to sharpen and strengthen that weak part of your life. It takes strength and strategy to practice self-control!

There are also times when I must put myself on a fast. The Bible says, "These things only come out by prayer and fasting." Fasting is a discipline that teaches you: (1) how to curb your appetite by replacing your hunger or desire with praying and reading the Word of God and (2) how to say "No" to something when you really want to say "Yes." Fasting is a principle that doesn't make you holier than everyone else but draws you near to God in a secret place. The purpose of fasting is to learn how to be more dependent on God. In the Bible, we see many accounts of fasting, including those of Moses, Esther, and even Jesus. Jesus discussed fasting when questioned by John the Baptist's disciples; He said that since He is no longer with us, He expects us to fast.

Fasting should be a normal discipline, a normal tool that we have in our toolbox. Fasting is for you. Everything we do to prepare our hearts for God's glory is for us, not God. He's already God! We're the ones trying to be more like Him, which is why we should make it a normal practice to pray, read the Bible, and fast. Fasting isn't meant to be easy! Its purpose is to promote spiritual maturity, helping you realize, "I don't need this." Whether your "this" is drinking, smoking, or excessive social media use, if you feel prompted to take a break, replace it with prayer and studying God's Word on the issue. This exchange will transform your heart.

Fasting can bring about a transformative "breaking" and "strengthening" process, breaking free from worldly attachments and strengthening your spiritual connection with God. If you struggle with harmful patterns like promiscuity, sex addiction, financial recklessness, or self-sabotage, consider fasting as a transformative tool. Focus your fast on breaking these cycles, seeking spiritual renewal and guidance. Focus on transformation by meditating on what the Bible says about your struggle and your identity in Christ, rather than fixating on the issue itself. For instance, if you desire to overcome fornication due to self-sabotage and unhealthy relationships, research Bible verses about fornication, biblical perspectives on sex, and most importantly, scriptures revealing your identity in Christ. Take the time to read about intimate relationships in the Bible.

Although there is so much to fasting that I can't cover in this chapter, fasting holds immense value for your faith—it's both beneficial and necessary for spiritual growth. By giving your body a break from food, you unlock its natural healing potential, allowing it to repair and rejuvenate itself through fasting. Explore the power of fasting by researching it online and delving into God's Word, discovering its biblical significance and transformative potential.

It is so important to have help along the way—counseling, prayer groups, accountability! Having individuals in our lives with whom we can be completely open and transparent is crucial, as they provide a safe space to discuss challenges, process emotions, and navigate life's complexities. You don't have to wait until something bad happens or your life is on the brink of ruin before you go to counseling. There are various counselors who specialize in addressing specific needs. Sometimes, you may not require processing a traumatic experience but rather guidance from a life coach to boost your self-confidence and unlock your potential to achieve a specific goal. You may need breathwork to help regulate your nervous system because you tend to be anxious. Whatever your need is, someone can help you achieve it. Don't try to do it on your own, and don't feel ashamed about people knowing your business. Jesus bore the shame on the cross, so you don't have to let shame control you.

Conquer the shame of your past experiences by courageously sharing your weaknesses with trusted individuals who can offer support, guidance, and unconditional love. Exercise discernment when choosing who to invite into your intimate space, seeking individuals who will prayerfully support and work with you toward healing. The Word of God tells us to confess our sins to one another and pray for one another so that we may be healed! There is power in confessing your weakness. The devil wants you to believe you are defined by shame, leading you to isolate yourself in darkness and separation. The Holy Spirit gently reminds you of your identity as a beloved son or daughter, empowering you to confide and confess rather than hide in shame. Satan is an accuser; he wants to convince you that you are whatever the act was. The Spirit of God lovingly rebukes your actions, reminding you, "This isn't who you're meant to be. You are redeemed, forgiven, and called to live differently."

I love worship! Worship refocuses my mind on Jesus, reminding me of my identity as more than a conqueror through His empowering love! Worship shifts the focus from you to God. It reminds you of who God is and allows Him to minister to you. Worship positions our hearts to believe and receive from God, allowing Him to work powerfully in our lives. Worshipping God, revering Him, opens the door for supernatural manifestation. The devil understands how important the concept of worship is.

When you go into your closet to worship God as your Prince of Peace, say to Him, "Thank You, God. Hallelujah! I worship You, Lord, for You are my peace. Your name is a strong tower where I can run to and be saved. Hallelujah! You told me to take heart because You have overcome the world. Hallelujah! I will be of good cheer and keep my mind fixed on You, for You promise to keep me in perfect peace when my thoughts are focused on You. So, as I worship You right now, I fix my mind on You. Hallelujah!

God, You are my peace. You are my peace! I praise You for Your perfect peace!" This prayer positions your heart, humbling your spirit before God, allowing you to cast your cares upon Him and make room for His perfect peace to manifest in every area of your life—body, finances, relationships, and wherever you need it. As you surrender, God begins to transform and strengthen your life, anchoring your heart in His unwavering peace. Worship God in whatever way you're equipped—through singing, dancing, prayer, or a beautiful blend of these, even singing in tongues—and confidently believe that you've already received His blessings.

I am big on affirmations. During my study time or private moments with God, I write out His Word to affirm His truth in my life and renew my mind. This study can be as simple yet profound as exploring my identity in Christ. Perhaps God is addressing emotional instability in my life, revealing how emotions can derail my faith, causing me to waver. Emotions fueled by reasoning can dictate my actions and undermine trust in God. Faith gives you reasons to trust God. I anchor myself in God's unchanging truth, learning to rely on His steadfast character rather than fleeting emotions. The proper emotions for our lives are joy and peace.

As you explore Scripture, the Holy Spirit may lead you to James 1:6-10, inspiring an affirmation like: "I will not sway back and forth between depression and joy, anxiety and peace. I am not double-minded; I am stable in all my ways and confidently expect good things from the Lord. When I declare a truth, I believe I've already received it!" Repeating affirmations about my identity in Christ and God's unconditional love renews my mind, teaching me to navigate life's challenges and internal struggles with faith and resilience.

I am a very sensitive person, and I've taken the time to understand my emotional triggers. Through self-reflection and spiritual growth, I've learned to recognize and surrender those triggers to God, practicing self-control and making room for His perfect love to transform my life. The devil will always present an opportunity for me to be rejected, but by developing a healthy habit—a routine of praying, reading, meditating on God's Word, and fasting—I am equipping myself to respond like Jesus, who, led by the Spirit into the wilderness, resisted the devil's temptations. He responded to the accuser of His identity with the truth.

We give the devil our worship when we believe we are what he says we are. When Satan accuses me of being rejected because someone or a group rejects me, I remind myself: "My Bible says God chose me, not the other way around (John 15:16). I may not meet their standards or fit their preferences, but I am chosen by God (1 Thessalonians 1:4–5). He will open doors of opportunity for me (Revelation 3:8) and draw people to me, causing them to recognize and seek me out (1 Corinthians 1:26-31)." That is me worshipping and thanking God for the transformative truth that releases me from the grip of rejection, establishes my footing on solid ground, and grants me the courage to endure with unshakable confidence

Avoid getting trapped by frustration and disappointment over your current circumstances. Don't let feelings of unfinished healing, age-related expectations (too old or too young), or frustration over unresolved issues ("I should be over this by now") hold you back from progressing. Embrace your journey, focusing on spiritual growth and perseverance. The path to prosperity and wholeness is a journey, not a destination. As you press on, healing and restoration will unfold. Decide now to persevere, for you are more than a conqueror through Christ Jesus. Instant deliverance may not occur, and tomorrow may not bring perfection. Yet, remember that God can work instant miracles and transformations. His power is not limited by time or circumstances. However, just in case there is a process, you must know that you are more than a conqueror through Christ Jesus.

Chapter 12

EMBRACING DELIVERANCE:
LIVING FREE FROM REJECTION AND REDISCOVERING WORTH

> "So do not fear, for I am with you; do not be dismayed, for I am your God. I will strengthen you and help you; I will uphold you with my righteous right hand"
> —Isaiah 41:10 (NIV)

In the journey of life, we often face rejection—whether it's from others, from situations, or even from our own selves. These feelings can weigh heavily on our hearts, leading us to question our worth and purpose. However, I've learned that we can cultivate disciplines in our lives to remind us that we are not rejected, but rather, we are accepted, loved, and valuable. This chapter will explore those disciplines and how they can help guard our hearts, cultivate our minds, and ensure that we survive our struggles and thrive beyond them.

Guarding Your Heart: Affirmations and Systems in Place

One of the most important disciplines I've established in my life is the practice of affirmations. Words have power, and the words we speak to ourselves shape our beliefs and perceptions. When faced with feelings of rejection or doubt, I turn to affirmations that reinforce my identity and worth. Phrases like "I am worthy of love and acceptance," "I am enough," and "I am a child of God, uniquely created for a purpose" have become my lifelines. But affirmations alone aren't enough. It's essential to have systems in place that serve as reminders of your value. For me, this means surrounding myself with a supportive community—friends, family, and mentors who uplift me and remind me of my worth.

I also intentionally consume positive media—books, podcasts, and videos that inspire and motivate me. These systems create a protective barrier around my heart, ensuring that I remain grounded in truth rather than succumbing to negative narratives.

Additionally, I practice mindfulness and reflection. Journaling has become a powerful tool for me to process my feelings and thoughts. When rejection surfaces, I write down my emotions and challenge any negative beliefs. By putting pen to paper, I can sift through my feelings and recognize that they do not define me. This practice allows me to confront my issues rather than bury them, helping me guard my heart against the weight of rejection.

Cultivating a Grounded Mindset

Cultivating a grounded mindset is essential for maintaining emotional and mental well-being. I've found that establishing daily routines can significantly impact my ability to stay focused and move forward. Morning rituals, such as meditation, prayer, or a simple moment of gratitude, set a positive tone for the day. They remind me to focus on the present rather than dwell on past rejections or future anxieties.

Staying grounded also involves nurturing my body. Physical health is closely tied to mental health. Regular exercise, balanced nutrition, and adequate rest are vital components of my self-care routine. When I take care of my body, my mind follows suit, allowing me to stay focused on my goals and aspirations.

Moreover, I prioritize continuous learning. Engaging in new experiences and acquiring knowledge keeps my mind sharp and open to possibilities. Whether through formal education, workshops, or casual reading, I embrace opportunities to grow. This commitment to learning enriches my life and empowers me to tackle challenges head-on, knowing that I have the tools to navigate whatever comes my way.

Moving Forward: The Power of Reflection and Intentionality

Moving forward rather than backward is an ongoing journey. It requires intentionality and self-reflection. I regularly assess my goals and aspirations, asking myself if I am taking steps toward them or allowing fear to hold me back. By setting clear, achievable objectives, I create a roadmap for my life that helps me stay on track.

I also practice gratitude. Each day, I make it a point to reflect on the blessings in my life. This simple act shifts my focus from what I lack to what I have, fostering a positive mindset. When I recognize my progress and achievements—no matter how small—I am reminded of my growth and the strength within me to continue moving forward.

Additionally, I seek feedback from trusted friends and mentors. Their insights provide valuable perspectives and help me stay committed to my goals. Constructive criticism is a tool for growth, and I embrace it as part of my journey toward self-improvement.

Maintaining Deliverance: Conquering Challenges

True deliverance is not merely surviving past challenges; it's about conquering them and ensuring they no longer plague us. I've learned that facing my struggles head-on is crucial to maintaining my freedom. This requires acknowledging the roots of my issues rather than glossing over them. I ask myself tough questions: "What did I learn from this experience? How can I ensure it doesn't define me moving forward?"

One of the most powerful ways to conquer a challenge is by reframing it as a lesson. I believe that every obstacle is an opportunity for growth. Instead of seeing rejection or failure as a reflection of my worth, I view them as stepping stones on my path. Each experience shapes me, strengthens my resolve, and equips me to face future challenges.

Moreover, I've found that sharing my experiences with others fosters healing. Vulnerability creates connection, and when I open up about my struggles, I not only help myself but also encourage others to confront their own challenges. In sharing, I find strength, and together we can support one another on our journeys toward true deliverance.

Conclusion: Embracing a Rejection-Free Life

In conclusion, the disciplines we cultivate in our lives shape how we respond to rejection and challenges. By implementing affirmations, creating supportive systems, and engaging in self-reflection, we can guard our hearts and cultivate a grounded mindset. Moving forward requires intentionality, but it also brings the promise of growth and transformation.

As we work to maintain our deliverance, let's remember that conquering our struggles is about more than just survival. It's about thriving, learning, and embracing the fullness of life that awaits us. By rejecting the labels of rejection and embracing our true selves, we open the door to a life filled with purpose, joy, and connection.

Your past does not define you; you are empowered by your experiences. Stand tall, embrace your journey, and remember that you are worthy of love, acceptance, and a life without the shadows of rejection. Let your story be a testament to the strength that resides within you, and may you continue to thrive in all that you do.

Chapter 13

"KEEP ON LIVING!"

> *"I will not die but live, and will proclaim what the Lord has done."*—Psalm 118:17 *(NIV)*

I hope that I have done a great job at being transparent. Everyone's story is different! There is purpose for your life, and I hope you believe that your life is good as you endure and move about life's swift transitions. Pain has a purpose and an expected end. Whatever your testimony, someone is waiting to hear your story. I would run into people who'd plant those seeds in me all the time, saying, "You should really write a book!" God gave me the desire of His heart, which was to write this book, but it took me so long because I didn't believe my story would bless someone. I was too afraid to share my story because of how raw it is! I honestly didn't want to share the details of my life in such an explicit way by writing a book, something that lives on forever. However, throughout the book-writing process, I felt a profound release and healing as I relived and shared these personal experiences in an intimate way. I have confidence that my testimony will help you overcome, break through, and break out, and I give God the glory for it all.

When we allow God to process us and begin giving us revelation about our lives, we come alive. It's like peeling an onion—as you reexamine your life and walk down memory lane with the help of the Holy Spirit, you'll cry as you peel back each layer, but you're only laying the layers down so you can chop them up and put them back in the Earth to season and flavor the life of someone else. Remember, we are the salt of the earth! Our lives are meant to add flavor to those around us, and with them witnessing our faith, they will then "taste and see that God is good."

I used to be very shy about speaking and being in front of people. Now, I continue to feel more liberated the more I tell my testimony. Your life is good! And very blessed! I get it—it's not easy telling your story. People will talk, but let them! People will ridicule you; you will be flabbergasted or maybe even downright appalled, but allow God to build you up in your most holy faith so that people will overcome by the blood of the lamb and the word of your testimony. There is an anointing to break yokes that flows from sharing your story, releasing freedom through the power of your testimony. I'm sure that people didn't receive Paul well because of his reputation as Saul, but he still shared his testimony.

This is just the beginning for me and for you as well. It isn't easy to be transparent when you have influence, but there is a holy intention behind opening your mouth and letting your story out. You know how people say "Shame on you"? Well, shame off of me and shame off of you! Yes, you may need to process what has happened in your life through therapy, journaling, or other methods, but know that it's worth it. Like cooking a delicious meal, it starts with all of these different ingredients, and there is a specific cooking strategy that will make all of these things come together and taste good! Ha! All things work together for the good of those who love God and believe they are called according to His purpose. That is your life. So much has happened in your life that may not taste good right now, but God has a way of mixing the ingredients of our lives to taste good, even when life doesn't feel good.

The goodness of our lives is attributed to how good God is, not how good or bad life is. Wooh, that is a tough perspective, but take it from someone who has tried to kill themselves. The best way to endure life is to believe that God is good and that He is working all things together for the good in a perfect and holy way. You are a conqueror! Keep telling yourself the truth of God's Word! I want to encourage you to write out the defining moments of your life that have gotten you where you are today and ask the Holy Spirit to guide you into all truth and holy perspectives as it pertains to your life. You have a purpose in this life! Keep on living!

Also, let me encourage you not to look back! Look in the mirror and practice positive self-talk, which is the scientific way of saying, "With the power of life in your tongue, speak life into yourself." Through the power of our words, we can shape our world based on what we believe. What we believe about our lives—our perspective—is what we rehearse. We often need help retraining our thought patterns and learning how to properly talk to ourselves. This doesn't mean denying, avoiding, or suppressing life's challenges or past experiences, but rather facing the truth with courage and learning to reframe our perspective.

Being a conqueror is about facing the truth with courage. Be bold, be courageous, for the Lord, your God, is with you! You are not stuck; you have too much power in you to not get up and live. Every morning, I read affirmations to myself:

"La Shawn, you have dealt with a lot, but right now, you are okay, and whatever isn't okay will be okay. You have conquered so much! Keep going!" Try your best to be intentional about fixing your perspective about life and believing that you are a conqueror. It is not an easy road, but I want to encourage you to write out the things that you've lived through and speak to those situations; speak to the person you were then, find closure, and resolve to move forward. It is time to get up. It is time to move on. Now is the time to keep on living. The time is now for you to tell your story.

Chapter 14

"DISCIPLINES OF THE HEART:
EMBRACING DELIVERANCE AND REJECTION-FREE LIVING"

> *"I will give you a new heart and put a new spirit in you; I will remove from you your heart of stone and give you a heart of flesh."*
> —Ezekiel 36:26 (NIV)

Our lives are woven from a tapestry of experiences, each one uniquely shaping us. Yet, in the midst of navigating life's triumphs and tribulations, it's easy to become self-focused, believing that every experience revolves around us. However, what if our experiences were not solely about our own growth, healing, or success? What if they were also meant to equip us to impact others, to foster empathy, and to reveal God's redemptive work in the world? This perspective shift can revolutionize our understanding of our experiences, transforming them from isolated events into catalysts for connection, compassion, and purpose.

The Ripple Effect of Our Stories

Life's challenges can often feel isolating, but it's essential to remember that our experiences serve a greater purpose. What we endure isn't just for our own benefit; it can resonate with others, offering them hope and encouragement. When we openly share our struggles, we create a space where others can feel seen and understood.

1. Personal Anecdote:

There was a time in my life when I faced significant challenges in my career. I had poured my heart and soul into a project, only to have it fail spectacularly. The feelings of inadequacy and self-doubt threatened to engulf me. However, in sharing this experience with a close friend, I discovered something powerful. She was struggling with her self-worth after a similar setback, and my transparency allowed her to open up about her feelings. Through my vulnerability, she found the courage to address her challenges. Together, we navigated our struggles, ultimately strengthening our friendship and fostering a sense of mutual support.

2. Scriptural Reference:

In 2 Corinthians 1:4, we are reminded, "He comforts us in all our troubles, so that we can comfort those in any trouble." This scripture underscores the cycle of support and healing. Just as God comforts us, we are called to extend that comfort to others. Our testimonies have the power to uplift and encourage, serving as a reminder that we are not alone in our struggles.

3. Reflection:

I encourage you to take a moment and consider your own experiences. Who in your life might benefit from hearing your story? Think about times when your struggles could provide insight, encouragement, or hope for someone else. Don't underestimate the power of your journey—your story could be the guiding light that someone else desperately needs.

Learning and Growth Through Adversity

Adversity forces us to confront our weaknesses and strengths. Each challenge we face becomes an opportunity for growth. It's through these moments that we often uncover the resilience that lies within us, leading to profound personal transformation.

Lessons Learned:

Throughout my trials, I have learned several vital lessons that have shaped my perspective on life. Here are a few of the most impactful ones:

- **Resilience is Built in the Struggle:** I learned that true strength is not the absence of hardship but the ability to rise each time we fall. Each setback has taught me to bounce back stronger, reminding me that I can face whatever comes my way.
- **Vulnerability is a Strength:** Sharing my struggles has shown me that vulnerability fosters connection. It's okay to ask for help, and doing so often opens the door to support and understanding from others.
- **Gratitude in Adversity:** I discovered that finding gratitude in my struggles has transformed my outlook. Even in the darkest moments, I learned to seek out the silver linings, shifting my focus from what I lack to what I have.

2. Practical Application:

To help you identify lessons learned from your struggles, I encourage you to engage in a self-reflection exercise. Here's a step-by-step guide to help you through this process:

- **Step 1: Find a Quiet Space**

  Set aside time in a comfortable, quiet space where you can reflect without distractions.

- **Step 2: Reflect on Your Challenges**

  Think about a significant challenge you have faced in your life. Write it down. What emotions did you experience during this time? How did it impact you?

- **Step 3: Identify the Lessons**

  Ask yourself: "What did I learn from this experience? How did it change me?" Write down at least three lessons you gained through this challenge.

- **Step 4: Consider the Impact on Your Life**

  Reflect on how these lessons have influenced your life. How have they shaped your decisions, relationships, or self-image? Write down your thoughts.

- **Step 5: Share Your Insights**

  Consider sharing your reflections with someone you trust. By articulating your lessons, you reinforce your growth and inspire others on their journeys.

By recognizing that our experiences are not solely for our benefit, we can transform our struggles into testimonies that uplift and empower others. Adversity becomes a catalyst for growth, teaching us resilience, vulnerability, and gratitude. Let's continue to embrace our journeys, understanding that what we overcome can light the way for those who walk alongside us.

The Journey Toward Purpose

Pursuing a greater purpose in life can involve enduring difficult seasons, but the outcome is worth the journey. This reality may sound discouraging, but it is essential to recognize that these challenges are often the crucible that refines us. It's in the depths of our struggles that we discover our true selves and our capacity for greatness.

Personal Anecdote:
There was a season in my life when it felt like I was walking through fire. I faced a series of challenges that seemed insurmountable—financial strain, the loss of a significant relationship, and the overwhelming weight of self-doubt. Each day felt heavier than the last, and I often questioned my purpose and worth. During this period, I vividly remember one night sitting on my bedroom floor, tears streaming down my face as I poured out my heart to God. I felt abandoned, as if all hope had slipped away. It was a moment of raw vulnerability, a point where I could have easily succumbed to despair. But in that dark moment, I felt a flicker of strength rising within me. I recalled the countless times I had faced adversity before and had come out stronger. I realized that this experience was an opportunity for growth and transformation, no matter how painful.

I began to reflect on what I wanted my life to represent. I forced myself to confront the emotions I had been trying to suppress—fear, anger, and sadness. It was a painful but necessary process. In doing so, I began to cultivate the resilience that would propel me forward. I started taking small steps toward healing, whether it was through prayer, journaling, or reaching out to friends for support. Each step reminded me that I was not alone in my struggles, and slowly but surely, I began to see the light at the end of the tunnel.

2. Scriptural Reference:

Romans 5:3-5 (NIV) states, "Not only so, but we also glory in our sufferings, because we know that suffering produces perseverance; perseverance, character; and character, hope. And hope does not put us to shame, because God's love has been poured out into our hearts through the Holy Spirit, who has been given to us." These verses have comforted and encouraged me during my toughest times. They remind me that our sufferings are not in vain; they are part of the process that shapes us into who we are meant to be. Each hardship I encountered became a stepping stone toward building resilience, deepening my character, and ultimately instilling hope within me. Through the lens of these scriptures, I learned to embrace my struggles as essential components of my journey toward purpose.

3. Empowerment:

To anyone reading this, I want to remind you that your struggles are not in vain. Every challenge you face is a crucial part of your journey toward your greater purpose. Embrace your journey, no matter how difficult it may seem. Understand that the pain you experience today can become the wisdom you share tomorrow. Your story can inspire others and show them that they, too, can overcome. Remember, every time you rise after a fall, you are building a legacy of resilience. You are equipping yourself with the tools needed to thrive, not just survive. So, when you find yourself going through hell, keep moving forward; your purpose awaits on the other side.

Building Resilience

Resilience is the ability to bounce back from adversity. It's not just about enduring hardships but also about learning and growing from them. Resilience can be cultivated over time through intentional practices and mindset shifts.

1. Practical Strategies:

Here are some practical strategies for building resilience:

- **Maintain a Positive Mindset:**
  Focus on the positives in any situation. Cultivating an attitude of gratitude can help you shift your perspective. Make it a habit to acknowledge at least three things you are thankful for each day. This practice can dramatically alter how you view your struggles and setbacks.

- **Seek Support from Others:**
  Surround yourself with people who uplift and encourage you. Whether it's friends, family, or mentors, having a strong support system can provide comfort and motivation when times get tough. Don't hesitate to reach out when you need help; vulnerability can be a strength.

- **Practice Self-Care:**
  Prioritize your physical, emotional, and mental well-being. Engage in activities that rejuvenate you, whether it's exercise, meditation, reading, or simply taking time to relax. Caring for yourself allows you to approach challenges with a clearer, more focused mind.

2. Reflection:

Take a moment to reflect on your own experiences of resilience. Think of a specific situation where you overcame adversity. How did you navigate that challenge? What strengths did you discover within yourself?

Consider these questions as you journal your thoughts:

- What did I learn from this experience?
- How did I feel during this time, and how did I cope?
- What positive changes resulted from my struggle?

By identifying these moments, you can empower yourself to recognize your growth and resilience in the face of adversity. Celebrate your victories, no matter how small, and acknowledge that you have the strength to conquer whatever comes your way.

Conclusion: Our Experiences Are Not Always About Us

To conclude this section, remember that going through hell to reach a bigger purpose is not just a daunting journey but a transformative one. Each experience, whether painful or joyous, shapes our character and helps us uncover our true selves. Remember that the struggles you endure today are preparing you for the greatness that lies ahead. Embrace the lessons learned, cultivate resilience, and allow your journey to inspire you and those around you. You are more than a conqueror through Christ Jesus, and your story is a powerful testament to the strength that resides within you.

Trusting the Process: God's Plan vs. Our Plan

Life is full of unexpected twists and turns, and it's easy to feel like we're navigating uncharted territory. But what if, instead of trying to control every outcome, we could learn to trust the process and surrender to God's sovereignty? In this section, we'll explore the transformative power of surrendering control and embracing the beauty of divine timing. By letting go of our own agendas and trusting in God's goodness, we can discover a deeper sense of peace, purpose, and fulfillment.

A. Surrendering Control

One of the hardest lessons we learn in life is that our plans are not always aligned with God's plans. Trusting the process means surrendering control and allowing God to lead us.

1. Personal Anecdote:

I remember a pivotal moment in my life when I meticulously planned my career path. I had set ambitious goals and envisioned the steps I needed to take to achieve them. I thought I had it all figured out until life threw me a curveball. A few months before a significant promotion I was expecting, I received the news that the position had been eliminated due to company restructuring. In that moment, I felt a wave of uncertainty wash over me. My plans were shattered, and I found myself grappling with feelings of confusion and disappointment. I questioned why this was happening to me and whether I was being punished for something.

After a period of frustration, I turned to prayer, seeking guidance and comfort. I realized that I had been so focused on my plans that I had neglected to seek God's will. I began surrendering my desire for control, acknowledging that God had a purpose in the unexpected turn of events. As I let go of my need for certainty, I started to feel a sense of peace wash over me. I began to see the situation not as a setback but as a divine redirection. God had a plan that I could not yet see.

2. Scriptural Reference:

Proverbs 16:9 (NIV) states, "In their hearts humans plan their course, but the Lord establishes their steps." This scripture reassured me that while I could create plans, God was ultimately the one guiding my journey. Realizing that my life was not solely dependent on my understanding but on God's perfect timing brought me comfort. It reminded me that even in uncertainty, I could trust that God was orchestrating my path for my good.

3. Encouragement:

I want to remind you that trusting the process can lead to unexpected blessings. Think about your own life—how often have you experienced moments when things didn't go as planned, only to find that God had something better in store for you? Reflect on those instances. Perhaps you were initially disappointed by a missed opportunity but later realized it led you to a path you never imagined. Trusting God's timing can bring peace amid chaos, and it can open doors you never knew existed.

B. The Beauty of Divine Timing

Divine timing is often different from our own expectations. Recognizing this can help alleviate frustration.

1. Personal Reflection:

Throughout my journey, I have encountered numerous instances where God's timing proved to be perfect, even when I didn't understand it at the time. One significant moment was when I applied for a leadership position that I felt would elevate my career. I prepared extensively, believing that this opportunity was meant for me. However, after the interview, I received a rejection email. I felt defeated and questioned why God had allowed me to pursue something that wasn't meant to be.

Weeks later, I was approached for a different role—one that aligned even more closely with my passions and strengths. I realized that the previous rejection was God's way of protecting me from a position that might not have been right for me. This experience taught me that sometimes, what feels like a setback is merely preparation for something greater. God's timing was perfect, even when it didn't align with my expectations.

2. Practical Application:

I encourage you to take a moment to journal about instances in your life when you experienced divine timing. Reflect on moments when you thought you knew what was best for you, only to later realize that God's plan was different—and better. Write about how these experiences shaped your faith and trust in God's process. Consider the lessons you learned and how they can be applied to your current situation.

Conclusion: Embracing the Journey of Trust

This section explored the importance of surrendering control and recognizing divine timing. Life may present challenges and disappointments, but when we trust the process, we open ourselves to the possibility of unexpected blessings. By reflecting on our experiences and journaling about the moments when God's timing proved perfect, we can cultivate a deeper understanding of His plan for our lives.

Let's embrace the journey ahead with confidence, knowing that every step—whether a leap forward or a step back—is part of the divine path laid out for us. Trusting in God's plan allows us to thrive, even amid uncertainty. Remember, you are never alone on this journey; God is with you, guiding your steps every step of the way.

Becoming an Authority Through Experience

Authority is not solely derived from knowledge or credentials but from the depth of one's experiences and the wisdom gained from navigating life's complexities. As we reflect on our journeys, we begin to recognize the value of our unique perspectives and the impact they can have on others. In this section, we'll explore how our personal experiences can shape us into authorities and why continued learning is essential to sustaining our growth and influence.

A. The Power of Personal Experience

Our experiences equip us to guide others through similar challenges. When we share our stories, we become authorities on the subjects we've lived.

1. Personal Anecdote:

As I reflect on my life, it's clear that each trial I've faced has shaped me into the person I am today. I vividly remember a particularly challenging period when I unexpectedly lost my job. At the time, it felt like the ground had been ripped out from beneath me. I was consumed by fear and doubt, questioning my worth and capabilities. However, that experience also opened doors I never expected. During the months of searching for a new position, I discovered my passion for coaching and mentoring others. I began volunteering to help job seekers refine their resumes and practice interview techniques. I quickly learned that I could make a meaningful impact by sharing my own experiences of loss, resilience, and eventual triumph.

Through this journey, I came to understand that my struggles were not in vain; they were preparing me to become an authority in helping others navigate their own adversities. I began to see how my story of overcoming challenges resonated with those I was helping. When I shared my personal anecdotes of doubt, fear, and perseverance, it not only built rapport but also provided hope and encouragement to others in similar situations. I learned that vulnerability is a strength, and sharing my journey allowed me to empower others to find their voices and navigate their paths with confidence.

2. Encouragement:

I encourage you to view your life experiences as valuable lessons that can benefit others. Every hardship you face is an opportunity to grow and learn, and by sharing your story, you can provide insight and encouragement to those walking similar paths. Reflect on your own experiences—what lessons have you learned? How have you overcome challenges? By becoming an authority through your experiences, you empower yourself and become a beacon of hope for others who may be struggling. Remember, your story can inspire, uplift, and transform lives.

B. The Importance of Continued Learning

Expanding your knowledge is essential for personal and professional growth.

1. Practical Strategies:
To become an authority in any area, especially in understanding adversity and resilience, it's crucial to continually educate yourself. Here are some practical strategies to consider:

- **Reading Books and Articles:** Explore literature on personal development, resilience, and overcoming adversity. Books written by individuals who have faced significant challenges often provide valuable insights and can serve as motivation.
- **Attending Workshops and Seminars:** Look for opportunities to attend workshops that focus on resilience, emotional intelligence, or personal growth. These events not only provide knowledge but also allow you to connect with like-minded individuals who can support your journey.
- **Connecting with Mentors:** Seek out mentors who have navigated similar challenges and can provide guidance. Learning from someone who has successfully walked the path can offer new perspectives and strategies that can enhance your understanding and approach.
- **Joining Support Groups:** Engage with community groups or online forums that focus on resilience and personal development. Sharing experiences and learning from others can deepen your understanding of your own journey while also providing valuable insights into the experiences of others.

2. Reflection:

I encourage you to take a moment to consider areas where you can deepen your understanding and expertise. What topics resonate with you? Are there specific challenges you've faced that you want to learn more about? Write down your thoughts and set goals for how you plan to educate yourself further. This could be as simple as committing to reading one book a month or attending a workshop every quarter.

As you expand your knowledge, remember that becoming an authority is a continuous journey. Embrace the learning process, and don't hesitate to share your insights with others. The more you learn, the more equipped you will be to guide and support those who look to you for encouragement and inspiration.

Conclusion: Embrace Your Authority

Becoming an authority through experience is a powerful and transformative process. Your struggles can serve as stepping stones for others, and your willingness to share your journey can inspire hope and healing. As you continue to learn and grow, remember that your experiences have equipped you to guide others on their paths. Embrace your authority and use it to empower those around you, knowing that you are contributing to a larger narrative of resilience and strength.

The Uniqueness of Your Story

Our lives are shaped by the intricate web of experiences, choices, circumstances, and relationships that intersect and influence one another. Within this intricate narrative, every individual has a distinct voice and perspective that deserves to be heard. As we explore the uniqueness of our stories, we'll discover why our narratives have the power to inspire, heal, and transform others. In this section, we'll delve into the significance of our personal narratives and provide guidance on crafting and sharing our stories in a way that resonates with others.

A. Your Narrative Matters

Each of us has a unique story, and it's essential to share it. Your trials and tribulations contribute to a larger narrative that shapes not only your life but also the lives of those around you.

1. Personal Anecdote:

A pivotal moment in my life occurred during a time of profound personal struggle. I had recently gone through a significant loss—a loved one had passed away unexpectedly, and I was drowning in grief. At that time, I felt isolated and unsure of how to cope. One evening, I decided to join a local support group for individuals who had experienced similar losses.

Sharing my story for the first time felt daunting, but as I opened up about my feelings, I could see the impact my words had on others in the room. I spoke about the confusion, pain, and anger I felt. To my surprise, many people nodded in understanding, and I could see tears in their eyes. In that moment, I realized that my experience resonated with them.

After sharing, several group members approached me, expressing how my story had given them the courage to share their own. It struck me that while I felt vulnerable and exposed, I was also creating a space for healing—not just for myself but for others. That evening marked the beginning of my journey into storytelling as a powerful tool for transformation. I learned that our narratives are not just for our own understanding; they have the potential to connect, inspire, and heal.

2. Encouragement:

I want to remind you that your story is important. Every experience you have—whether joyous or painful—contributes to who you are and can inspire change in others. Consider how many times you've found solace in hearing someone else's journey. Your unique experiences can offer hope, validation, and encouragement to those who may be struggling with similar issues. Embrace your narrative; it is your superpower! When you share your story, you not only honor your journey but also empower others to confront their own challenges. Your voice matters, and your experiences can make a difference.

B. Creating Your Narrative

Taking ownership of your story allows you to shape your narrative and take control of how you want to be perceived.

1. Practical Application:

To help you outline your own story, consider this guided exercise:

- **Identify Key Experiences:** Write down the most significant moments in your life—both positive and negative. Think about experiences that shaped your character, taught you lessons, or changed your perspective.
- **Highlight Transformative Lessons:** Next to each key experience, write down the lessons you learned. What did you take away from those moments? How did they contribute to your growth?
- **Connect the Dots:** Look for patterns or recurring themes in your experiences. Do you see a common thread in the lessons you've learned? This can help you understand the bigger picture of your narrative.

- **Craft Your Narrative:** Start crafting your narrative using your key experiences and lessons. Consider how these elements come together to form a cohesive story that reflects who you are.
- **Practice Sharing:** Once you have a draft of your narrative, practice sharing it. This could be with a trusted friend, in a support group, or even through journaling. The more you share your story, the more comfortable you will become.

2. Reflection:

Now, take a moment to reflect on how you can use your story to inspire others in your life. Ask yourself:

- How can I share my experiences with those around me?
- Are there particular people in my life who might benefit from hearing my story?
- What platforms or opportunities can I explore to share my narrative more broadly (e.g., writing, speaking engagements, social media)?

By taking the time to outline your story and reflect on its potential impact, you'll not only empower yourself but also open the door for others to connect with you and learn from your journey.

Conclusion: The Power of Your Narrative

Your story is unique and valuable. By sharing your trials and triumphs, you not only honor your journey but also pave the way for others to find strength and healing. Embrace the power of your narrative and recognize its potential to inspire change and transformation in the lives of those around you. Remember, you are not alone in your journey; your experiences can create connections that transcend struggles. As you learn to articulate and share your story, you become an authority in your life, offering hope and encouragement to others who may be facing similar challenges. So, go ahead—share your story. The world needs to hear it.

Setting Your Life Direction

As we navigate the complexities of life, it's easy to feel uncertain about our direction and purpose. However, the words we speak and the thoughts we entertain have a profound impact on our lives, shaping our perceptions, attitudes, and ultimately, our reality. In this section, we'll explore how the power of our words can be harnessed to set a positive direction for our lives and how speaking victory over our circumstances can help us overcome obstacles and achieve our goals.

A. The Power of Words

"Death and life are in the power of the tongue" (Proverbs 18:21). What we speak can shape our reality in profound ways. Words hold incredible power—they can uplift, encourage, and inspire, or they can belittle, discourage, and demoralize. Understanding this truth has been pivotal in my journey of self-discovery and growth.

1. Personal Anecdote:
For years, I struggled with negative self-talk. I often found myself in a loop of self-doubt, telling myself things like, "I'll never succeed," "I'm not good enough," or "I always mess things up." This internal dialogue influenced not only my self-esteem but also my decision-making and actions. The turning point came when I attended a workshop focused on personal development and the power of words. The facilitator emphasized the need to change our inner dialogue. I remember feeling a flicker of hope as she shared how her life transformed when she shifted her self-talk. Inspired, I decided to give it a try.

I started replacing negative thoughts with positive affirmations. Instead of saying, "I can't do this," I began telling myself, "I am capable and resilient." Initially, it felt unnatural, almost like I was lying to myself. However, as I continued to practice this new way of thinking, I noticed a significant change in my mindset. The more I affirmed my strengths and abilities, the more confident I became.

This shift in self-talk didn't just boost my self-esteem; it influenced my decision-making. I found myself taking on challenges I would have previously shied away from. I started setting and achieving goals, all because I had learned to speak life into my circumstances. This experience taught me the undeniable impact our words have on shaping our realities.

2. Practical Application:

To help you harness the power of your words, here are some affirmations you can incorporate into your daily life:

- "I am worthy of love and success."
- "Every day, I am growing stronger and more resilient."
- "I have the power to create positive change in my life."
- "I embrace new opportunities and challenges with confidence."
- "I am surrounded by love and support."
- "I choose to focus on the good in my life and the potential ahead."

Consider writing these affirmations down and placing them where you will see them daily—on your bathroom mirror, in your planner, or on your phone. Repeating these affirmations consistently will help shift your mindset and set a positive direction for your future.

B. Speaking Victory Over Your Life

Being intentional about the words we speak is crucial for creating the life we desire. When we consistently speak victory over our lives, we begin to manifest those victories in tangible ways.

1. Reflection:

Take a moment to reflect on your own self-talk. Are there negative patterns you've noticed? Perhaps you often find yourself thinking, "I'll never be successful," or "I'm always failing." Acknowledge these patterns without judgment. The first step to change is awareness. Now, consider the impact these negative thoughts may have had on your life. How have they influenced your choices, relationships, and overall outlook? After identifying these patterns, challenge them by creating positive counter-statements. For instance, if you catch yourself saying, "I always mess up," replace it with, "I am learning and growing from every experience."

2. Encouragement:

Remember, the words you speak have the power to shape your circumstances. Speaking life over yourself can lead to tangible changes in your situation. When you intentionally declare positive truths about your identity and future, you align your thoughts and actions with those affirmations.

As you practice speaking victory over your life, observe how your mindset shifts. Notice how your actions begin to reflect the confidence and empowerment you are cultivating. Surround yourself with supportive individuals who also speak life into their own circumstances and encourage you to do the same.

In summary, be intentional with your words. Embrace the power of positive self-talk and affirmations, and watch as your life begins to transform. You have the ability to set your life direction through the words you choose to speak, so choose wisely.

Conclusion: The Journey Forward

Setting your life direction begins with recognizing the power of your words. By consciously choosing to speak positively and affirmatively, you can transform your mindset and influence your reality. Embrace the opportunity to speak victory over your life and witness the incredible changes that unfold. Remember, you hold the pen to your own narrative, and the words you write can shape your destiny.

God Is Protecting Us

Life is unpredictable, and challenges can arise unexpectedly. In the midst of uncertainty, it's comforting to know that we're not alone. God's presence is a constant source of comfort and protection, even when we can't see or feel it. As we navigate life's ups and downs, it's essential to understand the nature of God's protection and how to recognize His plan unfolding in our lives. In this section, we'll explore the reassuring truth of divine protection and how to discern God's guidance during times of uncertainty.

A. Divine Protection

It's easy to feel alone during tough times, but God is always with us, guiding and protecting us through our trials. When we face adversity, we may question our circumstances and feel abandoned. However, it is in these moments that we can lean into our faith and recognize the protective hand of God in our lives.

1. Personal Anecdote:

I remember a particularly challenging period in my life when I felt overwhelmed and isolated. I was navigating a difficult job transition that left me uncertain about my future. The stress of impending change weighed heavily on my shoulders, and I found myself questioning whether I was truly on the right path.

One evening, after a long day of interviews and rejections, I drove home feeling defeated. As I approached an intersection, the traffic light turned yellow, and instinctively, I pressed the accelerator to make it through. Suddenly, a car sped through the red light, barely missing my vehicle. I could feel my heart racing as I pulled over to the side of the road, shaken by the close call. In that moment of fear and vulnerability, I sensed God's presence. It was as if He was saying, "I am here. I have protected you." The realization that I had been spared from what could have been a devastating accident filled me with gratitude and comfort.

Later that night, I sat in my living room, reflecting on the day's events. I realized that even in my moments of doubt and fear, God had been watching over me. It was a profound reminder that I was not alone and that His protection was always present, even when I couldn't see it.

2. Scriptural Reference:

Psalm 91:11 beautifully encapsulates this truth: "For he will command his angels concerning you to guard you in all your ways." This verse serves as a powerful reminder of God's protective nature. It assures us that we are not left to navigate life's challenges alone; instead, God has dispatched angels to guard us. When we face trials, we can hold onto this promise. It encourages us to trust that God is actively watching over us, orchestrating our paths, and ensuring our safety. This divine protection goes beyond physical safety; it encompasses emotional and spiritual protection as well. We can rest assured that God is our refuge, guiding us through every storm we encounter.

B. Recognizing God's Plan

Understanding that God's plan is often different from our own can be challenging, but it helps us to trust in His timing. Life can be unpredictable, and we may find ourselves in situations that seem impossible. Yet, it's crucial to remember that God has a greater purpose for us.

1. Reflection:

Take a moment to reflect on your own life. Can you identify instances where you felt God's protection and guidance? Perhaps there was a time when you faced a difficult decision, and while you might not have seen a way forward, God intervened in unexpected ways. Consider how you have navigated challenges and emerged stronger or wiser. Think about how certain closed doors have ultimately led you to better opportunities. Reflecting on these experiences can deepen your understanding of God's presence in your life and help you recognize the ways He has worked behind the scenes.

2. Encouragement:

Trust that God is orchestrating events for your good, even when the path ahead is unclear. Just as He guided me through difficult transitions and protected me in moments of vulnerability, He is doing the same for you. God's plan is often revealed in retrospect. In the moment, we may struggle to understand why certain things happen, but as we look back, we can see the fingerprints of His guidance.

Remember, you are a part of a divine plan. Your life has a purpose, and each challenge is an opportunity for growth. Embrace the uncertainty, knowing that God is in control and that He is shaping you for something greater.

Conclusion: Embracing God's Protection

God's protective hand is always upon us, guiding and shielding us from harm. As we navigate life's challenges, let us remain aware of His presence and trust in His plan. By recognizing God's protection in our lives and surrendering our own plans, we open ourselves to the beauty of His guidance.

You are not alone; God is with you, orchestrating your path and ensuring your safety. Embrace the journey, knowing that you are protected and loved, and trust that each step you take brings you closer to fulfilling His purpose for your life.

Your Destiny Is Unique

In a world where conformity and comparison can be tempting, it's easy to lose sight of what truly sets us apart. Yet, it's precisely our individuality that holds the key to fulfilling our deepest passions and purposes. As we journey through life, it's essential to tune into our inner guidance and celebrate what makes us unique. In this section, we'll explore the importance of embracing our distinctiveness and listening to our inner voice, that we may unlock our full potential and walk in the fulfillment of our one-of-a-kind destiny.

A. Embracing Your Uniqueness

We all have a unique purpose and destiny intricately woven into the fabric of our being. It's essential to embrace what makes us different, for those differences are often the keys to unlocking our true potential.

1. Personal Anecdote:
I vividly remember a pivotal moment in my life that shaped my understanding of uniqueness. It was during my early career days when I

found myself in a competitive work environment. Surrounded by talented individuals, I often felt the pressure to conform to the norms and expectations of my peers. I tried to mimic their styles, their approaches, and even their perspectives, believing that success meant fitting into a mold.

One day, I attended a leadership seminar where the speaker posed a thought-provoking question: "What makes you you?" At first, I was stumped. I had spent so much time trying to fit in that I had forgotten what made me unique. The speaker went on to share how embracing our individuality is not just beneficial but essential for true leadership and impact.

Inspired, I began to reflect on my experiences, skills, and passions. I realized that my background in event planning and my deep desire to empower others were gifts that set me apart. This was my moment of awakening—I understood that my uniqueness was not a barrier to success; it was the very foundation of my journey.

From that day forward, I made a conscious effort to embrace my individuality. I began to infuse my authentic self into my work, leading with creativity and passion. I discovered that when I honored my uniqueness, I not only felt more fulfilled, but I also inspired those around me to do the same. This realization shifted my perspective, allowing me to recognize that my differences were assets that could be harnessed for a greater purpose.

2. Encouragement:

Remember, your individuality is a gift that can be used for a greater purpose. Each of us is endowed with unique talents, experiences, and perspectives that contribute to our destinies. Embracing your uniqueness means recognizing that you have something special to offer the world.

When you honor your authentic self, you unlock doors to opportunities that align with your purpose. Celebrate what makes you different! It could be your creativity, your empathy, your analytical skills, or even your life experiences. Each piece of your identity plays a role in shaping your path and the impact you can have on others.

B. Listening to Your Inner Voice

The universe guides us in mysterious ways, but we must be attuned to our inner voice to follow that guidance. Learning to listen to this voice is crucial in navigating our paths and embracing our uniqueness.

1. Practical Strategies:

Here are some tips for practicing mindfulness and reflection to help you connect with your inner self:

- **Daily Meditation:** Spend a few minutes each day in silence, focusing on your breath. Allow your thoughts to settle and listen to what arises within. Meditation can help clear mental clutter and bring clarity to your inner voice.
- **Journaling:** Write down your thoughts, feelings, and experiences. Journaling is an excellent way to process emotions and gain insights into your inner self. Consider prompts like, "What makes me feel alive?" or "What do I truly desire in life?"
- **Nature Walks:** Spend time outdoors, immersing yourself in nature. The tranquility of nature can help you connect with your thoughts and feelings, allowing you to hear your inner voice more clearly.
- **Mindful Listening:** Practice active listening when you're in conversations with others. This not only strengthens your relationships but also helps you become more aware of your thoughts and reactions.

- **Seek Solitude:** Set aside time for solitude, free from distractions. Use this time to reflect on your journey, your goals, and your feelings. Solitude can be a powerful catalyst for self-discovery.

2. Reflection:

Consider moments when you listened to your intuition and how it led to positive outcomes. Maybe there was a time when you trusted your gut feeling to take a particular job, pursue a relationship, or make a significant life change. Reflect on how your inner voice guided you through uncertainty. What were the signs that led you to trust yourself? How did embracing your intuition contribute to your journey? Recognizing these moments can reinforce your ability to listen to your inner voice moving forward. The more you practice tuning into your intuition, the more confident you'll become in following its guidance.

Conclusion: Embrace Your Unique Destiny

Embracing your uniqueness and listening to your inner voice are essential steps in uncovering your unique destiny. Your individuality is not only a gift but a critical component in shaping your path. As you navigate life, remember to honor what makes you different and trust in the guidance of your inner voice.

Each experience, every lesson learned, and all the challenges faced contribute to your story. By embracing your authenticity, you open doors to possibilities you never thought existed. Your journey is uniquely yours, and as you embrace it, you empower not only yourself but also those around you.

Let your story unfold with confidence, knowing that your destiny is unique and worthy of celebration. Embrace the journey, trust in your path, and remember that your voice matters.

Lessons from Isolation

Life is full of unexpected twists and turns, and sometimes, those paths lead us to places of solitude. While isolation can be difficult to navigate, it can also be a catalyst for transformation. In this section, we'll explore how periods of isolation can be redeemed and repurposed for our good. We'll examine the ways in which isolation can be a gift, allowing us to focus inward and discover new aspects of ourselves. We'll also discuss how these seasons can be used to deepen our relationship with God, emerging stronger, wiser, and more resilient than before.

A. The Gift of Isolation

Periods of isolation can be incredibly challenging, often leaving us feeling lonely and disconnected. However, I have come to learn that these times can also serve as profound opportunities for growth and self-discovery.

1. Personal Anecdote:
I remember a particularly transformative period of isolation in my life. It was during the peak of the pandemic when everything around me was shifting, and the world felt like it had come to a standstill. Suddenly, I found myself alone at home, stripped of the usual distractions—no social gatherings, no events to plan, no bustling daily routines.

Initially, this isolation was jarring. I felt a sense of loss, a disconnection from the world I had always been a part of. I missed the energy of collaboration, the joy of community, and the simple pleasure of human interaction. However, as the weeks turned into months, I began to view this isolation as an opportunity for self-reflection.

With all the noise of life silenced, I had the chance to dive deep into my thoughts and feelings. I started journaling my experiences, fears, and hopes.

What emerged was a clearer understanding of my purpose and desires. I found that I had been so busy fulfilling roles and responsibilities that I had neglected to truly consider what I wanted for myself.

Through this time of solitude, I began to reconnect with my passions. I revisited hobbies I had long forgotten, such as painting and writing, allowing my creativity to flow freely. I realized that this period of isolation was a gift—a chance to rediscover who I was beyond my roles as a mother, a businesswoman, and a community leader. It became a time of significant personal growth.

2. Encouragement:

I want to remind you that isolation can be a time of reflection and renewal. While it may feel uncomfortable, these moments allow us to step back from the chaos of life and gain clarity about our true selves. If you find yourself in a similar situation, embrace it. Use this time to explore your thoughts, reflect on your experiences, and reconnect with your passions. Remember, periods of isolation are not meant to punish us but to prepare us for what is next. They can lead to newfound strength, creativity, and self-awareness. Lean into the discomfort and allow it to guide you toward growth and understanding.

B. Building a Relationship with God

Isolation provides a unique opportunity to deepen our relationship with God. In the stillness, we can hear His voice more clearly, connect with His presence, and seek His guidance in our lives.

1. Practical Strategies:

To make the most of these periods of solitude, consider engaging in the following practices:

- **Daily Prayer:** Use this time to communicate with God. Share your thoughts, feelings, and desires. Pour out your heart to Him and listen for His guidance in return. Establish a routine that incorporates prayer into your daily life.
- **Meditation and Mindfulness:** Spend time in silence, focusing on your breath and being present in the moment. Use this time to clear your mind and listen for God's voice. Meditation can help center your thoughts and bring peace to your spirit.
- **Bible Study:** Dive into Scripture during your moments of isolation. Choose passages that resonate with you and seek to understand their meanings. Journaling your thoughts on these passages can enhance your understanding and deepen your relationship with God.
- **Worship and Praise:** Engage in worship, whether through singing, listening to music, or creating your own expressions of praise. Worship allows you to connect with God on a deeper level and invites His presence into your life.
- **Serve Others from Afar:** Even in isolation, you can find ways to serve others. Write letters of encouragement, call friends to check on them, or volunteer virtually. Serving others allows you to extend God's love and compassion even when you're physically apart.

2. Reflection:

Take a moment to consider how you can cultivate a deeper connection with God during challenging times. Reflect on your past experiences of isolation. How did you respond? Did you lean into your faith, or did you withdraw?

Think about the ways you can intentionally engage with God during future periods of solitude. Perhaps you can create a prayer journal, set aside specific times for reflection, or establish a routine that fosters a connection with Him.

God desires a relationship with you, and periods of isolation can be the perfect opportunity to draw near to Him. Embrace these moments as a chance to deepen your faith and understanding of His love for you.

Conclusion: Embracing the Journey and Lessons of Isolation

Lessons from isolation can be invaluable. In reflecting on the lessons learned during periods of isolation, we recognize that these moments, often perceived as lonely or daunting, can actually serve as profound opportunities for growth and self-discovery. Just as we face adversity, we also encounter the gift of solitude, allowing us to connect more deeply with ourselves and our Creator.

Overcoming adversity requires strength, resilience, and faith, and isolation often becomes a catalyst for these qualities to flourish. It is within these challenging times that we can hear God's voice more clearly, allowing us to realign our paths and deepen our relationship with Him. Embracing the journey means understanding that every struggle, every moment of silence, holds the potential for transformation.

As we navigate life's ups and downs, let us remember that our experiences are not solely for our benefit; they are also meant to inspire and uplift those around us. The insights we gain during isolation equip us to support others in their journeys, creating a ripple effect of hope and encouragement.

When you find yourself in a season of solitude, trust that you are being prepared for something greater. God's plan is unfolding, and there is a purpose behind every moment of isolation. Embrace this time as a chance to reflect, grow, and connect with God in ways you may have never thought possible.

So, as you continue on this journey, remember, you are not alone. Your story is a powerful testament to the strength that resides within you. Embrace the challenges, learn from your trials, and celebrate your victories, knowing that this is where you truly come alive. May your journey inspire others and bring light to those who are navigating their own periods of darkness.

Together, let us rise, embracing the lessons from our isolations and sharing the hope that emerges from our experiences. This is just the beginning of a life filled with purpose, joy, and connection.

Chapter 15

BRING IT ON HOME:
THIS IS WHERE WE COME ALIVE!

> "So if the Son sets you free, you will be free indeed."
> —John 8:36 *(NIV)*

"Bring it on home!" This phrase resonates deep within my spirit, igniting a fire of determination and purpose. It's not just a call to action; it's a declaration that life, with all its ups and downs, challenges and triumphs, is meant to be embraced with fervor. This is where we come alive!

Life can often feel like a rollercoaster ride, with its twists, turns, and unexpected drops. It's easy to get lost in the chaos and feel overwhelmed. But I believe every trial we face is an opportunity to rise, grow, and truly live. When we grasp this truth, we begin to see that each moment—both joyous and painful—is part of a greater narrative that is unfolding.

In this final chapter, we will explore the power of belief, the journey toward wholeness, and the unwavering promises of God. We will delve into the concept of perseverance and how it plays a vital role in our stories. This is not how your story ends! You have a destiny waiting to be fulfilled, and it's time to bring it on home.

Believe That You Have a Future

Belief is the foundation of our lives. It shapes our thoughts and actions—and, ultimately, our futures. The first step in overcoming challenges is to believe that you have a future—a bright, hopeful future filled with possibilities.

The Power of Vision

Having a vision for your future is crucial, especially when life throws challenges your way. It's easy to get bogged down by the present and forget that our circumstances can change. I often reflect on the times in my life when I felt stuck, unsure of what was next. During those moments, I had to remind myself that God had a plan for me, one that was greater than my current struggles.

1. Personal Anecdote:

There was a season in my life when I felt completely lost. I was navigating a tumultuous period filled with uncertainty and self-doubt. It was around the time I faced a significant career transition. I had poured my heart and soul into my work, and suddenly, it seemed like everything I had built was crumbling around me. I remember sitting in my living room, feeling paralyzed by fear and anxiety about my future. What was I going to do next? How could I move forward when it felt like I was at a dead end?

In that moment of despair, I took a deep breath and closed my eyes. I began to pray, asking God for clarity and direction. As I sat in stillness, I felt a flicker of hope ignite within me. It was as if a gentle whisper was reminding me that this was only a chapter in my story, not the entire book. I began to visualize what my future could look like—embracing new opportunities, pursuing my passions, and ultimately leading a life filled with purpose. That vision brought me comfort and allowed me to see beyond my current circumstances.

I realized that my feelings of being stuck were temporary and that God had already laid out a path for me to follow. I began to write down my goals, sketching a roadmap of where I wanted to go and who I wanted to become. This simple act of visualizing my future reignited my passion and motivated me to take actionable steps toward my dreams.

2. Scriptural Reference:
Jeremiah 29:11 states, "For I know the plans I have for you, declares the Lord, plans to prosper you and not to harm you, plans to give you hope and a future." This verse has been a guiding light in my life, especially during difficult times. Whenever I felt overwhelmed by uncertainty, I would recite this scripture, reminding myself that God's plans are good and filled with hope.

It became clear to me that my vision for the future wasn't solely based on my ambitions or desires but on trusting God's faithfulness. He knows the intricacies of my journey and has equipped me with the strength to navigate each twist and turn. This knowledge helped me to let go of my fears and embrace the future with anticipation.

Reflection:
As you reflect on your own life, consider the importance of having a vision. Are there times when you felt lost or uncertain about your future? How did you navigate those feelings? Embrace the power of your vision and allow it to guide you through life's challenges. Remember that your circumstances can change, and with God's guidance, you can move toward a future filled with hope and purpose.

Cultivating a Growth Mindset

To believe in your future, you must cultivate a growth mindset. This means recognizing that challenges are not roadblocks but stepping stones on your journey. A growth mindset allows you to view setbacks as opportunities for growth and improvement. It empowers you to approach life with curiosity and resilience, knowing that every experience contributes to your personal and professional development.

1. Practical Application:
Here are some strategies for developing a growth mindset:

- **Embrace Failure:** Understand that failure is not a reflection of your worth but a crucial part of the learning process. When you encounter setbacks, ask yourself, "What can I learn from this experience?" Reframe failure as feedback rather than defeat. Each mistake provides insights that can propel you forward.
- **Seek Challenges:** Step outside of your comfort zone. Pursue new opportunities, take on tasks that seem daunting, and challenge yourself to grow in areas where you feel less confident. Remember that the most significant growth occurs when you stretch your capabilities.
- **Cultivate Curiosity:** Approach life with a sense of wonder. Ask questions, explore new interests, and be open to different perspectives. A curious mind is more likely to adapt to change and find innovative solutions to problems.
- **Surround Yourself with Growth-Oriented Individuals:** Build a network of supportive friends, mentors, and colleagues who inspire you to grow. Engaging with others who share a growth mindset can encourage you to adopt similar beliefs and practices.

- **Practice Gratitude:** Focus on the positives in your life, even during difficult times. Maintaining a gratitude journal can help you appreciate your progress and the lessons learned along the way.

2. Affirmations:

Daily affirmations can reinforce your belief in your future and your ability to grow. Incorporate these affirmations into your routine, whether through journaling, meditation, or speaking them aloud:

- "I am capable of achieving my dreams."
- "I embrace the possibilities that lie ahead."
- "Every challenge I face helps me grow stronger."
- "I learn and improve with every experience."
- "I am open to new opportunities and adventures."
- "I trust the journey and know that my future is bright."

Reflection:

As you cultivate a growth mindset, reflect on how your perspective can shape your future. Consider how you can embrace challenges, seek learning experiences, and practice affirmations that reinforce your potential. By adopting this mindset, you empower yourself to navigate life's ups and downs with confidence, transforming obstacles into opportunities for growth.

Do You Want to Be Made Whole?

Wholeness is a state of being that goes beyond mere survival. It encompasses physical, emotional, and spiritual well-being. To achieve this state, we must actively seek it out and be willing to do the work required.

Understanding Wholeness

Wholeness is not just the absence of problems; it is the presence of peace, joy, and fulfillment in every aspect of our lives.

1. Personal Anecdote:
My journey toward wholeness has been anything but straightforward. There was a time when I felt fragmented, trying to piece together different aspects of my life that seemed disconnected. I was navigating through the chaos of my past, carrying emotional baggage that weighed heavily on me. I remember feeling like I was merely surviving, going through the motions of life without truly living.

The first significant challenge I faced was acknowledging my pain. I had been through a series of traumatic experiences that left me emotionally scarred. For years, I buried those feelings, thinking that if I didn't acknowledge them, they would simply fade away. However, I soon realized that ignoring my pain only allowed it to fester. It wasn't until I faced my struggles head-on—through therapy, journaling, and deep self-reflection—that I began to understand what wholeness truly meant.

In my quest for wholeness, I learned the importance of self-care. I started to prioritize my physical health by eating well and exercising regularly. I incorporated mindfulness practices into my daily routine, focusing on meditation and prayer. These practices became essential tools for grounding myself and finding balance amidst the chaos.

Spiritually, I sought to deepen my relationship with God. I began to see wholeness as not just a personal goal but a divine calling. I realized that God wanted me to experience abundance in every area of my life. Through prayer and studying Scripture, I began to cultivate a deeper understanding of my identity in Christ, recognizing that I was worthy of love, healing, and wholeness.

2. Self-Assessment:

To help you reflect on your own state of wholeness, I invite you to consider the following questions. Take some time to journal your thoughts and feelings as you explore these areas of your life:

- **Physical Well-being:** How do you feel about your physical health? Are there areas where you feel strong and areas where you feel weak or unwell? What steps can you take to improve your physical health?
- **Emotional Well-being:** Are there unresolved emotions or traumas that you need to address? How do you typically cope with stress or emotional pain? What healthier coping mechanisms can you adopt?
- **Spiritual Well-being:** How connected do you feel to God or your spiritual beliefs? Are there practices that nurture your spiritual life, such as prayer, meditation, or attending services? What steps can you take to strengthen this aspect of your life?
- **Mental Well-being:** How do you perceive your mental health? Are there negative thought patterns that hold you back? What strategies can you implement to cultivate a more positive mindset?
- **Social Well-being:** How fulfilled do you feel in your relationships? Are there connections in your life that are toxic or draining? What boundaries can you establish to protect your emotional energy?

Reflecting on these questions can provide clarity about where you currently stand on your journey toward wholeness. Remember, wholeness is an ongoing process that requires dedication and self-compassion.

The Process of Healing

Healing is not an overnight process; it requires time, effort, and patience. Just as physical wounds take time to mend, emotional and spiritual wounds need time to heal as well. It's essential to approach healing with the understanding that it's a journey, not a destination. Each step forward is a victory, and every setback is a part of the process.

1. Practical Strategies for Healing:
Here are some actionable steps you can take to begin your healing journey:

- **Seek Professional Help:** Consider working with a therapist or counselor who specializes in trauma or emotional healing. Professional support can provide you with valuable tools and insights to navigate your feelings. Therapists can help you unpack your experiences, develop coping strategies, and encourage you to confront unresolved emotions.
- **Join Support Groups:** Connecting with others who have gone through similar experiences can be incredibly beneficial. Support groups provide a safe space for sharing, understanding, and encouragement. Hearing others' stories can remind you that you're not alone in your journey.
- **Practice Self-Care:** Make self-care a priority in your daily routine. This could include simple practices like taking walks, practicing yoga, or spending time in nature. Find activities that rejuvenate your spirit and bring you joy.
- **Engage in Journaling:** Writing about your thoughts and feelings can be a powerful tool for processing your emotions. Set aside time each day to journal about your experiences, reflections, and hopes for the future. Allow yourself to write freely, without judgment or fear of how it sounds.

- **Incorporate Meditation and Mindfulness:** Mindfulness practices, such as meditation or deep breathing exercises, can help center your thoughts and bring you peace. These practices enable you to focus on the present moment, reducing anxiety and promoting emotional clarity.
- **et Realistic Goals:** Healing is a journey, and setting achievable goals is important. These goals can be small, such as attending therapy once a week, or larger, such as completing a self-help book on healing. Celebrate your progress, no matter how small it may seem.

2. Scriptural Reference:

In John 10:10, Jesus states, "I have come that they may have life, and have it to the full." This powerful verse emphasizes that God desires for us to experience abundant life. He wants us to heal, thrive, and live fully in every aspect of our lives.

When we embrace the journey of healing, we open ourselves up to the fullness of life that Jesus promises. God does not want us to remain in a state of brokenness; He longs for us to be whole, free from the shackles of our past. Reflect on this promise and allow it to encourage you as you navigate your healing process. Trust that, with God's guidance, you are moving toward a life filled with purpose, joy, and fulfillment.

The Journey Through Trials

Life is a tapestry woven with threads of joy and sorrow, triumphs and tribulations. Each trial we encounter is not merely a roadblock but a stepping stone on the path to our purpose. When we learn to embrace our struggles, we discover the potential for growth and transformation that lies within them.

1. Personal Anecdote: My Journey Through Adversity

One of the most significant challenges I faced occurred during a particularly tumultuous period in my life. I was at a crossroads, feeling the weight of multiple responsibilities while grappling with personal losses and health issues. It felt like everything was spiraling out of control, and I was drowning in a sea of uncertainty. Amidst this chaos, I was faced with a daunting decision regarding my career. I had poured years of hard work into my job, but changes in leadership left me feeling undervalued and overlooked. Despite my dedication, it became increasingly clear that I needed to prioritize my well-being and seek a new path. However, making such a drastic change felt terrifying. What if I failed? What if I regretted leaving the stability I had?

After much prayer and soul-searching, I decided to take a leap of faith. I resigned from my job and focused on my health and personal development. At first, this decision felt like a monumental risk. The uncertainty loomed over me like a dark cloud, and I often questioned whether I had made the right choice. But as I navigated through this challenging transition, I began to discover newfound strengths within myself. I started exploring my passions and pursuing opportunities I had previously overlooked. I engaged in self-care practices, embraced a healthier lifestyle, and connected with a supportive community that uplifted me during this time.

The journey was not without its struggles; there were moments of doubt and fear. Yet, each step I took led me to unexpected growth. I learned the importance of resilience, the value of believing in myself, and the beauty of embracing uncertainty. Eventually, I found a career that aligned more closely with my passions and values, one that allowed me to serve others while fulfilling my purpose.

Looking back, I can see that this challenging season was not the end but a necessary part of my journey. It shaped me, refined me, and ultimately positioned me for the opportunities that lay ahead. I emerged from that trial stronger, more self-aware, and ready to embrace the fullness of life that God had in store for me.

2. Reflection: Embracing Your Own Challenges
Now, I encourage you to take a moment to reflect on your own journey through trials. Consider the challenges you have faced in your life—those moments that felt overwhelming, discouraging, or insurmountable. What lessons have you learned from those experiences? How have they shaped who you are today?

Ask yourself:

- "What personal strengths did I discover during my trials?"
- "How did I grow or change as a result of these experiences?"
- "What opportunities for transformation arose from the challenges I faced?"
- "How can I use my past struggles to inspire others who may be going through similar situations?"

Remember, every trial is an opportunity for growth, and every challenge serves a purpose. As you reflect on your journey, hold on to the belief that there is an "after this." Just as the sun rises after the darkest night, there is hope on the horizon, waiting for you to embrace it. Your story is still being written, and each chapter adds depth to your narrative of resilience and triumph.

God's Promises

In a world filled with uncertainty and change, one thing remains constant: God's promises. He is a faithful God, and His Word never fails. During our darkest moments, we can find solace in the assurance that He will never leave us nor forsake us. Understanding and embracing these promises can transform our perspective and bring hope, even when faced with adversity.

1. Scriptural Reference: Isaiah 41:10
One scripture that has profoundly impacted my life is Isaiah 41:10, which states: "So do not fear, for I am with you; do not be dismayed, for I am your God." This verse serves as a powerful reminder that we are never alone in our struggles.

I vividly recall a particularly challenging time when this verse became a lifeline for me. I was overwhelmed by feelings of anxiety and fear, caught in the grip of uncertainty about my future. It felt as though the weight of the world was on my shoulders, and I couldn't see a way out. In those moments of despair, I turned to Scripture, and Isaiah 41:10 leaped off the page. The promise that God is with us, that He is our God, brought an overwhelming sense of peace. I realized that my fears and worries did not define my reality. Instead, I could lean into the truth of God's presence, knowing that He was walking alongside me every step of the way. This realization was transformative; it allowed me to shift my focus from my circumstances to the steadfastness of God's love and faithfulness.

2. Encouragement: Embracing God's Faithfulness
I want to encourage you to hold on to the promises of God in your own life. Remember that His faithfulness is constant, even when life feels chaotic or overwhelming. You may be facing trials, but God is right there with you, offering comfort and strength.

Reflect on the moments when you have experienced His faithfulness. Perhaps it was a time when you felt lost but suddenly found direction or when you felt alone but sensed His presence in a profound way. Acknowledge those moments as reminders of His unwavering commitment to you.

There is always hope for restoration, no matter how dire your situation may seem. God can turn your trials into triumphs and your setbacks into setups for something greater. Trust that His promises will sustain you; allow them to guide you through the darkest valleys. Embrace the truth that you are never alone—God is with you, and His faithfulness will see you through.

God Will Restore: Hope for the Future

Restoration is not just a concept; it is a powerful promise woven throughout the fabric of Scripture. God specializes in restoration, taking what has been lost or broken and bringing it back to life. Whether it's in our relationships, finances, or personal growth, the assurance that God can restore us offers profound hope for the future.

A. The Nature of God's Restoration

Understanding how God restores can completely transform our perspective on loss and suffering. When we experience pain, it's easy to feel as though we are beyond repair, but God sees us differently. He sees the potential for healing and renewal, and He invites us into a journey of restoration.

1. Personal Anecdote: My Journey of Restoration

I remember a time in my life when everything felt shattered. After my felony case and subsequent bankruptcy, I felt like I was living in a constant state of defeat. My relationships were strained, my financial situation was dire, and

I was struggling with feelings of inadequacy. I had lost so much—my reputation, my self-worth, and even my faith in myself.

However, it was during this painful season that I began to seek God with a fervor I had never experienced before. I found solace in His presence and began to pray for restoration in every area of my life. Slowly but surely, I started to see glimpses of hope. Relationships that had been strained began to heal; friends and family rallied around me, offering support and love when I needed it most.

Financially, things began to turn around as I developed better habits and sought counsel on how to manage my money. I learned the importance of stewardship and became intentional about my spending. What once seemed impossible—restoring my financial stability—slowly became a reality.

Through this journey, I came to understand that restoration is not merely about returning to a previous state; it's about being made new. God took my broken pieces and crafted something beautiful from them, revealing a strength and resilience within me that I never knew existed.

2. Scriptural Reference: Psalm 23:3

Psalm 23:3 states, "He restores my soul." This verse is a profound reminder of God's desire to restore us from the inside out. The context of this scripture is incredibly rich; it paints a picture of a shepherd who cares deeply for his sheep, tending to their needs and leading them to green pastures and still waters.

When David wrote this Psalm, he was expressing his complete dependence on God's guidance and care. The act of restoring the soul involves renewing our minds, healing our hearts, and revitalizing our spirits. It is an invitation to experience God's grace and mercy, no matter the circumstances we find ourselves in.

In moments of despair, I have often turned to this verse as a reminder that my soul can be restored, regardless of the challenges I face. God's restoration is holistic; it encompasses our emotional, spiritual, and physical well-being. He has the power to mend what is broken, heal what is hurting, and renew what has been lost.

B. Embracing the Process of Restoration

The journey of restoration is not always easy, but it is always worth it. It requires us to let go of our past hurts, embrace God's healing, and actively participate in the process.

1. Practical Strategies: Here are some steps to facilitate your own restoration journey:

- **Seek God's Presence**: Spend intentional time in prayer and worship, inviting God into your pain and asking Him for restoration.
- **Journaling**: Write down your thoughts, feelings, and prayers. Reflect on your journey and acknowledge the areas where you seek restoration.
- **Connect with Others**: Surround yourself with a supportive community that encourages your healing process. Share your experiences and allow others to walk alongside you.

2. Reflection: Take a moment to consider areas in your life where you desire restoration. What losses or brokenness have you experienced? How might God be inviting you into a process of healing and renewal? Write down your reflections and share them with a trusted friend or mentor who can support you on your journey.

Trusting in the Process

Restoration is a journey that unfolds over time, and one of the most important aspects of this journey is learning to trust God's timing. It can be challenging to remain patient, especially when we desire immediate results, but understanding that restoration is a process helps us navigate our struggles with hope and resilience.

1. Practical Strategies for Remaining Patient and Faithful

Here are some tips to help you remain patient and faithful during your restoration process:

- **Document Your Journey:** Keep a journal to record your thoughts, feelings, and the progress you make along the way. Writing can provide clarity and serve as a reminder of how far you've come. Reflecting on your journey can help you recognize patterns and learn from your experiences.

- **Set Small Goals:** Break your restoration journey into smaller, achievable goals. Celebrate each victory, no matter how minor it may seem. Recognizing progress—like forgiving someone, letting go of a past hurt, or making a healthier choice—can boost your motivation and provide encouragement.

- **Practice Gratitude:** Cultivating an attitude of gratitude can shift your focus from what you lack to what you have. Each day, write down three things you are thankful for. This practice can help you find joy in the present moment and remind you of God's blessings, even amid challenges.

- **Stay Connected:** Surround yourself with supportive individuals who uplift and encourage you. Engage in community—whether it's through a church group, support network, or close friends—who can walk alongside you during your restoration process. Sharing your struggles and successes can create a powerful bond of support.

- **Focus on Prayer and Meditation**: Dedicate time daily to connect with God through prayer and meditation. This practice helps center your thoughts and reinforces your trust in Him. Seek His guidance and ask for patience as you wait for His restoration.

- **Learn from Scripture**: Dive into God's Word for encouragement. Verses like Psalm 27:14, "Wait for the Lord; be strong and take heart and wait for the Lord," remind us to be patient and trust in His timing. Reflecting on such scriptures can provide comfort during difficult moments.

2. Encouragement: God's Restoration Comes in Unexpected Ways

It's important to remember that God's restoration often comes in ways we don't expect. We may have a specific idea of what we want or need, but God sees the bigger picture. His plans for restoration may not align with our own expectations, yet they are always rooted in His goodness and love. Here are some practical steps to guide you:

- **Stay Open to Surprises**: Be receptive to the unexpected ways God may choose to work in your life. Restoration sometimes comes through new relationships, opportunities, or paths we never imagined. By remaining open to these possibilities, we create space for God to move in our lives.

- **Trust the Process**: Understand that the waiting period is part of the journey. Trusting God means believing that He is working behind the scenes, even when you can't see it. Just as a seed must be buried before it can grow, our restoration often requires time beneath the surface before we see the fruits of our labor.

- **Reflect on Past Experiences**: Consider past instances where you've experienced God's unexpected provision or restoration. Reflecting on these moments can bolster your faith as you navigate your current situation, reminding you that God has been faithful in the past and will be in the future.
- **Embrace the Journey**: Lastly, acknowledge that the restoration process is just as important as the outcome. Each step you take is an opportunity for growth, learning, and deepening your relationship with God. Embrace the journey, knowing that it is shaping you into the person God has called you to be.

The Conqueror in You

We are all conquerors through Christ, a powerful truth that can radically transform our lives. This section focuses on embracing our identity as victors in Christ and recognizing the inherent strength that comes with that identity.

A. Understanding Your Identity

When we understand who we are in Christ, we can face life's challenges with confidence, knowing that we have already won the ultimate battle.

1. Personal Anecdote: Embracing My Identity as a Conqueror

There was a pivotal moment in my life when I fully embraced my identity as a conqueror. It was during a particularly challenging season—a time marked by trials that seemed insurmountable. I was grappling with personal and professional setbacks that left me feeling defeated and questioning my worth. As I reflected on my circumstances, I realized that I had allowed the chaos around me to overshadow the truth of who I am in Christ.

One evening, I sat down with my journal, desperate for clarity and direction. As I wrote about my struggles, I began to recall the victories I had experienced in my life—moments when I had overcome obstacles, defied expectations, and risen above challenges. Each of these instances served as a reminder of the strength that God had placed within me. I wrote, "I am not defined by my failures; I am defined by my victories."

That night, I felt a shift within me. I began to speak affirmations over my life, declaring my identity as a conqueror. I repeated to myself, "I am more than a conqueror through Christ who loves me. I can overcome anything because He is with me." With each affirmation, I felt the weight of doubt and fear lifting, replaced by a newfound confidence and strength.

From that moment on, I consciously chose to embrace my identity as a conqueror. No longer would I allow my circumstances to dictate my worth. Instead, I would remind myself daily that I am a child of God, equipped with His power to overcome any challenge. This shift in perspective changed how I viewed my struggles and inspired me to take action. I began to set goals, pursue opportunities, and embrace the future with hope and determination.

2. Scriptural Reference: Romans 8:37

Romans 8:37 declares, "No, in all these things we are more than conquerors through him who loved us." This verse is profound in its simplicity and power. It reminds us that our identity as conquerors is not based on our own abilities or strength but on the love of Christ that empowers us to overcome.

When we recognize that we are more than conquerors, we can face adversity with a different mindset. This verse serves as a reminder that even in the midst of challenges, we have the assurance of victory. It's not just about surviving; it's about thriving, knowing that we are supported by the One who has already won the battle.

The significance of this verse in our daily lives is immense. It calls us to live boldly, to approach challenges with the confidence that we are equipped to handle whatever comes our way. When we internalize this truth, we shift from a mindset of defeat to one of empowerment. We no longer see ourselves as victims of our circumstances but as victors in Christ, ready to take on the world.

Embracing Your Identity as a Conqueror
Understanding your identity as a conqueror means embracing the fullness of who you are in Christ. It involves recognizing that:

- **You are Loved**: God's love for you is unconditional and unwavering. It's this love that empowers you to face challenges and rise above them.
- **You are Equipped**: You have been given the tools and strength needed to overcome any obstacle. This includes the Holy Spirit, who guides and empowers you.
- **You have Purpose**: Your life is filled with purpose, and your experiences, both good and bad, contribute to that purpose. Every trial is an opportunity for growth and transformation.
- **You can Impact Others**: As a conqueror, you are not only meant to overcome for yourself but also to inspire and uplift others. Your story has the power to encourage those around you to embrace their own identities as conquerors.

Moving Forward as a Conqueror
As you continue to embrace your identity as a conqueror, remember to:

- **Speak Life**: Use affirmations to remind yourself of your strength and worth. Speak positively about your future and the possibilities that lie ahead.

- **Reflect on Your Journey**: Take time to reflect on past victories. Remind yourself of the challenges you've overcome and the strength you possess.
- **Surround Yourself with Support**: Engage with a community that encourages and uplifts you. Share your journey with others and allow their stories to inspire you.
- **Trust in God's Plan**: Always return to the truth that God has a purpose for your life. Trust that He is guiding your steps and working all things for your good.

Conclusion

You are more than a conqueror through Christ. Embrace your identity, recognize your strength, and approach life with confidence and hope. Regardless of your challenges, remember that you have the power to overcome. Allow this truth to guide you as you navigate your journey, and may you always rise above, living a life that reflects your identity as a conqueror.

Embracing Your Strength

Every person has strength within them, waiting to be unleashed. Recognizing and embracing this inner strength is crucial for overcoming obstacles and pursuing our goals. It empowers us to face challenges with confidence and resilience, allowing us to navigate life's ups and downs with grace.

1. Practical Strategies: Identifying and Leveraging Your Strengths

Here are some exercises that can help you identify your strengths and leverage them in your life:

A. Strengths Inventory

- **Self-Reflection:** Take a moment to reflect on your past experiences. Consider times when you felt most proud of yourself. What strengths did you exhibit during those moments? Write down specific qualities or skills that helped you achieve those successes.
- **Feedback from Others:** Sometimes, we may not see our strengths as clearly as others do. Ask friends, family, or colleagues to share what they believe your strengths are. You might be surprised by their insights and observations.
- **Strengths Assessment Tools:** Consider taking a strengths assessment, such as the Gallup StrengthsFinder or VIA Survey of Character Strengths. These tools can provide valuable insights into your inherent strengths and help you understand how to leverage them in various areas of your life.

B. Setting Strengths-Based Goals

- **Align Goals with Strengths:** Once you've identified your strengths, set specific goals that align with them. For example, if you have a strength in communication, consider goals that involve public speaking, writing, or mentoring others.
- **Create an Action Plan:** Develop an action plan that outlines the steps you'll take to leverage your strengths. This could include seeking opportunities that allow you to use your strengths, such as joining a club, volunteering, or pursuing professional development.
- **Celebrate Small Wins:** As you work toward your goals, take time to celebrate your achievements, no matter how small. Recognizing and appreciating your progress will reinforce your strengths and motivate you to keep moving forward.

C. Strengths Reflection Journal

- **Daily Journaling**: Create a journal dedicated to reflecting on your strengths. Each day, write down instances where you utilized your strengths, how they helped you overcome challenges, and the positive outcomes that resulted. This practice will help reinforce your understanding of your capabilities and encourage you to continue embracing your strengths.

2. Encouragement: You Possess the Strength to Overcome

As you embark on this journey of embracing your strength, remember that you possess the ability to overcome any obstacle, no matter how daunting it may seem. Challenges may appear overwhelming at times, but by acknowledging and leveraging your strengths, you can navigate through them with resilience. Here are some practical steps to guide you:

- **Believe in Yourself**: Trust that you have the strength within you to face life's challenges. The same qualities that have helped you succeed in the past will continue to support you as you move forward.
- **Stay Persistent**: Life is filled with ups and downs, and it's essential to remain persistent in your pursuit of growth and success. Embrace the journey, and don't be discouraged by setbacks. Each obstacle is an opportunity for learning and development.
- **Draw Inspiration from Others**: Look to others who have overcome challenges and embraced their strengths. Their stories can serve as a source of inspiration and motivation for your own journey.
- **Reach Out for Support**: Surround yourself with individuals who uplift and encourage you. Seek out mentors or join supportive

communities that foster personal growth. Together, you can celebrate each other's strengths and achievements.

Conclusion

Embracing your strength is a vital step toward overcoming challenges and achieving your goals. By identifying your strengths, setting strengths-based goals, and reflecting on your journey, you will cultivate a deeper understanding of your capabilities. Remember that you have the power to face any obstacle and emerge victorious. Embrace your strength and let it guide you on your path to success!

Keep Going: Your Story is Not Over

Life's journey is filled with twists and turns, and while the road may sometimes feel daunting, it's crucial to keep moving forward. Each step we take, no matter how small, brings us closer to our goals and helps us grow. In this section, we will explore the significance of perseverance and its transformative power in our lives.

A. The Importance of Perseverance

Perseverance is not merely about pushing through obstacles; it's about embracing the process of growth and understanding that setbacks are often stepping stones toward success. It's the determination to keep going, even when faced with challenges, that shapes our character and strengthens our resolve.

1. Personal Anecdote: A Time When Perseverance Was Crucial

Let me take you back to a time in my life when perseverance became my lifeline. I was working on a significant project that meant a lot to me—a community initiative aimed at empowering young women in my area. I had poured my heart and soul into planning, fundraising, and organizing workshops that would provide valuable resources and mentorship.

As the project launch date approached, I faced numerous hurdles. Key speakers canceled at the last minute, funding fell through, and community support dwindled. I felt overwhelmed and questioned whether I should continue or throw in the towel.

I remember sitting at my kitchen table one night, surrounded by stacks of paperwork, feeling utterly defeated. I had invested so much time and energy into this initiative, yet it seemed like everything was falling apart. But amidst the turmoil, a flicker of determination ignited within me. I realized that giving up would mean denying not only myself but also the young women who were counting on this program.

I made a decision that night to persevere. I reached out to my network, seeking help and support. I revisited my original vision, adjusting my plans to accommodate the unforeseen challenges. Through countless late nights, meetings, and brainstorming sessions, I rallied a team of passionate individuals who believed in the cause.

The day of the event finally arrived, and it was a resounding success! The turnout exceeded my expectations, and the impact on the young women in attendance was profound. Seeing their smiles and hearing their stories made every obstacle worthwhile. It was a powerful reminder that perseverance pays off, and sometimes, the greatest victories come from the hardest battles.

2. Reflection: Encouraging Readers to Think About Their Own Perseverance

Now, I want to encourage you to reflect on your own experiences with perseverance. Think about a time when you faced a challenge that seemed insurmountable. What did you learn about yourself during that journey? Did you find the strength to push through, or did you need to seek support from others?

Here are a few questions to guide your reflection:

- What was the challenge you faced, and how did it make you feel?
- What steps did you take to overcome that challenge?
- How did your perseverance shape the outcome?
- What lessons did you learn that you can apply to future challenges?

By taking the time to reflect on your experiences, you can gain valuable insights into your capacity for perseverance. Each challenge you face becomes a part of your story—a testament to your resilience and determination. Remember that every setback is an opportunity for growth and learning.

Conclusion

Perseverance is a powerful force that propels us forward, even in the face of adversity. It's the commitment to keep going, to embrace the journey, and to trust that your story is far from being over. As you navigate life's challenges, hold onto the belief that you possess the strength and resilience to overcome anything that comes your way.

Let your experiences with perseverance serve as a reminder of your capabilities. Continue to move forward, knowing that every step you take brings you closer to your dreams and aspirations. Your story is still being written, and it's filled with potential, hope, and the promise of a brighter tomorrow. Keep going; you are not alone on this journey.

The Power of Testimony

Every challenge we face can lead to a powerful testimony. When we navigate difficult seasons in our lives and come out on the other side, we gain a story that not only reflects our journey but also highlights the faithfulness and goodness of God. Our testimonies can serve as beacons of hope for others who may be experiencing similar struggles.

1. Personal Anecdote: A Testimony of God's Faithfulness
I'd like to share a personal testimony that exemplifies God's unwavering faithfulness in my life. A few years ago, I went through a significant period of turmoil. I was managing multiple responsibilities at that time, including my work, family, and personal projects. The pressure began to mount, and I felt as though I was balancing on a tightrope.

In the midst of this chaos, I encountered a financial crisis that left me feeling utterly hopeless. Unexpected expenses emerged, and despite my best efforts to manage my budget, I found myself facing mounting debt. I remember lying awake at night, overwhelmed by worry and fear about how I would make ends meet.

In those moments of desperation, I turned to prayer. I cried out to God, seeking His guidance and provision. I had to remind myself of His promises and the countless times He had come through for me in the past. As I prayed and sought His wisdom, I felt a sense of peace wash over me, even amidst the uncertainty.

A few days later, I received an unexpected phone call from a former client who wanted to hire me for a project I had previously worked on. This opportunity not only alleviated my financial burden but also reminded me of the power of divine timing and God's faithfulness. Through that project, I was able to pay off my debts and restore my financial stability.

This experience taught me that even in our darkest moments, God is at work behind the scenes, orchestrating events for our good. It was a profound reminder that He cares for us and provides for our needs, even when we can't see a way forward.

2. Encouragement: Sharing Our Stories

I want to encourage you to reflect on your own experiences and consider sharing your testimony with others. Your story holds power. Testimonies have the ability to inspire and uplift those around us, reminding them that they are not alone in their struggles.

Think about a challenge you've faced and how God has been faithful in your life. Perhaps it's a story of healing, restoration, or guidance through difficult circumstances. When we share these experiences, we foster connections and create spaces for empathy and understanding. Here are some ways to share your testimony:

- **Journaling**: Write down your experiences and reflect on how God's hand has guided you through each challenge.
- **Social Media**: Use your platforms to share snippets of your journey. Your honesty may resonate with someone who needs encouragement.
- **Small Groups or Community**: Share your story in a supportive setting where others can relate to your struggles and victories. It creates a sense of community and understanding.

By sharing your testimony, you not only honor your journey but also inspire others to recognize God's work in their lives. Remember that your experiences are valid, and your voice matters. Let us embrace the power of testimony, knowing that through our struggles, we can uplift and encourage others on their journeys. You never know who might need to hear your story today.

Staying Faithful

Faithfulness is a choice we make daily, and it is a vital aspect of our journey toward overcoming adversity and achieving our purpose. Staying faithful requires intentionality and commitment, especially in the face of challenges that may tempt us to stray from our paths.

1. Practical Strategies for Maintaining Faithfulness

To cultivate faithfulness in our lives—spiritually, emotionally, and relationally—we can implement several practical strategies:

A. Spiritual Faithfulness:

- **Daily Devotions:** Set aside time for prayer, meditation, and Bible study each day. This can help you draw closer to God and stay grounded in His Word.
- **Join a Community:** Engage with a church or spiritual group where you can fellowship with others who share your beliefs. Being part of a supportive community can reinforce your faith and provide encouragement during difficult times.
- **Accountability Partners:** Find a friend or mentor who shares your faith and can hold you accountable. Regular check-ins can help you stay focused on your spiritual goals.

B. Emotional Faithfulness:

- **Self-Care Practices:** Prioritize self-care by engaging in activities that promote mental and emotional well-being. This could include exercise, journaling, or creative hobbies.
- **Healthy Boundaries:** Establish boundaries in your relationships to protect your emotional health. Learn to say "No" when necessary and surround yourself with people who uplift and support you.

- **Reflect and Journal:** Take time to reflect on your emotions and experiences. Journaling can help you process your feelings and maintain clarity about your emotional needs.

C. Relational Faithfulness:

- **Open Communication:** Foster healthy communication in your relationships. Be honest and open with those you care about and encourage them to do the same. This creates a foundation of trust and understanding.
- **Quality Time:** Spend quality time with loved ones, prioritizing connection and engagement. Make a conscious effort to nurture your relationships through shared experiences and meaningful conversations.
- **Practice Forgiveness:** Understand that no one is perfect, and conflicts may arise. Cultivate a spirit of forgiveness and grace toward yourself and others, allowing relationships to heal and grow.

Incorporating these strategies into your life can help you cultivate a spirit of faithfulness, leading to a deeper relationship with God and stronger connections with those around you. By choosing faithfulness every day, you can navigate life's challenges with grace and resilience, knowing that you are running the race marked out for you.

2. Scriptural Reference: Perseverance in Our Journey

Hebrews 12:1 states, "Therefore, since we are surrounded by such a great cloud of witnesses, let us throw off everything that hinders and the sin that so easily entangles. And let us run with perseverance the race marked out for us." This verse serves as a powerful reminder that we are not alone in our journey. The "great cloud of witnesses" refers to those who have gone before us, enduring their own trials and maintaining their faithfulness. Their stories inspire us to run our race with perseverance, despite the challenges we may face.

- **Encouragement for the Journey:** As we stay faithful, we must remember to keep our eyes fixed on our purpose and the path God has laid out for us. There will be distractions, obstacles, and moments of doubt, but faithfulness empowers us to keep moving forward.

How Long Will You Dwell at This Mountain?

Mountains symbolize the significant obstacles we encounter in our lives—those challenges that seem towering and insurmountable. While it's easy to feel overwhelmed and stuck when faced with these mountains, the truth is that we have the power to confront and overcome them. This section will challenge you to reflect on your obstacles and encourage you to move beyond your limitations.

A. Confronting Your Mountains

As you prepare to face your mountains head-on, remember that the journey to overcoming them begins with a single step—acknowledging the obstacles that stand in your way.

1. Personal Anecdote: Overcoming Stagnation

There was a time in my life when I felt entirely stuck, as if I were standing at the foot of a towering mountain, unable to find a way to climb it. This was during a particularly challenging period in my career when I felt unfulfilled and frustrated. I had been working hard, but it seemed like no matter how much effort I put in, I was not making the progress I desired. The weight of my circumstances felt heavy, and I found myself questioning my abilities and purpose.

During this time, I often reflected on the mountain before me—the fear of failure, the worry of judgment, and the overwhelming feeling of being trapped in my situation. It wasn't until a mentor encouraged me to confront my fears that I realized I had to take action. I began by identifying the specific obstacles that held me back. This process required me to confront my limiting beliefs, recognize my strengths, and develop a plan to move forward.

With each small step I took—whether it was seeking new opportunities, attending workshops, or networking with others—I began to feel a sense of empowerment. I was no longer dwelling at the base of the mountain; I was actively climbing it. Eventually, the mountain that once loomed large before me became a series of smaller hills I could conquer one at a time.

2. Reflection: Identifying Your Mountains

Now, I invite you to take a moment to reflect on your own life. What mountains are you currently facing? Consider the obstacles that make you feel stuck or paralyzed. Are they related to your career, relationships, health, or self-doubt? Take some time to journal about these mountains. Write down the feelings they evoke and how they impact your life. Once you've identified them, ask yourself:

- "What steps can I take to confront these obstacles?"
- "What resources or support do I need to move forward?"
- "How can I shift my mindset to see these mountains as opportunities for growth rather than insurmountable barriers?"

B. Moving Beyond Limitations

Now that you've acknowledged the mountains that stand in your way, it's time to shift your focus from the obstacles themselves to the possibilities that lie beyond them.

1. Practical Strategies for Confronting Your Mountains

Moving beyond your limitations requires action. Here are some actionable steps to help you confront your mountains:

- **Set Clear Goals:** Break down your challenges into smaller, manageable goals. By setting specific, achievable objectives, you can create a clear path forward.
- **Seek Support:** Don't be afraid to reach out to others for help. This can be friends, family, mentors, or support groups. Sharing your challenges can provide new perspectives and encouragement.
- **Embrace Change:** Change can be daunting, but it's often necessary for growth. Be open to new opportunities and experiences that can lead you away from your current limitations.
- **Practice Resilience:** When faced with setbacks, remind yourself of your past victories. Resilience is built through experience, and recognizing your ability to overcome challenges can empower you to keep going.
- **Cultivate a Positive Mindset:** Focus on what you can control and choose to see challenges as opportunities. Practice daily affirmations to reinforce your belief in your ability to overcome obstacles.

2. Encouragement: God Is with You

Remember, as you confront your mountains, you are not alone. God is with you every step of the way, guiding and supporting you through the challenges you face. In times of doubt, hold on to the promise found in Isaiah 41:10, which reminds us, "So do not fear, for I am with you; do not be dismayed, for I am your God. I will strengthen you and help you; I will uphold you with my righteous right hand." This promise serves as a reminder that you have divine support as you move forward. Every step you take, no matter how small, brings you closer to conquering the mountains in your life.

As you reflect on your journey, let go of the fear that holds you back and embrace the strength and courage that lie within you. You have the power to move beyond your limitations and emerge victorious on the other side. Let your story be one of overcoming and thriving, and remember—how long will you be stuck on this mountain? It's time to take that first step forward.

Tell Yourself How You're Going to Feel

The words we speak to ourselves hold immense power. Our self-talk, whether positive or negative, shapes our emotions, influences our actions, and ultimately determines the trajectory of our lives. In this section, we will explore the significance of positive affirmations and how they can transform your mindset, helping you cultivate a more empowering and uplifting inner dialogue.

A. The Power of Positive Affirmations

As you embark on this transformation journey, you must equip yourself with the tools that will help you overcome self-doubt, build confidence, and unlock your full potential. Positive affirmations are one such powerful tool.

1. Personal Anecdote: Transforming My Mindset

I vividly remember a time in my life when negativity seemed to be my constant companion. I found myself entrenched in self-doubt, often berating myself for perceived failures. Whether it was related to my career, relationships, or personal goals, I had developed a habit of speaking harshly to myself.

One day, during a particularly challenging period, a friend handed me a small card filled with positive affirmations. Skeptical but curious, I began to incorporate these affirmations into my daily routine. At first, it felt strange to declare things like "I am capable" and "I am worthy of love and success." However, I committed to the practice, repeating these affirmations every morning as I stood in front of the mirror.

As the days turned into weeks, I started to notice a shift in my mindset. Each time I recited an affirmation, I felt a flicker of hope and positivity ignite within me. Slowly but surely, the negative self-talk that had previously dominated my thoughts began to diminish. Instead of focusing on what I lacked or where I had fallen short, I found myself embracing a newfound sense of confidence and resilience.

The turning point came when I faced a significant challenge—a job interview for a position I desperately wanted. Instead of succumbing to anxiety and self-doubt, I stood in front of the mirror, looked myself in the eye, and declared, "I am prepared. I am qualified. I am ready for this opportunity." When I walked into that interview, I felt empowered and confident, knowing that I had changed my narrative—and it was a success.

The positive affirmations became more than just words; they became a lifeline. This experience taught me that our internal dialogue is not merely a reflection of our circumstances but a powerful force that can shape our reality.

2. Practical Strategies: Daily Affirmations for Empowerment

Incorporating positive affirmations into your daily routine can significantly enhance your mindset and overall well-being. Here's a list of affirmations you can adopt to help shape your thoughts and emotions:

- I am enough. I have everything I need within me to succeed.
- I choose to focus on the positive aspects of my life.
- I am deserving of love, joy, and abundance.
- I embrace challenges as opportunities for growth.
- I am in control of my emotions and reactions.
- I attract positive energy and people into my life.
- I am resilient, capable, and strong.
- I trust the timing of my life and surrender to the process.
- I am constantly learning and evolving.
- I celebrate my achievements, no matter how small.

To make the most of these affirmations, consider the following practical strategies:

- **Daily Practice:** Choose a specific time each day—morning, afternoon, or evening—to recite your affirmations. Consistency is key.
- **Visual Reminders:** Write your affirmations on sticky notes and place them where you will see them frequently (e.g., on your bathroom mirror, computer, or fridge).
- **Affirmation Journaling:** Dedicate a journal to your affirmations. Each day, write them down and reflect on how they make you feel.
- **Affirmation Meditation:** Incorporate affirmations into your meditation practice. As you meditate, focus on your affirmations, allowing them to resonate deeply within you.

- **Share with Others:** Encourage friends or family members to join you in practicing affirmations. Sharing your affirmations can foster a supportive environment for personal growth.

By integrating positive affirmations into your daily life, you can cultivate a mindset that empowers you to overcome challenges, embrace opportunities, and foster emotional well-being. Remember, the words you speak to yourself are powerful—so choose wisely and tell yourself how you're going to feel!

Shaping Your Emotions

Our emotions are often the product of our thoughts and beliefs. They can shift dramatically based on the narratives we create in our minds. Understanding this connection is vital for anyone looking to cultivate a healthier emotional landscape.

1. Reflection: Identifying Negative Patterns

To begin shaping your emotions positively, it's essential to first take stock of your self-talk. Consider setting aside some time to reflect on the following questions:

- **What do you tell yourself on a daily basis?** Take note of the language you use. Are you more critical or encouraging?
- **How do you react in challenging situations?** Do you find yourself spiraling into negative thoughts, or do you try to find a silver lining?
- **What recurring themes do you notice in your self-talk?** Are there specific phrases or beliefs that seem to pop up regularly, especially during times of stress or uncertainty?

As you reflect on these questions, keep a journal to jot down your insights. This process of self-awareness is the first step toward recognizing any negative patterns that may be holding you back from experiencing emotional wholeness. For example, you might realize that you often tell yourself you're not good enough when you make a mistake, or you might notice that you consistently compare yourself to others, leading to feelings of inadequacy. Recognizing these patterns allows you to understand how your thoughts can shape your emotions.

2. Encouragement: Changing Your Narrative

Once you've identified any negative patterns, it's time to embrace the empowering truth that you have the power to change your narrative. Here are some encouragements to help you shift your mindset:

- **Acknowledge Your Power:** Remember that you have the ability to influence your emotional state through your thoughts. By consciously choosing to speak positively to yourself, you can reshape how you feel and respond to life's challenges.

- **Reframe Your Thoughts:** Instead of focusing on what went wrong, consider what you can learn from the experience. For example, if you made a mistake at work, remind yourself, "I'm growing and learning, and this experience is an opportunity for improvement."

- **Practice Gratitude:** Cultivating an attitude of gratitude can help shift your focus away from negative self-talk. Each day, write down three things you're grateful for. This practice can help you recognize the positive aspects of your life and improve your overall emotional state.

- **Surround Yourself with Positivity:** Engage with uplifting content—whether it's inspirational books, motivational podcasts, or encouraging friends. Surrounding yourself with positive influences can help counteract negative thoughts and feelings.

- **Affirm Your Worth:** Regularly remind yourself of your value and capabilities. Use the affirmations we discussed earlier; personalize them to resonate with your experiences and aspirations. For instance, if you often feel unworthy, you might affirm, "I am deserving of success and happiness."

By actively working to reshape your emotional landscape through positive self-talk, gratitude, and supportive environments, you will find that your emotional well-being improves significantly. Remember, you hold the pen to your life's narrative—choose to write a story filled with positivity, resilience, and hope!

Nourishment for the Journey Ahead

The journey of life can be arduous and unpredictable. In the midst of challenges, it's easy to feel depleted and uncertain about what lies ahead. Just as God nourished Elijah for his long journey in 1 Kings 19, we, too, need spiritual nourishment to sustain us through life's trials. This section will delve into the importance of seeking God's provision, understanding how He equips us for the path ahead, and recognizing the blessings that come from prioritizing our relationship with Him.

A. Seeking God's Provision

God is aware of our needs long before we even voice them. His provision is not limited to our material wants; it also encompasses emotional, spiritual, and relational nourishment. By aligning our hearts with His will, we open ourselves to the abundance He desires for us.

1. Personal Anecdote: Experiencing God's Provision

I vividly remember a challenging season in my life when I felt overwhelmed and directionless. After a series of personal and professional setbacks, I found myself questioning my purpose and doubting whether I could continue on my journey. My finances were tight, and I was struggling to balance the responsibilities of being a single mother while pursuing my dreams.

One particular day, after a sleepless night filled with worry, I decided to take a walk to clear my mind. I remember feeling the weight of uncertainty pressing down on me. As I walked, I prayed for guidance and provision, desperately seeking reassurance that I would be okay. To my surprise, I stumbled upon a small local café that I had never noticed before. With just a little change in my pocket, I stepped inside. As I sat down, I noticed a flyer for a community event that focused on empowerment and entrepreneurship—something I had been yearning for but felt was out of reach.

That evening, I attended the event and met several incredible individuals who inspired me with their stories of overcoming adversity. One woman, in particular, took me under her wing and offered mentorship, guiding me toward resources that helped me rebuild my confidence and establish my business. Through this experience, I realized that God's provision came in unexpected ways, often through the people and opportunities He places in our paths.

Scriptural Reference: Seeking the Kingdom First

In Matthew 6:33, we are reminded, "But seek first his kingdom and his righteousness, and all these things will be given to you as well." This scripture emphasizes the importance of prioritizing our relationship with God and trusting that He will provide for our needs.

When we focus on seeking God and aligning our lives with His will, we open ourselves to the blessings He has in store for us. Our spiritual nourishment becomes a priority, which in turn prepares us to face the challenges ahead with strength and resilience.

B. Understanding God's Provision

God's provision may not always align with our expectations, but it is always sufficient for the journey. He knows what we need before we even ask and often provides in ways we least expect.

1. Recognizing God's Blessings

Reflecting on the times when I've felt God's provision reminds me to be aware of the blessings around me. Whether it's a kind word from a friend, unexpected financial help, or a moment of clarity during prayer, these blessings serve as reminders of God's faithfulness.

To cultivate this awareness, I encourage you to keep a gratitude journal. Each day, jot down at least three things you are grateful for. Over time, this practice can shift your perspective, allowing you to see how God is actively providing for you, even in the small things.

2. Trusting in God's Timing

Just as God nourished Elijah with food and rest before sending him on his journey, we must be patient and trust in His timing. There have been instances in my life when I felt like I was in a holding pattern—waiting for the right opportunity or clarity on my next steps. In those moments of waiting, I had to remind myself that God was preparing me for what was to come.

C. Practical Steps for Spiritual Nourishment

To ensure that we are spiritually nourished and ready for the journey ahead, we must actively seek God's provision and cultivate our relationship with Him. Here are some practical steps to help you on this journey:

1. **Daily Prayer:** Make time each day to connect with God through prayer. Share your concerns, desires, and gratitude. Prayer is an essential way to seek God's guidance and nourishment.
2. **Bible Study:** Spend time reading and meditating on Scripture. The Word of God provides the spiritual food we need to grow and thrive. Consider joining a Bible study group to deepen your understanding and gain insights from others.
3. **Fellowship:** Surround yourself with a supportive community of believers. Engage in conversations that uplift and encourage you in your faith.
4. **Service:** Find ways to serve others in your community. Acts of service can nourish your spirit and provide a sense of purpose while allowing you to witness God's provision in the lives of others.
5. **Self-care:** Remember to care for your physical and emotional health. Engage in activities that replenish your energy and spirit, such as exercise, meditation, or spending time in nature.

Conclusion: Embracing God's Provision for the Journey

As we navigate life's challenges, let us be reminded of God's unwavering provision. Just as He nourished Elijah for his journey, He is eager to provide for us—body, mind, and spirit. By seeking Him first, embracing His timing, and recognizing the blessings He bestows, we can move forward with confidence and purpose.

Trust in God's plan for your life and remember that you are never alone on your journey. With faith as your foundation, you can embrace the nourishment that God provides and boldly step into the future He has in store for you.

Practical Steps for Spiritual Nourishment

Cultivating habits that nourish our spirits is essential for navigating life's challenges and embracing the journey ahead. Just as we prioritize our physical health with nutrition and exercise, we must also tend to our spiritual well-being. Here are some practical strategies and reflective exercises to help you develop daily spiritual practices that will sustain and empower you.

1. Practical Strategies for Daily Spiritual Practices

A. Prayer

Prayer is a powerful way to connect with God and nourish your spirit. It allows you to communicate your thoughts, feelings, and desires and provides a space for divine guidance. Here are some tips for establishing a consistent prayer life:

- **Set Aside Dedicated Time:** Choose a specific time each day for prayer, whether in the morning to set the tone for your day or in the evening to reflect and give thanks.
- **Create a Prayer Journal:** Write down your prayers, thoughts, and reflections. This practice can help you track your spiritual growth and see how God answers your prayers over time.
- **Incorporate Different Types of Prayer:** Use various forms of prayer, such as thanksgiving, supplication, and intercession. This variety keeps your prayer life engaging and meaningful.

B. Reading Scripture

Engaging with the Word of God is vital for spiritual nourishment. Here's how to make Scripture reading a daily practice:

- **Establish a Reading Plan:** Choose a Bible reading plan that fits your schedule. Whether you read a chapter a day or follow a topical study, consistency is key.
- **Meditate on Scripture:** Take time to reflect on a specific verse or passage. Consider its meaning and how it applies to your life. This deep engagement fosters a richer understanding of God's Word.
- **Memorize Verses:** Choose a few key verses to memorize. Having Scripture in your heart allows you to recall God's promises and truths during challenging times.

C. Worship

Worship is an essential aspect of spiritual nourishment. It helps shift your focus from life's challenges to the greatness of God. Here are some ideas for incorporating worship into your daily routine:

- **Listen to Worship Music:** Create a playlist of songs that uplift your spirit and draw you closer to God. Allow yourself to sing along and express your feelings through worship.
- **Participate in Corporate Worship:** Attend church services regularly or engage in small group worship settings. Community worship fosters connection and accountability in your spiritual journey.
- **Worship in Nature:** Spend time outdoors, appreciating the beauty of God's creation. Take moments to worship Him in silence, expressing gratitude for His handiwork.

2. Reflection: Creating a Spiritual Growth Plan

To ensure you are nourished for the journey ahead, it's essential to create a spiritual growth plan. Here's a step-by-step guide to help you establish your plan:

A. Assess Your Current Spiritual State

- Take a moment to reflect on your current spiritual practices. What habits are nourishing your spirit? Are there areas where you feel stagnant or disconnected from God?

B. Set Specific Goals

- Based on your assessment, set achievable spiritual goals. For example, you might aim to pray for 15 minutes daily, read one chapter of the Bible each day, or attend a weekly Bible study.

C. Choose Practices to Implement

- Identify specific practices you want to incorporate into your daily life. This could include prayer journaling, memorizing Scripture, or setting aside time for worship each week.

D. Schedule Your Practices

- Create a daily or weekly schedule to integrate these practices into your routine. Consistency is key to forming new habits and ensuring spiritual nourishment.

E. Evaluate Your Progress

- Regularly evaluate your spiritual growth and the effectiveness of your practices. Are they helping you feel more connected to God? Adjust your plan as necessary to ensure it remains meaningful.

F. Seek Accountability

- Share your goals with a trusted friend or mentor who can help keep you accountable. Having someone to walk alongside you can provide encouragement and support in your spiritual journey.

Conclusion: Nourishment for the Journey Ahead

As we conclude this exploration of spiritual nourishment and personal growth, it's essential to remember that the journey is ongoing. By incorporating practical strategies and creating a spiritual growth plan, you can cultivate habits that enrich your spirit and prepare you for the road ahead. Spiritual nourishment is not a one-time event; it is a lifelong commitment that requires intentionality and effort.

Deepening your relationship with God will empower you with the strength, wisdom, and guidance necessary to navigate life's challenges. Each day brings new opportunities for growth and transformation, so embrace the journey. Trust that God will provide the nourishment you need to flourish at every step and remain open to the lessons that come your way.

Conclusion: Bringing It On Home

In bringing it on home, remember that you are equipped to face whatever life throws your way. This is the moment to fully embrace the strength that resides within you. Life is filled with challenges but also with opportunities for triumph. As you reflect on the journey ahead, ask yourself, "Do I want to be made whole?" The resounding answer is yes!

Embrace your journey with faith, hope, and unwavering determination. Remember that there is an "after this." Your current struggles are not the end of your story; they are merely chapters in a much larger narrative. God will restore what has been lost, and His unwavering presence will sustain you. You are a conqueror, and your story is far from over.

Stand firm in your faith, persevere through your trials, and continue moving forward with courage. You have a destiny waiting to be fulfilled, and your testimony holds the power to inspire others on their journeys. Now is the time to step into the fullness of life. Embrace your calling and live boldly and unapologetically. The journey may have its ups and downs, but with God by your side, you will rise to meet every challenge with grace and strength.

So, bring it on home because this is where we truly come alive! You are ready to shine and make your mark on the world. Your journey has just begun, and it holds incredible promise. Embrace it with open arms and a joyful heart!

A Call to Action for Readers

As I conclude this chapter, I invite you to reflect on your own journey. What drives you? What are the passions that stir your soul? Are you living in alignment with your purpose, or are there areas where you need to recalibrate? Remember that discovering and embracing your purpose is not a destination but a dynamic process that unfolds over time.

The path to purpose may not always be easy, but it is undoubtedly worth it. You have the power to shape your narrative, to rise above challenges, and to lead a life filled with meaning and impact. As you embark on this journey, lean into your faith, trust the process, and remain open to the divine guidance that surrounds you. Let your purpose be the North Star that guides you through the storms and celebrations alike. Embrace the journey, honor your story, and step boldly into the calling that awaits you.

In the end, remember this: Purpose drives everything. It is the heartbeat of The Global Strategist, LLC, and the foundation upon which I build my life and work. Together, let us embark on a journey of empowerment, growth, and transformation as we collectively strive to make the world a better place one empowered leader at a time.

Epilogue

BUILDING YOUR SPIRITUAL HOUSE

When you start to take steps of faith and see God's favor, it's amazing how that can stir up other people's jealousy, criticism, gossip, and slander. But God has put greatness in you. He's called you to stand out, be a difference maker, and take your family to a new level. You're going to have to be thick-skinned and determined not to waste your time trying to win over people who are not happy when you succeed. Just stay focused on what God has called you to do.

In Bible times, city walls had one main purpose: to keep the enemy out and to keep the people inside safe. In some ways, those who belong to God are like a strong wall—not to keep people out but to keep evil out and give people a safe, happy place where they can get to know God. But unlike the heavy stones that were used to build city walls, we are living stones shaped to fit perfectly in the place that God has chosen for us. Together with other believers, we are becoming a spiritual house, a temple for His presence. "You also, like living stones, are being built into a spiritual house" (1 Peter 2:5).

God has made each of us different and special so that we can use our abilities to help each other. In this way, we all need and depend on each other. This is what makes the wall—or building—strong: when each of us fills our place, and the love between us holds us tightly together. "In Him, the whole building is joined together and rises to become a holy temple in the Lord" (Ephesians 2:21).

The Legacy of Job: Faith in the Midst of Trials

As we look further into the Old Testament, we can learn about the life of Job. While most of us are likely familiar with the tragedies that befell Job, how many of us remember his abundant wealth? Job is introduced to us in Scripture as the wealthiest man in the land (Job 1:3). He was blessed beyond measure, a man of integrity and faith. Yet, in a moment, he lost virtually everything—his livestock, his seven sons, and three daughters, among other possessions. But here's the beauty of Job's story: after enduring unimaginable testing and trials, the Lord restored him and blessed him even more than he had before. Job 42:10 tells us that "the Lord restored his fortunes and gave him twice as much as he had before." This reminds us that the abundance from the Lord is not something to be maligned or feared. God can and does bless those who serve and love Him wholeheartedly. Job stands as a testament to the reality that our trials do not dictate our worthiness of God's blessings.

A Call to Embrace Your Purpose

As you close this chapter in your life, I encourage you to embrace your purpose fully. Reflect on the lessons learned throughout this journey. Understand that every struggle has shaped you into the person you are today. You have faced the storms, weathered the trials, and emerged not just as a survivor but as a conqueror.

Remember that your purpose is intricately woven into the fabric of your experiences, both joyous and painful. Each setback has been a setup for your comeback. You have the tools and the tenacity to rise above any challenges that lie ahead. Don't allow the naysayers to dim your light. Instead, let your journey inspire others to find their own path.

As you continue to build your spiritual house, keep in mind that it is not done alone. Seek out your community. Surround yourself with those who uplift and support you. Lean into the relationships that encourage your growth and celebrate your successes. Together, as living stones, we can create a structure that withstands the pressures of the world, offering refuge and strength to ourselves and others.

Looking Ahead: The Future is Bright

The road ahead may not always be smooth, but trust that God has a plan for your life. Just like Job, you may face moments of despair, but also know that restoration is possible. God can turn your mourning into dancing and your ashes into beauty. Your story isn't finished yet; it's just beginning.

As I poured my heart into this book, I prayed that every word would resonate with you and touch your spirit. I hope that through sharing my journey, you find inspiration to confront your challenges and rise up to your purpose. Each page was written with the intention to empower you, remind you of your inherent worth, and encourage you to embrace the unique calling that God has placed on your life. So, go forth with confidence. Pursue your dreams with passion. Use your voice to inspire and uplift those around you. Stand firm in your faith, knowing that you are a living testament to God's love and grace. You are destined for greatness, and your purpose is waiting to be fulfilled.

Thank you for embarking on this journey with me. May your life be filled with purpose, passion, and the unwavering knowledge that you are loved beyond measure. Keep building your spiritual house, and let your light shine brightly for all to see.

ACKNOWLEDGEMENTS

First and foremost, I want to thank my Father God in Heaven. I thank you for all the adversities that I have experienced to date. I would not be who I am if I had not experienced these trials.

Thank you for healing all the voids in my life and gifting me an opportunity to use the voice that you have given me to change the nation. I know this is just the beginning but I am grateful that you chose me. Your love, patience, grace and mercy will forever be the reason I continue to soar.

God you are good, all of the time and all of the time God is good.

My life thus far has been shaped by the people and the events I have described throughout this book. I have learned so much about myself and are proud of the accomplishments I have made.

To my father, my true ride or die. Daddy, you have given me more love and support than I deserve or could ever repay. Thank you for always being my behind-the-scenes support and guiding light in everything I do. I am forever grateful and thank you from the bottom of my heart.

To my mother, Mom thank you for love that you have given me over the years. Thank you for being part of the journey that shaped me into the person I am today. While our relationship hasn't always been easy, I am grateful for the lessons it taught me about perseverance, self-worth, and seeking my own path. I continue to hold hope for a deeper connection and to one day experience the love of a mother in the way I've always longed for.

To my baby brother Kevin, we've been riding this thing together since birth. I love you and I thank you for all that you do. Your presence in my life reminds me of the importance of family and unconditional love. Whether it's through your laugher, your wisdom, or just knowing you've got my back, you've been a rock for me in ways you may not even realize.

Katherine, Caden and Justin, you bring so much joy to my life and make being called Auntie such an honor. Your laughter, energy and love remind of how much family truly means. I'm so proud of each of you and blessed to have you in my life. Keep shining!

To my aunts, uncles and cousins, thank you for being a vital part of my journey. Each of you holds a special place in my heart, and I treasure the role you've played in shaping who I am today. Thank you!

Dr. Apostle Gigi Palmer, words cannot express the depth of my gratitude for your unwavering love, guidance, and prayer. Thank you for never giving up on me, for standing in the gap when I needed it most, and for allowing God to use you as a vessel to speak life and purpose into me. Being ordained by you and completing your Bible College has been a transformative experience that I will cherish forever. I am profoundly blessed by your support and will always hold your impact on my life close to my heart.

Writing the chapters about friendships reminded me of how deeply blessed I am by God's goodness, shown through the incredible an unconventional women I have the privilege of doing life with. In every season, through every high and low, I'm grateful to always have a place to turn.

To my incredible community of supporters, thank you for pouring into me with your love, prayers, and encouragement. Your unwavering belief in me has been a source of strength and inspiration through every season. I am endlessly grateful for the way you've lifted me up, cheered me on, and stood by my side. This book is as much a reflection of your impact as it is of my journey. Thank you for being my village and my blessing.

While I may have authored this book, it took an incredible tea of dedicated individuals to bring my vision to life. Thank you for your unwavering commitment to making this book a reality and for providing me the support I needed to see it through completion.

To you, the reader, thank you again for joining me on this journey. I hope the words on these pages inspire, uplift and empower you.

P.S. To my future husband: I'm becoming the woman God designed me to be- just for you. I know you are worth the wait. Can't wait for two hearts to become one.

ABOUT THE AUTHOR

DR. LA SHAWN DENISE WITT,
THE GLOBAL STRATEGIST™

Dr. La Shawn Denise Witt, known as The Global Strategist ™ was born January 3, 1977. A native of Los Angeles, California, Dr. Witt worked in the field of education for over 22 years as a Director, Principal, Assistant Principal, Middle School Teacher and Teacher on Special Assignment. Dedicated to her personal educational advancement, she has earned two Bachelor degrees from Loyola Marymount University in Biology and African American studies, a Masters degree in Education including her secondary teaching credential from Pepperdine University, administrative credential with special education leadership certification in the Masters of Education ISLA program from Loyola Marymount University, as well as a Doctorate in Educational Leadership from Argosy University. In addition, she has completed graduate level courses in the Masters of Human Services and Personnel Counseling program at Mount Saint Mary's College.

In 2017, she decided to step out on faith and live her dream of inspiring others and follow the steps that God called her to walk in. She coined her journey as, "The year of 40" and began strategizing to make her dream a reality.

A serial-entrepreneur, Dr. Witt owns *Divine Diva Events* (DDE), a wedding and special event business based out of Beverly Hills, CA with satellite locations throughout the country. It has always been her dream to provide clients around the country quality, trustworthy event planning at an affordable rate. She has worked in the event industry for 22 years and has established a respectable rapport with many of her clients, successfully producing over 720 events. She maintains working relationships with many of Los Angeles' top event industry professionals. Dr. Witt sees each event as a unique opportunity to design the experience of a lifetime and gives each client an elegantly personalized affair. She is also the proud owner of *Fabulous Divas and Gents*, a first- class travel management group that specialized in hosting group travel events around the world for predominantly African-American women and couples.

During the holiday season, Dr. Witt provides special-made dishes to clients across the country under the auspices of *Divas Fabulous Fixins'*. She enjoys sharing stories about her childhood in the kitchen with her grandmother, mother and aunt. She takes joy in preparing these dishes, knowing that families are blessed with traditions that she once shared with her family.

Over the course of her life, Dr. Witt has faced and overcome many obstacles that have shaped her into who she is today. In the fall of 2024, she will finally release her first book appropriately entitled, "*The Diva Herself: I Survived My Mess*". In her book, she will discuss how being a silent rape survivor at age 15 contributed to abusive and failed relationships, poor handling of finances, long bouts of depression, struggling with validation and acceptance, and multiple attempts of suicide. She will share how her journey to "The year of 40" opened the door to walk into a more fulfilled purpose and produced her first Women's Spiritual Retreat under *My Sister's Keeper*. This retreat convened in May 2018 and celebrated diversity, spiritual experience, and healing of women from all walks of life. This event has led to many speaking engagements for women-based events around the country and continues today known as The Wonder Woman Conference.

Dr. Witt has recently launched an initiative through My Sister's Keeper to fund transitional recovery homes in the city of Los Angeles. She founded Charity House, LLC and her mission is to end homelessness for women, families and communities and assist with providing them with second chance opportunities in life and to restore self-sufficiency and dignity. She is currently in the beginning stages of overseeing a partnership merge to open transitional housing in Los Angeles. Under this same umbrella, she has launched Rahab's Daughters. It is her desire to provide resources and support to end prostitution in the city of Los Angeles.

Rounding out her entrepreneurial talents, Dr. Witt launched an Educational Consulting business, Witt & Associates, LLC. Her boutique firm is dedicated to driving transformational change in school districts and higher education institutions. The company targets school districts to provide strategic planning and professional development that are facing teacher shortages and retention challenges, as well as facilitating administrative retreats for executive leadership team. She specializes in coaching new administrators, empowering minority leaders through personalized coaching and leadership development, and addressing organizational efficiency. Dr. Witt's innovative approach and inspiring presentation style make her a sought-after speaker globally, renowned for her ability to elevate leadership, enhance organizational culture and foster visionary leadership.

With a passion for empowering women and a commitment to holistic well-being, Dr. Witt is a dynamic transformational speaker who delivers captivating keynote presentations, workshops, and seminars. Armed with a wealth of knowledge and personal experiences, she inspires her audiences to unlock their potential, overcome obstacles and lead fulfilling lives.

She is an active and committed member of Delta Sigma Theta Sorority, Incorporated, holding various leadership roles at both local and regional levels, with aspiration of becoming a National Leader. She is also a Life Associate member of Jack and Jill of America, Incorporated. She is a member of several esteemed organizations, including Tabahani Book Circle, National Sorority of Phi Delta Kappa, National Association of University Women, The Links Incorporated, and a host of other professional organizations, showcasing her dedication to community service, education and leadership development across multiple platforms.

She is also active in the African American Alumni Association at Loyola Marymount University (LMU). She has served on the AAAA Ambassadors for the last 10 years. This involvement includes serving on the planning committees for various engagement events for alumni as well as financially supporting the goals of AAAA to provide scholarships for current students. In 2019, she was elected to serve on the board for the African American Alumni Association.

Dr. Witt recently graduated from Regency the School of Leadership and Theological Studies where she earned certificates in Biblical Studies, Advanced Ministry and Leadership and Leadership and Theological Studies. She is the recipient of The President's Award and is now an ordained Evangelist.

Outside of her professional commitments, she indulges in her passions of traveling, reading, shopping, attending live concerts and participating in community service.

Dr. Witt currently resides in Inglewood, California where she enjoys spending time with the love of her life, her adult daughter Morgan, a graduate of Howard University. Her famous Shih Tzu's Dolce & Gabbana have gone on to be with the Good Lord.

La Shawn is "The Global Strategist" and one of her mantra's acclaims "God is within her she will not fail."

For more information on Dr. Witt, please visit her hub at: http://globalstrategist.info

www.ingramcontent.com/pod-product-compliance
Lightning Source LLC
Chambersburg PA
CBHW050518100526
44581CB00001B/26